The Evolution of Military Power in the West and Asia

This book investigates how states in both the West and Asia have responded to multi-dimensional security challenges since the end of the Cold War, focusing on military transformation.

Looking at a cross-section of different countries, this volume assesses how their armed forces have responded to a changing international security context. The book investigates two main themes. First, how the process of military 'transformation' – in terms of technological advances and new ways of conducting warfare – has impacted on the militaries of various countries. These technologies are hugely expensive and the extent to which different states can afford them, and the ability of these states to utilise these technologies, differs greatly. Second, the volume investigates the social dimensions of military transformation. It reveals the expanding breadth of tasks that contemporary armed forces have been required to address. This includes the need for military forces to work with other actors, such as non-governmental agencies and humanitarian organisations, and the ability of armed forces to fight asymmetric opponents and conduct post-conflict reconstruction tasks. The conflicts in Iraq and Afghanistan exemplified how important the relationship between technological and social transformation has become.

This book will be of much interest to students of strategic studies, military innovation, Asian politics, security studies and International Relations.

Pauline Eadie is Assistant Professor in International Relations at the University of Nottingham, UK, and is author of *Poverty and the Critical Security Agenda* (2005).

Wyn Rees is Professor of International Security at the University of Nottingham, UK, and is author or editor of 13 books.

Routledge Global Security Studies
Series Editors: Aaron Karp and
Regina Karp

Global Security Studies emphasizes broad forces reshaping global security and the dilemmas facing decision-makers the world over. The series stresses issues relevant in many countries and regions, accessible to broad professional and academic audiences as well as to students, and enduring through explicit theoretical foundations.

Nuclear Proliferation and International Security
Edited by Morten Bremer Maerli and Sverre Lodgaard

Global Insurgency and the Future of Armed Conflict
Debating fourth-generation warfare
Terry Terriff, Aaron Karp and Regina Karp

Terrorism and Weapons of Mass Destruction
Responding to the challenge
Edited by Ian Bellany

Globalization and WMD Proliferation
Terrorism, transnational networks, and international security
Edited by James A. Russell and Jim J. Wirtz

Power Shifts, Strategy, and War
Declining states and international conflict
Dong Sun Lee

Energy Security and Global Politics
The militarization of resource management
Edited by Daniel Moran and James A. Russell

US Nuclear Weapons Policy after the Cold War
Russians, 'rogues' and domestic division
Nick Ritchie

Security and Post-Conflict Reconstruction
Dealing with fighters in the aftermath of war
Edited Robert Muggah

Network Centric Warfare and Coalition Operations
The new military operating system
Paul T. Mitchell

American Foreign Policy and the Politics of Fear
Threat inflation since 9/11
Edited by A. Trevor Thrall and Jane K. Cramer

Risk, Global Governance and Security
The other war on terror
Yee-Kuang Heng and Kenneth McDonagh

Nuclear Weapons and Cooperative Security in the 21st Century
The new disorder
Stephen J. Cimbala

Political Economy and Grand Strategy
A neoclassical realist view
Mark R. Brawley

Iran and Nuclear Weapons
Protracted conflict and proliferation
Saira Khan

US Strategy in Africa
AFRICOM, terrorism and security challenges
Edited by David J. Francis

Great Powers and Strategic Stability in the 21st Century
Competing visions of world order
Edited by Graeme P. Herd

The Globalisation of NATO
Intervention, security and identity
Veronica M. Kitchen

International Conflict in the Asia-Pacific
Patterns, consequences and management
Jacob Bercovitch and Mikio Oishi

Nuclear Proliferation and International Order
Challenges to the Non-Proliferation Treaty
Edited by Olav Njølstad

Nuclear Disarmament and Non-Proliferation
Towards a nuclear-weapon-free world?
Sverre Lodgaard

Nuclear Energy and Global Governance
Ensuring safety, security and non-proliferation
Trevor Findlay

Unipolarity and World Politics
A theory and its implications
Birthe Hansen

Disarmament Diplomacy and Human Security
Regimes, norms and moral progress in international relations
Denise Garcia

Causes and Consequences of Nuclear Proliferation
Edited by Robert Rauchhaus, Matthew Kroenig and Erik Gartzke

Why Did the United States Invade Iraq?
Edited by Jane K. Cramer and A. Trevor Thrall

Regional Powers and Security Orders
A theoretical framework
Edited by Robert Stewart-Ingersoll and Derrick Frazier

A Perpetual Menace
Nuclear weapons and international order
William Walker

Iran's Nuclear Programme
Strategic implications
Joachim Krause

Arms Control and Missile Proliferation in the Middle East
Edited by Bernd Kubbig

The National Politics of Nuclear Power
Economics, security and governance
Benjamin Sovacool and Scott Valentine

Arms Controls in the 21ˢᵗ Century
Between coercion and cooperation
*Edited by Oliver Meier and
Christopher Daase*

Reconceptualising Deterrence
Nudging toward rationality in
Middle Eastern rivalries
Elli Lieberman

Psychology, Strategy and Conflict
Perceptions of insecurity in
International Relations
Edited by James W. Davis

**Nuclear Terrorism and Global
Security**
The challenge of phasing out highly
enriched uranium
Edited by Alan J. Kuperman

**Ballistic Missile Defence and US
National Security Policy**
Normalisation and acceptance after
the Cold War
Andrew Futter

**Economic Statecraft and
Foreign Policy**
Sanctions, incentives and target
state calculations
*Jean-Marc F. Blanchard and
Norrin M. Ripsman*

**Technology Transfers and Non-
Proliferation**
Between control and cooperation
Edited by Oliver Meier

**Northern Security and Global
Politics**
Nordic-Baltic strategic influence in a
post-unipolar world
*Edited by Ann-Sofie Dahl and
Pauli Järvenpää*

Geopolitics and Security in the Arctic
Regional developments in a
global world
*Edited by Rolf Tamnes and
Kristine Offerdal*

**Precision Strike Warfare and
International Intervention**
Strategic, ethico-legal, and
decisional implications
*Edited by Mike Aaronson, Wali Aslam,
Tom Dyson and Regina Rauxloh*

**Nuclear Proliferation and the
Psychology of Political Leadership**
Beliefs, motivations and perceptions
K.P. O'Reilly

**Nuclear Weapons and International
Security**
Collected essays
Ramesh Thakur

**International Relations Theory and
European Security**
We thought we knew
*Edited by Lorenzo Cladi and
Andrea Locatelli*

**The Evolution of Military Power in
the West and Asia**
Security policy in the post-Cold
War era
Edited by Pauline Eadie and Wyn Rees

**Regional Peacemaking and Conflict
Management**
A comparative approach
*Edited by Carmela Lutmar and
Benjamin Miller*

**Nonproliferation Policy and Nuclear
Posture**
Causes and consequences for the
spread of nuclear weapons
*Edited by Neil Narang, Erik Gartzke
and Matthew Kroenig*

The Evolution of Military Power in the West and Asia

Security policy in the post-Cold War era

Edited by
Pauline Eadie and Wyn Rees

LONDON AND NEW YORK

First published 2016
by Routledge
2 Park Square, Milton Park, Abingdon, Oxon OX14 4RN

and by Routledge
711 Third Avenue, New York, NY 10017

Routledge is an imprint of the Taylor & Francis Group, an informa business

British Library Cataloguing in Publication Data
A catalogue record for this book is available from the British Library

Library of Congress Cataloging in Publication Data
The evolution of military power in the West and Asia : security policy in the post-Cold War era / edited by Pauline Eadie and Wyn Rees.
pages cm -- (Routledge global security studies)
Includes bibliographical references and index.
1. Asia--Armed Forces. 2. National security--Asia. 3. Asia--Military policy.
4. Western countries--Armed Forces. 5. Western countries--Military policy.
6. National security--Western countries. 7. Military art and science--
Technological innovations. 8. Security, International. I. Eadie, Pauline,
1965- editor. II. Rees, Wyn, editor.
UA830.E93 2015
355'.03301821--dc23
2015014034

ISBN: 978-1-138-88623-0 (hbk)
ISBN: 978-1-315-71498-1 (ebk)

Typeset in Times New Roman
by Taylor & Francis Books

MIX
Paper from
responsible sources
FSC
www.fsc.org FSC® C013604

Printed and bound by CPI Group (UK) Ltd, Croydon, CR0 4YY

Contents

List of illustrations   ix
Acknowledgements   x
List of contributors   xi
Abbreviations   xiii

1 **Introduction**   1
   PAULINE EADIE AND WYN REES

PART I
Diversification of tasks and cross-sectorial engagement   15

2 The military and the humanitarian capacities challenge: new
   dimensions of partnerships in a fragile world   17
   RANDOLPH KENT AND CHARLOTTE STONE

3 Post-conflict reconstruction: concepts, issues and challenges   34
   ALPASLAN ÖZERDEM

PART II
The West   59

4 The United States and transformation   61
   WYN REES

5 Western European armed forces and the modernisation agenda:
   following or falling behind?   79
   DAVID J. GALBREATH

6 Military transformation in Russia   96
   KEIR GILES

PART III
Asia   **117**

  7 Great power identity, security imaginary and military
     transformation in China   119
     REX LI

  8 Japan's military transformation: catching up on 'traditional'
     security agendas via 'non-traditional' justifications?   148
     CHRISTOPHER W. HUGHES

  9 Indian military transformation in the twenty-first century   167
     RAJAT GANGULY

 10 Smart power, military transformation and the US-Philippine joint
     Balikatan exercises   189
     PAULINE EADIE

 11 Conclusion   210
     PAULINE EADIE AND WYN REES

     Index   217

Illustrations

Figures

7.1 China's GDP growth rate, 1993–2013   127
7.2 China's official defence budget, 2000–14   132

Table

5.1 Snapshot analysis of force transformation in Europe   86

Acknowledgements

The idea for this book came from a conference jointly organised in June 2013 between the Institute of Asia Pacific Studies and the Centre for Conflict, Security and Terrorism, both of which are in the School of Politics and International Relations at the University of Nottingham. The conference was called 'The Transformation of Western and Asian Military Forces'. We would like to thank the speakers and delegates who helped to make the conference thought provoking and informative. Many of the papers in this collection originated as presentations at that conference. We would also like to thank the Centre for Advanced Studies (CAS) at the University of Nottingham for funding the conference via their Integrating Global Society funding scheme.

We would also like to thank our research assistant, Vladimir Rauta, for his attention to detail in the final formatting of this book.

Contributors

Pauline Eadie is an Assistant Professor at the University of Nottingham. She is Deputy Director of the Institute of Asia Pacific Studies (IAPS) at the University of Nottingham. She is currently working on a project investigating the aftermath of Typhoon Yolanda, which monitors the effectiveness of the Typhoon Yolanda relief efforts in the Philippines in relation to good governance and building sustainable routes out of poverty. This project focuses on urban risk, vulnerability and resilience in the aftermath of Yolanda, and has been awarded an ESRC/DFID Poverty Alleviation grant (ES/M008932/1).

David J. Galbreath is Professor of International Security and AHRC-ESRC Conflict Theme Lead Fellow for the Partnership for Conflict, Crime and Security (PACCs). He is also Director of the Centre for War and Technology, and Editor-in-Chief of both *European Security* (since 2009) and *Defence Studies* (since 2014).

Rajat Ganguly is based in the School of Management & Governance at Murdoch University, Perth, Australia. He is the founding editor of the *Journal of Asian Security and International Affairs* (Sage).

Keir Giles is an Associate Fellow of the International Security Department and Russia and Eurasia Programme of Chatham House, the Royal Institute of International Affairs. He is also a director of the Conflict Studies Research Centre, a group of subject matter experts in Eurasian security.

Christopher W. Hughes is Professor of International Politics and Japanese Studies in PAIS, a Research Associate at the Centre for the Study of Globalisation and Regionalisation, and Head of the Department of Politics and International Studies. Professor Hughes is also co-editor of the *Pacific Review.*

Randolph Kent is a Visiting Senior Research Fellow at King's College, London. Until March 2014, he had directed the Humanitarian Futures Programme at King's College London. The programme, established at the end of 2005, was designed to help enhance the adaptive and anticipatory capacities of humanitarian organisations to deal with the types of threats that need to be faced in the future.

Rex Li is Reader in International Relations and Director of East Asian Security and Peace Project, Liverpool John Moores University, UK. He is a Research Associate of the East Asian Peace Programme, Department of Peace and Conflict Research at Uppsala University, Sweden. He has served as an Associate Editor of *Security Dialogue*, International Peace Research Institute, Oslo/Sage. He has also lectured regularly at the UK Defence Academy. A frequent participant and speaker at high-level policy conferences and Track-Two meetings in the UK, Europe, Asia and the US, Dr Li has published widely on Asia-Pacific security and China's international relations. His work has appeared in a range of scholarly and policy journals, including *Journal of Strategic Studies, Contemporary Politics, Pacifica Review, Global Change, Peace & Security, The Asan Forum, Journal of Contemporary China, Asia Pacific Business Review, The World Today, World Defence Systems*, and elsewhere. He has contributed chapters to many edited volumes and is the author of *A Rising China and Security in East Asia: Identity Construction and Security Discourse* (London: Routledge, 2009).

Alpaslan Özerdem is Co-Director of the Centre for Trust Peace and Reconciliation Studies (CTPRS). He specialises in the politics of humanitarian interventions, disaster response, security sector reform, reintegration of former combatants and post-conflict state building. He has also taken an active role in the initiation and management of several advisory and applied research projects for a wide range of national and international organisations. Professor Özerdem leads the CPRS Turkey – Peace and Security Studies research group and organises the annual Istanbul Human Security Conference series. He is also President of the Centre for Strategic Research and Analysis (CESRAN) and edits the online, open-access *Journal of Conflict Transformation and Security* (JCTS).

Wyn Rees is a Professor in the School of Politics and International Relations. He teaches and researches in the broad field of International Relations and specialises in International Security. He was a Visiting Professor at the College of Europe, Bruges. Wyn Rees is a member of the British International Studies Association, the Political Studies Association and the University Association for Contemporary European Studies.

Charlotte Stone has over six years' experience in international affairs research, policy and project management, and has had roles at the Planning from the Futures Project and Humanitarian Futures Programme, King's College London; Help for Heroes; Chatham House; and Policy Exchange. Charlotte has a BA in History and International Relations from the University of Exeter and an MA in International Security from the University of Reading.

Abbreviations

A2AD	asymmetric anti-access area denial
ADIZ	Air Defence Identification Zone
AFP	Armed Forces of the Philippines
AFRICOM	United States Africa Command
AFSPA	Armed Forces Special Powers Act
AIFV	armoured infantry fighting vehicle
AJT	Advanced Jet Trainer
AMN	Afghan Mission Network
AOR	area of responsibility
APC	armoured personnel carrier
ASAT	anti-satellite
ASBM	anti-ship ballistic missile
ASCM	anti-ship cruise missile
ASDF	Air Self-Defence Force
ASEAN	Association of Southeast Asian Nations
ASG	Abu Sayaff Group
ASW	anti-submarine warfare
BDF	Basic Defence Force
BJP	Bharatiya Janata Party (India)
BMD	ballistic missile defence
BOA	bulle operationnelle aéroterrestre (air-land operational bubble)
C4ISR	command, control, communication, computers, intelligence, surveillance, reconnaissance
C4ISTAR	command, control, communication, computers, intelligence, surveillance, targeting acquisition and reconnaissance
CBI	Central Bureau of Investigation
CCP	Chinese Communist Party
CIA	Central Intelligence Agency
CIP	combat infrastructure platform
CIS	communication and information system
COIN	counterinsurgency
CRTR	Commission for Reception, Truth and Reconciliation
CSIS	Centre for Strategic and International Studies

xiv Abbreviations

CSTO	Collective Security Treaty Organisation
CUP	Capability Uplift Programme
DCDC	Development, Concepts and Doctrine Centre
DDF	Dynamic Defence Force
DDG	guided missile destroyers
DDH	destroyer-helicopter (warships)
DDR	disarmament, demobilisation and reintegration
DGA	Direction générale de l'armement (French defence armaments procurement agency)
DII	Defence Information Infrastructure
DPJ	Democratic Party of Japan
DRDO	Defence Research and Development Organization
DSACEUR	NATO Deputy Supreme Allied Commander Europe
EB(A)O	effects-based (approach to) operations
ECOWAS	Economic Community of West African States
EFR	Emergency First Response
ESDI	European Security and Defence Identity
ESDP	European Security and Defence Policy
FCS	Future Combat System
FFG	guided missile frigate
FGA	fighter ground attack
FOFA	Follow-on-Forces-Attack
FRES	Future Rapid Effects System
GDP	gross domestic product
GNP	gross national product
GPA	Governance and Public Administration pillar
GPS	global positioning systems
GPV	*Gosudarstvennaya programma vooruzheniya* (State Armaments Programme)
GSDF	Ground Self-Defence Force
HADR	humanitarian assistance and disaster relief
HAER	Humanitarian Assistance and Emergency Rehabilitation pillar
HAL	Hindustan Aeronautics Limited
HUMINT	human intelligence
IA	Indian Army
IAF	Indian Air Force
IBG	integrated battle groups
ICBM	intercontinental ballistic missile
IED	improvised explosive device
IFOR	Implementation Force
IN	Indian Navy
INTERFET	International Force in East Timor
IOR	Indian Ocean Region
IPCL	International Peace Cooperation Law

IS	Islamic State
ISAF	International Security Assistance Force
JCS	Joint Chiefs of Staff
JDA	Japan Defence Agency
JDCC	Joint Doctrine and Concepts Centre
JSDF	Japan Self-Defence Forces
JSP	Japan Socialist Party
KFOR	Kosovo Force
LACM	land-attack cruise missile
LDP	Liberal Democratic Party (Japan)
LOC	Line of Control
MBT	main battle tank
MCM	mine counter-measures
MDIE	Multinational Digitised Interoperability Exercises
MIC	Multinational Interoperability Council
MILF	Moro Islamic Liberation Front
MIRV	multiple independently targetable re-entry vehicle
MNLF	Moro National Liberation Front
MoD	Ministry of Defence
MoF	Ministry of Finance
MOOTW	military operations other than war
MRAP	mine-resistant, ambush-protected vehicle
MSDF	Maritime Self-Defence Force
MUNISTAH	United Nations Stabilisation Mission in Haiti
NATO	North Atlantic Treaty Organization
NCO	non-commissioned officer
NCW	network-centric warfare
NDA	National Democratic Alliance
NDPG	National Defense Program Guidelines
NEB	numerisation de l'espace de bataille
NEC	network-enabled capabilities
NGO	non-governmental organisation
nm	nautical miles
NPA	New People's Army
NSC	National Security Council (Japan)
NSNW	non-strategic nuclear weapons
ODA	official development assistance
PDR	Philippine Defense Reform
PGM	precision guided munitions
PKOs	peacekeeping operations
PLA	People's Liberation Army
PLAAF	People's Liberation Army Air Force
PLAN	People's Liberation Army Navy
PRC	People's Republic of China
PRT	provincial reconstruction team

QDR	Quadrennial Defense Review
R2P	responsibility to protect
RMA	Revolution in Military Affairs
RPAS	remotely piloted aerial system
RUF	Revolutionary United Front
SADC	Southern African Development Community
SAM	surface-to-air missile
SCF	système de contact de futur
SDPJ	Social Democratic Party of Japan
SDR	Strategic Defence Review
SFOR	Stabilisation Force
SICAT	Systéme informatique de communication de l'armée de terre
SIGINT	signals intelligence
SIPRN	Secret Internet Protocol Router Network
SLA	Sierra Leone Army
SLOC	sea lines of communication
SSBN	nuclear-powered ballistic-missile submarine
SSGN	nuclear-powered guided-missile attack submarine
SSN	nuclear-powered submarine
TPED	tasking, processing, exploiting and dissemination
TsVSI	*Tsentr Voyenno-Strategicheskikh Issledovaniy* (Russian Centre for Military-Strategic Research)
UAV	unmanned aerial vehicle
UN	United Nations
UNAMET	United Nations Mission in East Timor
UNAMSIL	United Nations Mission in Sierra Leone
UNCLOS	United Nations Convention on the Law of the Sea
UNMIK	United Nations Interim Administration Mission in Kosovo
UNMIT	United Nations Integrated Mission in Timor-Leste
UNOCHA	United Nations Office for the Coordination of Humanitarian Affairs
UNTAET	United Nations Transitional Administration in East Timor
UPA	United Progressive Alliance
USA	United States of America
USAID	United States Agency for International Development
USSR	Union of Soviet Socialist Republics
VDV	*Vozdushno-desantnye voyska* (Russian Airborne Assault Forces)
VFA	Visiting Forces Agreement
VKO	*Voyenno-kosmicheskaya oborona* (Russian New Aerospace Defence Command)
WFP	World Food Programme
WYSIWYG	what you see is what you get

1 Introduction[1]

Pauline Eadie and Wyn Rees

Since the end of the Cold War there has been a period of rapid change in international security. The entrenched certainties characterised by the risk of inter-state, East–West conflict gave way to a much more fluid and unpredictable environment. The East–West focus diminished and Western armies, postured hitherto for high-intensity war-fighting, looked less relevant. Two principal pressures have been evident on Western and Asian militaries. First, the removal of superpower confrontation made it possible to re-focus attention on security challenges that had previously been overshadowed. This book seeks to investigate how states in the West and Asia have responded to these multi-dimensional challenges. This has been symbolised by the counter-insurgency conflicts fought in Iraq and Afghanistan and the debates about asymmetric warfare that have raised questions about the dominance of the US military. The global economic crisis exacerbated these tensions by squeezing military budgets and leading to major spending cuts in countries. Consequently, competition for funding between different branches of the armed forces is a recurring theme throughout these chapters.

A second pressure has been military modernisation and the changing roles for armed forces. Armed services have been required to retain their effectiveness amidst a rapidly evolving threat environment. This has placed a premium upon the ability to respond to security challenges in innovative and agile ways. At the same time, the roles demanded of armed forces have changed. Rather than use military power in an uncontrolled manner, militaries have been called upon to be more selective in their application of violence. They have also been required to undertake humanitarian and peacekeeping operations, as well as rebuild states in whose internal issues they have intervened. This is the second aspect of this book.

A changing security environment

The security environment of the last two decades has witnessed conflicts over a variety of issues. Recent conflicts, especially those involving Western powers, have not concerned national survival but have rather been 'wars of choice' in which countries have engaged in expeditionary operations far from their own shores. The grounds for these conflicts have included the preservation of territorial integrity and combating terrorism. Humanitarianism has also been a justification, although critics would contend that more selfish interests, such as resources, frequently belie the public rhetoric. The first Gulf War was fought over the territorial integrity of Kuwait, after Saddam Hussein attempted to seize the oil and the wealth of that nation. The conflicts in the Balkans started as civil conflicts but then drew in Western powers in an attempt to preserve the rights of Muslim-majority populations against the expansionist designs of their Orthodox Serb neighbours. The wars in Afghanistan and then in Iraq took place in the context of the US-declared 'war on terror'. In Afghanistan, a Western coalition fought to eject an extremist government that was harbouring a terrorist organisation. In the 2003 war against Iraq, the USA justified the conflict on the pretext of weapons of mass destruction and alleged links between Saddam and al-Qaeda, but at heart the campaign was a desire to change regimes hostile to American interests within the Middle East.

Western militaries have found themselves fighting against a variety of adversaries. In conflicts such as Kosovo and Libya, Western air forces were deployed against state forces and paramilitaries, whereas in Afghanistan, and most recently against the forces of Islamic State in occupied parts of Iraq, Western militaries have found themselves fighting insurgents and terrorists rather than the representatives of nation-states. This experience in the West has contrasted with that of many countries in Asia that have remained focused on preparations for large-scale inter-state warfare. The possibility of war between India and Pakistan, North and South Korea, and growing Chinese tensions with Japan have preoccupied the attention of policymakers. The possibility of inter-state war has seemed remote in post-Cold War Europe. This may, however, only have been an anomaly of history (Strachan and Scheipers 2011: 10). The conflict in Ukraine has brought this threat back onto the agenda: the North Atlantic Treaty Organization (NATO) has sought to signal to the Russian government that any provocations against the Baltic states, for example, would involve a confrontation with the forces of the Alliance.

Just as the pretexts for conflict have been more complex, so have the roles performed by armed forces. Post-Cold War tasks for the military have ranged from preparations for high-intensity warfare at one end of the spectrum, to peacekeeping and post-conflict stability operations at the other. The Balkans witnessed the beginning of this broadening of military roles as Western forces were called upon to impose a peace settlement on the warring parties. The Dayton Accords in Bosnia involved peace-enforcement operations in which the factions were threatened with large-scale violence by NATO forces if they returned to the use of force. In Afghanistan, the International Security Assistance Force (ISAF) was mandated by the United Nations (UN) to provide a secure environment so that post-conflict reconstruction efforts could take place. Asian powers such as Japan have contributed forces to post-conflict reconstruction tasks and China has made contributions to peacekeeping operations.

The equipment and the training required to perform different military tasks varies significantly. For inter-state warfare, the premium is upon sophisticated weapons platforms that can provide a technological advantage over an adversary, such as tanks, combat aircraft and naval vessels. Equipment and training for tasks like peace enforcement may require well-armed combat forces in case of the break out of military hostilities, and armed forces may be required to conduct offensive operations. At the other end of the spectrum, tasks such as post-conflict stabilisation, peacekeeping and reconstruction demand forces equipped and trained differently. These are more politically sensitive environments where the threat of force may destabilise a situation. These situations call for troops that can resist provocation, that travel around in soft-skinned vehicles and carry only light weapons. Humanitarian tasks, such as post-disaster reconstruction, involve skills and equipment associated with civilian operations and may require the military to interface with non-governmental organisations (NGOs).

The chapters in this book look at how a selection of leading Western and Asian countries have been configuring their armed forces to cope with these post-Cold War security challenges. The choice of countries reflects a cross-section of some of the leading military powers. The USA has remained the world's dominant security actor throughout the period and has served as the framework for other countries to determine their appropriate levels of military capability. Three key European countries – the United Kingdom, France and Germany – complement the Western perspective. Along with the USA, these countries are contrasted with the experiences of Russia. Although not normally regarded as part of the 'West', the process of Russian military change over the last two decades has been intimately involved with its response to perceived Western dominance.

At the heart of this collection is an attempt to contrast the experiences of Western countries (including Russia) with those of states from the Asia-Pacific region. China and India, as growing military powers both within their own regions as well as globally, present fascinating case studies. Two more unusual choices are Japan and the Philippines. The former is an advanced military power that has operated hitherto under self-imposed constraints. This may now be coming to an end as the Abe government in Tokyo reassesses the strategic context for Japan. The Philippines represents a much less developed state that occupies a strategic location and enjoys a strong historical relationship with the USA.

In the case of non-Western powers, there has been much less willingness to engage in expeditionary operations. Russia and China have been extremely critical of the Western propensity to use force outside their borders. Russia has used force in the post-Cold War period but only in conflicts within its so-called 'near abroad', such as against Georgia in 2008 and more recently in Ukraine. India has remained preoccupied with the risk of conflict with rivals in its neighbourhood and the risk of over-spill from the conflict in Afghanistan.

Transformation

The second theme of this book is 'transformation' and how it has impacted on the militaries of both Western and Asian countries. Transformation has arisen in different ways and has impacted unevenly on states around the world. Western countries have led technological transformation, which has arisen largely from the influence of civil technologies, such as digitisation, upon the military. Asian countries have reacted to trends that have originated within the West. The impact of transformation has occurred within a complex strategic environment in which states around the world have been forced to plan not only to fight other state actors, but also non-state actors such as militias and private security companies. Military forces have also been increasingly involved in reconstruction and humanitarian efforts in post-conflict and post-disaster environments. Two key aspects of transformation are addressed in the following chapters – one technological and the other social.

Technological transformation

The USA has been the pioneer of the concept of 'transformation', defined as the application of high-technology, 'effects-based' operations and an expeditionary orientation to modern warfare. American technology has been central to transformation and the conduct of its military operations has showcased its power and given other states a model to which they can both aspire and react. This was exemplified by various national reactions to the technological sophistication shown by the USA during the first Gulf War. A new period in warfare had dawned and Western forces, led by the USA, were going to be difficult to challenge in this type of conflict. The experience of this conflict posed some fundamental questions both for Western states as well as for their potential adversaries.

However, transformation is understood to be more than just military modernisation. It is the extent to which militaries have exploited new technologies to change the way in which they think about, plan for and conduct military operations (Terriff et al. 2010: 1). It consists, on the one hand, of the technological sophistication of the platforms and weapon systems that may be acquired by a state. No single technology has become dominant; rather, there have been significant improvements in existing technologies. New technologies have provided the ability to see things on the battlefield, making things harder to detect, and ensure that weapons are more accurate. Micro-electronics, information processing, innovative materials and new sensors have been applied to weapon systems and resulted in major steps forward in precision targeting, communications and lethality. This was talked about as representing a 'Revolution in Military Affairs' – a major leap forward in the capability of Western armed forces (Freedman 2006).

For transformation to be absorbed effectively, it should have an effect on doctrine and organisation. All of these technologies need to be married to doctrinal thinking that enables them to be exploited. Only when there are changes within military structures can it be said that significant innovation has occurred. In the words of one group of commentators, transformation is 'the organisational implementation of significant change […] visible both in process and in consequence' (Sapolsky et al. 2009: 6).

Analysts such as Admiral William Owens have argued that transformation should facilitate substantial enhancements in military capability (Owens 2001). It should enable better-informed and faster decision making, provide the ability to strike at greater range and with more confidence of destroying the target, and render friendly forces less vulnerable to retaliation. It should also enable the decentralisation of authority, by enabling units at lower levels to obtain an overview of the battle space (Owens 2001: 23). However, at the same time, transformation enables high-level commanders to exert tighter oversight over tactical situations. This exemplifies both how technology can facilitate radically different outcomes, as well as the importance of political choices over the technology.

Yet these technologies are hugely expensive and states vary in the extent to which they can afford to procure them. Even for a country as rich as the USA, these exotic technologies incur crippling price tags. There has been extensive debate within the US armed services over the appropriate procurement programmes needed to realise the concept of transformation. There has also been fierce inter-service rivalry over types of equipment and their compatibility with the other armed services.

For America's European allies there has been the question of whether their threat perceptions justify such defence spending. If Europe failed to invest in similar technologies then it would be difficult to work alongside US forces in a meaningful way. For example, failure to be able to communicate with their American counterparts would result in European armies being unable to operate in proximity to US forces. Yet ensuring that their forces remain interoperable with the USA imposes massive burdens on European militaries. It has required them to reconfigure their forces away from the large manoeuvre formations of the past to the smaller and more agile forces capable of expeditionary operations. The result, as witnessed in Afghanistan, has been disappointing. Countries have been unwilling to spend the money necessary to change their forces and reluctant to engage in expeditionary operations. This led the former US Secretary of Defense Donald Rumsfeld to be openly sceptical of the value to the USA of fighting with allies (Rumsfeld 2002: 31).

Under pressure from the USA, NATO sought to address the growing gap amongst its own members concerning transformation. At the NATO Prague Summit in 2002 it was agreed to replace the old Atlantic Command based in Norfolk, Virginia. In its stead was inaugurated Allied Command Transformation, led by its first commander, US Admiral Edmund Giambastiani. The aim was to draw the European nations into closer alignment with the USA. Key shortfalls in NATO capabilities were identified, including command and control, intelligence-gathering assets and communications.

In addition, more emphasis was placed on long-range transportation and shaping logistical capacities that could support forces fighting in distant theatres.

Social transformation

Military transformation is not just technological, it is also social. The statement of General Chang Ting-Chen, of Mao Zedong's central committee, that revolutionary war was 80 per cent political action and only 20 per cent military has gained traction in recent years. The implication is that both counter-insurgency and post-conflict operations must be guided by socio-political, as opposed to merely war-fighting, strategies. Specifically, 'military actions executed without properly assessing their political effects at best result in reduced effectiveness and at worst are counterproductive' (Petraeus 2007: 40). Cross-sectorial engagement and the notion of 'shifting centres of gravity' away from 'spoilers' towards both civilian and military peace builders are, thus, essential for sustainable peace. Technology can win wars but it cannot build positive peace.

The idea of social transformation follows the notion that counterinsurgency is about winning the support of the population as opposed to the control of territory. Successful conflict resolution involves winning hearts and minds. Similarly, post-conflict reconstruction requires the involvement of a range of actors including multilateral organisations as well as non-governmental agencies. The military find themselves as contributors, albeit important ones, in a much larger mosaic. As David Galea notes, 'war is not a chess game but a vast social phenomenon with an infinitely greater and ever expanding number of variables, some of which elude analysis' (Galea 1964: xi). Consequently social military transformation involves both cross-sectorial learning and community-level trust building.

Over the last decade, attention has been devoted to social transformation, as a result of the conflicts in Iraq and Afghanistan. How to fight non-state actors and how to rebuild war-ravaged societies has occupied military attention. Yet this focus has been changing with the return of more traditional threat perceptions. The rise of China as a military power and Russian policy in Ukraine has placed a spotlight on the risk of major inter-state competition. Asia is likely to be a theatre of great power competition in the future. While asymmetric conflict has not gone away, it is no longer the sole consideration.

One of the objectives of this book is to explore the relationships, both positive and negative, between technological and social transformation. This has taken place simultaneously in a variety of countries with differing levels of capabilities and resources. It has resulted in different outcomes. Social learning seems to be one of the hardest challenges facing the military. Across the cases examined in this book a default mindset is that more or better weapons will bring security, even when the arsenals in question are unsuited to the threats faced. It is also shown that states plan on the basis of past and imagined threats, as opposed to future and real ones.

PART I: Diversification of tasks and cross-sectorial engagement

The two opening chapters in this book serve to illustrate the complex dynamic that is driving the social transformation of military activity. They seek to create a context for the subsequent chapters. The first, by Randolph Kent and Charlotte Stone, investigates the diversity of roles that militaries carry out and how this impacts upon transformational processes, with a particular emphasis on the evolution of the military towards humanitarian action. This chapter argues that it is important to go beyond ethical questions of military intervention in disaster situations and complex emergencies. It is proposed that the civil and military sectors could be well served by developing a dialogue that would allow military expertise to be fully utilised by humanitarian agencies – that is, a process of social learning between the two sectors. This chapter brings together themes of trust and the changing, complex and sometimes catastrophic nature of actual and perceived threats and risks to humanity. Kent and Stone argue that the military has much to offer the humanitarian sector in terms of strategic vision, capacity building and programme management. However, hierarchy is identified as a contentious issue. Hierarchy is embedded in military ethos and is essential for effective operations but can also be a threat to the administrative equity that underpins some civil agencies.

Alpaslan Özerdem's chapter also assesses the notion of cross-sectorial engagement. Özerdem argues that post-conflict construction is a relatively new phenomenon that poses fundamental political and developmental challenges for those seeking to build 'positive' peace in post-conflict environments. Özerdem challenges the prevailing orthodoxy that market-driven democracy can act as a cure all for societies that have little or no previous ideological affinity with this mode of social organisation. However, it is argued that effective post-conflict reconstruction and peace building are both underpinned by security-sector reform, including disarmament and the reintegration of former combatants into society, the establishment of effective governance including respect for human rights and the rule of law, socio-economic recovery programmes and justice and reconciliation initiatives.

Özerdem argues that cross-sectorial coordination is essential for both the physical delivery of reconstruction efforts and to stabilise and secure social regeneration in the post-conflict environment. This is a complex task that involves altering threat perceptions amongst previous warring factions. Consequently, it is essential that sustainable 'peace dividends' are evident early in the reconstruction process, and that local people are fully engaged in the delivery of these dividends. Özerdem explains why community relations are just as important as cross-sectorial relations in post-conflict environments. His chapter offers a useful analysis of the complex social and physical demands faced by the military in contemporary post-conflict environments with specific reference to failings in Iraq and Afghanistan.

PART II: The West

This section looks at the way militaries within the West have responded to the challenges of transformation, led by the USA, as well as the variety of roles that military forces have been called upon to perform. Some of these challenges have been compounded by strategic shifts in policy arising from the American pivot towards Asia and NATO's withdrawal from Afghanistan at the end of 2014. The USA has been the focus of the debate about transformation: its allies have weighed how far to emulate it, whilst its enemies have sought ways to circumvent its capabilities. Countries in Europe have engaged with the concept of transformation to varying extents, but the USA has grown critical that some of them have appeared to slide towards demilitarisation. For its part Russia has lacked the resources to compete with the USA in any meaningful way. Nevertheless, it continues to regard its own military forces as vital to its status both regionally and internationally.

Wyn Rees explores the manner in which the USA has led military transformation. He relates US military transformation to, but goes beyond, the Revolution in Military Affairs (RMA), arguing that advanced weaponry alone does not transform military capacity. He links advances in technology to new ways of fighting and innovative military doctrines. This marriage of technology to new conceptual approaches offers greater capability which in turn limits US casualties and preserves political support at home. America has also experienced changing threat perceptions since the end of the Cold War – a theme that runs throughout the chapters in this book.

Whilst there has been technological and strategic adaptation, there has been no wholesale change in the mission profile of the US military. The USA has operated within the mindset of inter-state, as opposed to intra-state, war. After the end of the Cold War it imposed cuts across all branches of the armed forces and US strategy shifted from an emphasis on firepower towards smaller, more agile military capabilities. This was typified by the use of strategic airpower during the first Gulf War. The devastation brought by US airpower meant that the enemy was unable to withstand the subsequent land campaign that was over within 100 hours. After the terrorist attacks on the USA on 11 September 2001 (9/11), the funding constraints that helped dictate US military transformation were reversed and all branches of the armed forces embraced technological change, not least to justify their own existence. The USA became unchallengeable as a conventional military power. However, the problem for the USA is that it faces non-conventional conflicts. Despite its technological capacity the USA cannot dictate the ways that wars are fought.

The USA continues to labour under the Powell Doctrine which dictates that wars should only be entered into when the exit route is clearly defined and vital interests are at stake. This has left the USA poorly equipped to deal with the aftermath of the Afghanistan and Iraq wars and the demands of low-intensity conflict and post-conflict reconstruction. Technological learning far outpaced the social transformation of US forces and the failure to develop effective cross-sectorial relations. Rees argues that technological supremacy has been undermined by lagging military social transformation in post-conflict situations.

David Galbreath opens his chapter by noting the shifting role of Europe in US geo-political ambitions. Galbreath interrogates the US-European relationship by focusing on whether the United Kingdom, France and Germany have followed or fallen behind the lead of US military transformation. He argues that the extent to which European states have chosen to engage with security matters in the world beyond Europe dictates policy choices. Galbreath examines the types of wars that European armies are now expected to fight and a shift in the military mindset away from inter-state war. National interest or even regional interests are no longer synonymous with territorial defence and this has forced the European powers to follow US involvement in conflicts beyond their borders. NATO emerged as a natural vehicle for the US/European debate over military transformation. Galbreath argues that whilst the Europeans were initially intrigued by US developments, such as Full Spectrum Dominance and Joint Vision 2010, these ultimately failed to take root in Europe. He notes that Europe was alienated by the 'keep up or give up' stance of the USA towards transformation.

Moving East, Keir Giles argues that whilst Russian forces are undergoing a process of transformation, the drivers behind this are fundamentally different from those seen in the West. According to Giles, Russia has premised technological transformation over the social transformation of the military. Budget limitations have seriously hindered the transformative capacity of the Russian military and until very recently reform has simply meant downsizing. Russia's threat perceptions have focused on the USA and its allies, particularly their aerospace systems and long-range precision weapons. The perception that there will be a sharp rise in China's strategic nuclear capabilities over the next few years has simply served to compound the Russian obsession with aeronautics and nuclear parity. However, public utterances of China as a threat are limited possibly because there is a fear that the USA would capitalise on any real or perceived Sino–Russian tensions.

Giles argues that the actual, as opposed to imagined, threats that face Russia are much closer to home and likely to emerge from destabilisation in Southern and Central Asia, the Near and Middle East, and the North and South Caucasus. Privately Russia has been profoundly affected by Western interventions in the Arab Spring, the fate of North African leaders such as Gaddafi, and the belief that socio-economic instability will lead to a feeding ground for radical Islam. However, despite these real threats, counterinsurgency training, discussed elsewhere in this collection in relation to the social transformation of the military, is Russia's lowest funding priority. Russia has shown little interest in funding or developing military capabilities beyond its immediate environs. Problems are also identified in the funding, training, conscription and retention of military personnel. Traditionally the salaries of the foot soldiers of the Russian military have been pitiful. Demographic change and the need for specialist operational training dictates that the Russians can no longer operate on this basis.

PART III: Asia

In addition to countries in Asia having either adversarial or allied relations with the USA, many also have tense relations with each other. This makes for a highly complex threat environment. There is also great diversity amongst states in Asia regarding their ability to modernise or transform their militaries; many lack the resources to be able to fund technological development or to purchase it from abroad. This may drive weaker states into alliances with the 'great' powers that could distort or compound the strategic environment. Asian transformation, like that of Europe and Russia, occurs against a global backcloth.

All of the chapters in this book make reference to the relationship between China and the USA and its impact on military modernisation. Rex Li's chapter analyses how changes in China's military doctrine and its force modernisation have been heavily influenced by US military transformation. Li firmly situates China's military modernisation within the context of great power aspiration and its attendant threat perceptions. He adopts both a neo-realist and a con-structivist theoretical framework to explain the US-Chinese relationship. In neo-realist terms China has sought military transformation in the face of US meddling in territorial disputes in the East and South China Seas. In the face of the 'Asian pivot', also discussed by Christopher Hughes and Pauline Eadie, Chinese military transformation was regarded as a necessity. In contrast to this, constructivism draws on 'security imaginaries' that evoke the historical memory and lessons of past territorial disputes. Consequently, the legacy of the 'century of national humiliation', during which the Chinese were defeated by the Western powers and the Japanese, is significant in Chinese security discourse. The perception of inadequate defensive capabilities at that time shapes how the Chinese view the future. The legacy of Chinese humiliation feeds into the 'China Dream' (BBC 2013) of a powerful nation.

Based on President Hu Jintao's notion of 'three provides and one role', Li argues that the strategic priorities of China are to maintain stability at home and to defend economic development both at home and abroad. However, China also seeks to contribute to world peace and conduct 'military operations other than war'. This is the notion of social military transformation emerging. Meanwhile, the technological transformation of the Chinese military is premised on the belief that future wars will be short, geographically limited and specific in military and political objectives. The Chinese have sought to emulate US technological developments in response to this belief, including the use of new technology and the integration of command and control and combat systems.

The Chinese are aiming for 'jointness' (the ability of all branches of the armed forces to operate together) in a way that is also identified by Rees in reference to the USA. China has aspirations as a great maritime power given its various maritime territorial disputes and the need to protect trade and energy supplies. The Chinese have allocated funds to aeronautical modernisation but maritime security has been their primary concern.

A history of defeat and humiliation also explains Japanese military history. After its defeat at the end of World War II Japan was effectively a demilitarised power under the auspices of US control. It is within this context that Christopher Hughes's chapter addresses military transformation in Japan. For Japan the end of the Cold War heralded a new strategic environment in which to review its national security. The demilitarisation of Japan during the Cold War means that it is now playing catch-up in terms of its military doctrine, alliances and capabilities. Hughes argues that the Japanese will continue this approach in relation to traditional security interests and 'normal power'. Japan will work towards military 'legitimacy' by focusing its efforts on non-traditional security concerns such as human, developmental or environmental security.

In common with other countries the 1991 Gulf War was a shock to Japan, not least because the USA requested a human contribution to the war effort. In the event, Japan made only a financial contribution. Nevertheless this event triggered a full-scale national security debate which was reignited in the wake of 9/11. Japan was now faced with reconsidering its relationship with the USA in light of the 'war on terror' and regional problems such as the nuclear status of North Korea and Chinese encroachments on Japanese territories in the East China Sea. The modernisation of the Chinese military, in the aeronautical, maritime and cyber spheres, fuelled Japanese fears over Chinese intentions.

Debates emerged within Japan on breaching the ban on collective self-defence and renaming Japan's Self-Defence Forces (JSDF) the 'National Defence Military'. Both of these debates threaten to change Japanese anti-militaristic principles. Hughes identifies moves that have been made by Japanese policymakers towards a more proactive defence posture. Japan owns some of the most sophisticated military technology in the world and has worked on logistical support alongside the USA in Afghanistan and Iraq. JSDF engagement with peacekeeping operations has been limited but symbolic. Similarly, the Japanese focus on non-security concerns has allowed its military to regain legitimacy whilst avoiding war-fighting. The transformation of its military is therefore a truncated and unique process. Transformation has come about not just in terms of technological or social and cross-sectorial change but in the identity of the Japanese nation and its operational capabilities as a sovereign power.

India ranks behind only the USA, Russia and China as the largest military in the world and Rajat Ganguly's chapter offers an insight into its relative strengths. According to Ganguly, India emerged as a major military power in the world at the start of the twenty-first century. Military spending, 50 per cent of which goes to the army, was US$65.4 billion in 2013, and 40 per cent of this amount, across all three forces, has been spent on arms and infrastructure. This is a significant spending spree in a country with widespread yet declining rates of poverty (312 million absolute poor; World Bank 2013). Its modernisation has been driven by worries over its neighbours, specifically China, whose accelerated defence spending on high-tech equipment rang alarm bells in India. It also has a long history of friction with Pakistan which has recently been linked to Afghanistan.

India has sought to consolidate its position by building a series of bilateral defence agreements. Relations with the USA have thawed, and Washington and Delhi have held joint military exercises and established a positive strategic dialogue. India procures weapons from where it can and Russia continues to be its major supplier. Japan and Australia have also sought strategic convergence with India in the face of the perceived China threat. India's leaders understand national security in primarily political, as opposed to military, terms and this has meant that its extensive military spending has been haphazard. More is not necessarily better, as corruption and incompetence have tainted India's military initiatives.

The military influence of the USA on Asia is furthered explored in the last chapter, on the Philippines, by Pauline Eadie. Whilst China, Japan and India can be seen as major players in Asian military transformation, this is less true of the Philippines, which remains largely reliant on the USA in terms of outward-facing military capacity. Like Japan, the Philippines has an enduring relationship with the USA, albeit one that was forged under different circumstances. Now the relationship is no longer a one-way street as the Philippine archipelago is strategically important to the USA as a gateway to the Pacific and Muslim South-East Asia and within reach of China.

This chapter focuses on smart power – that is, the idea that soft and hard power can be combined effectively as a process of both carrots and sticks to achieve desired foreign policy outcomes. This idea is tested through an analysis of the joint US-Philippines Balikatan (shoulder-to-shoulder) military training exercises in which social military transformation and cross-sectorial engagement have been important elements. The Balikatan exercises have been used as a testing ground for strategies that have later been rolled out in Iraq and Afghanistan. Counterinsurgency in the Muslim south of the Philippines has been characterised by the deployment of US-supplied hardware and the creation of infrastructure that both aids the development of the local population and facilitates the movement of troops. Meanwhile, soft power initiatives have included the development of cross-sectorial engagement and the provision of schools and medical care in areas threatened by insurgents. Eadie argues that the Balikatan exercises operate in a multifaceted sense in relation to smart power. Internally they deploy both hard and soft power that is designed to 'attract' the local population away from the influence of insurgents. Outwardly the Balikatan exercises can be seen as a display of hard power and are primarily aimed at China: they are both a show of force and an illustration of commitment. Like Japan, the Philippines fears Chinese encroachments on its maritime territories and it seems to be no coincidence that recent Balikatan exercises have been designed as a show of maritime strength.

The Conclusion seeks to draw out the similarities and contrasts behind the technological and social transformations between Western and Asian military forces. It seeks to wrestle with the question of the relative successes of social and technological transformation in the countries concerned. The various national experiences are placed within a comparative context. It argues that Western countries have led the transformation process. This has resulted from the fact that they have been the originators of the military technology, as well as the states engaged in social transformation, due to their expeditionary operations. Nevertheless, Asian states have responded to these challenges and have brought new perspectives to bear on these issues. Rather than emulate Western examples, they have developed their own unique policies.

The Conclusion attempts to look into the future to discern the trajectories of transformation thinking across the world. New developments such as biotechnology, robotics and nanotechnology are likely to have profound military implications. The international security environment looks set to become more complex with the return of great power rivalries and the risk of interstate war. The need to understand transformation, in both its technological and social dimensions, has never been more pressing.

Note

1 The following chapters are drawn from the proceedings of the 'Transformation of Western and Asian Military Forces' conference held at the University of Nottingham, UK, on 13–14 June 2013. The Institute of Asia Pacific Studies (IAPS) and the centre for Conflict Security and Terrorism (CST) organised the conference, both of which are based in the School of Politics and International Relations.

Bibliography

BBC (2013) 'What Does Xi Jiping's China Dream Mean?' *BBC News*, 13 June. http://www.bbc.co.uk/news/world-asia-china-22726375 (accessed on 18 May 2014).

Freedman, L. (2006) *The Transformation of Strategic Affairs*, Adelphi Paper 379, March.

Galea, D. (1964) *Counterinsurgency Warfare Theory and Practice*, Westport: Praeger.

Owens, W. (2001) *Lifting the Fog of War*, Baltimore: Johns Hopkins University Press.

Petraeus, D. et al. (2007) *The US Army/Marine Corps Counterinsurgency Field Manual, Issues 3–24*, Chicago: University of Chicago Press.

Rumsfeld, D. (2002) 'Transforming the Military', *Foreign Affairs*, Vol. 81, No. 3, pp.20–33.

Sapolsky, H., Green, B. and Friedman, B. (eds) (2009) *US Military Innovation since the Cold War: Creation without Destruction*, London: Routledge.

Strachan, H. and Scheipers, S. (2011) 'Introduction', in Strachan, H. and Scheipers, S. (eds) *The Changing Character of War*, Oxford: Oxford University Press.

Terriff, T., Osinga, F. and Farrell, T. (eds) (2010) *A Transformation Gap: American Innovations and European Military Change*, Stanford: Stanford Security Studies.

World Bank (2013) *India Achievements and Challenges in Poverty.* http://web.worldbank.org/WBSITE/EXTERNAL/TOPICS/EXTPOVERTY/EXTPA/0,contentMDK:20208959~menuPK:435735~pagePK:148956~piPK:216618~theSitePK:430367~isCURL:Y~isCURL:Y,00.html (accessed 19 May 2014).

PART I

Diversification of tasks and cross-sectorial engagement

2 The military and the humanitarian capacities challenge

New dimensions of partnerships in a fragile world

Randolph Kent and Charlotte Stone

Introduction

In May 2012, the World Food Programme (WFP), in collaboration with the Southern African Development Community (SADC) and the United Nations Office for the Coordination of Humanitarian Affairs (UNOCHA), organised and ran the Pandemic Preparedness and Response Exercise in South Africa. The purpose of the simulation exercise, built around the potential threat of a pandemic, was to promote disaster preparedness planning across the region and within the government ministries of participating countries. UN agencies and non-governmental organisations (NGOs) were eager to be part of the process in ways that linked regional and national plans with community-based organisations. Barclays Bank, amongst other private-sector organisations, also attended the exercise to determine what would be required to ensure business continuity in the event of a pandemic, and how it would therefore have to fit into relevant pandemic plans.

Key to the exercise, however, was the issue of planning – strategic planning to support SADC members' ministries in preparedness planning. This was the role of United States Africa Command (AFRICOM), which, well versed in strategic planning, was willing to share its experience because it, too, realised that a pandemic in West Africa could potentially be a security threat to the USA. In a very fundamental sense the WFP-led pandemic preparedness exercise could be considered an example of the way in which the military's role in humanitarian action is increasingly evolving and moving beyond traditional operational support and towards activities related to prevention and preparedness.

This chapter proposes that the role of the military in humanitarian action will, by necessity, continue to evolve and move beyond purely operational assistance. In doing so, it acknowledges the often essential role the military performs in providing assistance in disasters and complex emergencies (Whiting 2012; Metcalfe 2011) and considers how the role of the military might evolve to support more effective humanitarian prevention, preparedness and response.

At the same time, this chapter also reflects geo-political and cultural distinctions between militaries in the West and in the East when it comes to humanitarian planning and action. The attitudes and responsibilities of each differ in approaches and attitudes. In part, this is due to a world in which post-Western hegemonic military capacities are in a state of flux and in which various non-Western militaries' involvement is increasing when it comes to humanitarian as well as security agendas. In part, the difference between West and East in this context has also to be seen as what had been Western imperviousness to a modern tradition in the East that linked military response to humanitarian crises far more than the Western-dominated 'international humanitarian sector' did.

Be it the militaries of the East or the West, this chapter will put forward its key premise – that the global community is faced with a *humanitarian capacities challenge*. This is a challenge that will require the humanitarian sector to look to the capacities of 'non-traditional' actors such as the military to support them in becoming more anticipatory, innovative and strategic.

There is no doubt that the extent and form of military involvement in disaster and complex emergency contexts remains contentious, and fraught with stereotypes. Nevertheless, when it comes to international intervention in humanitarian crises, military involvement is often deemed essential. This is clearly the case in Asia as reflected in the 2005 Association of Southeast Asian Nations (ASEAN) agreement on disaster management, and increasingly so in terms of 'Western' responses, as evidenced by the 2014 response to the Ebola crisis in West Africa. Whilst examples such as these illustrate the military's contribution to humanitarian intervention, this contribution has generally focused upon a relatively limited number of response activities, deemed to reflect the operational comparative advantages of the military. These include facilitating humanitarian access for civilian relief workers in times of conflict, protection of civilians in armed conflict, providing logistical support and lift capacity, and offering supplemental humanitarian assistance such as medical relief.

To date, the humanitarian sector has not adequately explored the full range of military capacities that could help it address aspects of the capacity challenge. The current debate about the role of the military in humanitarian action has been limited to issues pertaining to the protection of humanitarian space and the integrity of humanitarian principles. While there is understandable concern that military involvement in humanitarian action may reflect the increasing politicisation of humanitarian assistance, the interface between the military and humanitarian sector's needs, at the same time, is to be viewed from an alternative perspective. Rather than seeking to better understand processes of civil-military cooperation, coordination or integration, this chapter proposes that humanitarian and military actors need to move beyond the operational and devote more resources to improving dialogue across the two sectors to explore how the military and its changing role might support more effective humanitarian action. Indeed, despite considerable efforts to bring the humanitarian and military sectors together, there are few initiatives that have enabled both sectors to explore the value-added of military capacities to support humanitarian prevention, preparedness and response in more systematic and consistent ways.

The evolving strategic context

The humanitarian capacities challenge

The global community is faced with an ever-expanding number of humanitarian threats – their dimensions and dynamics growing in many instances exponentially. Those with humanitarian roles and responsibilities will increasingly lack the capacities and resources required to deal with such threats, and the implications of these emerging deficits will inevitably lead to increased instability and conflict, as well as impacting upon the lives and livelihoods of untold numbers around the world – East, West, North and South. As this book seeks to contrast Western and Asian experiences, can any general comments be made about their contrasting or similar experiences?

In this most fundamental sense the global community will have to prepare to address a *humanitarian capacities challenge*, requiring a different concept of humanitarian actors and actions and a different concept of risk. This challenge has to be seen in at least five contexts: (i) the changing nature of humanitarian crisis threats; (ii) political and socio-economic changes in a post-Western hegemonic age; (iii) a new vulnerability paradigm cutting across all sectors of society; (iv) emerging opportunities to offset even some of the most extreme crisis drivers; and (v) institutional constraints that will have to be overcome to ensure effective means of dealing with ever-more complex crisis drivers.

It is from this perspective that the military's role might change in ways that can meet what might be called the *humanitarian capacities challenge* – a challenge that will require a different concept of 'humanitarian actor' and 'humanitarian actions' and a different concept of 'humanitarian threat'. While one has to acknowledge that the starting points for military intervention in humanitarian crises are different, there is a growing global awareness that the military will have to have a more active role in humanitarian response. Certainly the importance of the military as 'principal providers' had been recognised in India and China and in many other parts of South and South-East Asia and the Far East for many decades. In that sense, the West is only catching up. Nevertheless, there can be little doubt that militaries around the world are reviewing their roles in anticipation of greater and more systematic engagement in humanitarian action.

A spectrum of catastrophic risks

That the numbers of disasters are growing and their impacts intensifying are well-substantiated facts. As the World Bank (2013) and others have suggested, disasters are increasing rapidly and having ever more impact on lives as well as livelihoods. The military is well versed in horizon scanning of future risks and threats, and recognises that the types, dimensions and dynamics of humanitarian crises are expected to increase, and so too might their potential role in supporting related operations (Ministry of Defence 2008).

The missing component in these analyses, however, is the increasing complexity of a growing number of such crisis drivers. The March 2011 tsunami in Japan that subsequently led to equipment failures at the Fukushima nuclear power plant which in turn resulted in a nuclear meltdown was a devastating but good example. The interface between technology, natural hazards, demographic patterns and societal choice will, in other words, be a feature of more and more humanitarian crisis drivers and humanitarian crises. In that sense there is a spectrum of catastrophic risks, from those that are recognised as risks to those that seem relatively implausible, or 'unknown'. Along that spectrum there has been a standard formula for decision makers and planners to determine and prioritise possible humanitarian threats – namely, those risks that demand more immediate attention and those that do not. That formula distinguishes between those risks that have a high probability of occurring but with relatively low impact, and those with low probability and high impact.

The formula is convenient, but flawed. In the first place, as a growing number of those involved in complexity theory are demonstrating, systems are inherently 'non-linear'. Their dynamics reflect myriad factors that in and of themselves do not ensure consistency and predictability. With that in mind, it is worth noting that many leading thinkers believe that modern complex systems research has a lot to say about the world we live in, characterised as it is by interconnectedness, networks, emergence, non-linear change, phase transitions and tipping points, intelligent actors adapting to their circumstances and each other, and systems that evolve together over time (Ramalingam 2013: 142).

Furthermore, the formula supports a tendency to look at risk in terms of crisis drivers that are known, that are already identified and for which there are established response mechanisms. In so doing, decision makers and planners limit their understanding of both the problem and the solution, and reinforce the inclination to deal with such threats in terms of their own pre-programmed responses. It is, however, becoming increasingly evident that decision makers and planners are failing to appreciate fully the types, dimensions and dynamics of future risks, and that while preparing for known threats is laudable, preparing for future threats – for the *what might be*'s – will be increasingly essential for dealing with those catastrophes at the existential end of the spectrum, and this, in turn, will call for new approaches to partnerships, to innovations and to organisations' ability to adapt.

The spectrum's dimensions

There are various ways to plot a spectrum of catastrophic risks. Degrees of impact upon affected populations, a typology of crisis drivers, geographical and economic distributions, all can be plotted on a spectrum of risks. For the purposes of this chapter, the spectrum will reflect differing degrees of complexity and uncertainty. In other words, at one end of the spectrum, 'standard' crisis drivers such as droughts, floods, earthquakes and volcanoes are recognised and definable threats. This is not to imply that they are necessarily predictable, though increasingly they are, or that their causes and impacts do not reflect complex interactions. Rather, it is to suggest that decision makers and planners recognise the destructive power of standard crisis drivers, and indeed the complicated dynamics that lead one crisis driver to trigger others, and ultimately to expose different sorts of vulnerabilities. They are attuned to such threats, and focus their attention on measures for mitigating their impacts or at least for dealing with their impacts. Hence, at one end of the disaster spectrum, those that might be regarded very broadly as the 'knowns' reflect more often than not natural disaster types that are challenging, potentially catastrophic, and for which considerable national and international efforts are made to monitor and address them.

Disasters resulting from technological causes are increasingly emerging on that spectrum of risks. Such technology-driven incidents are not new, as evidenced by the 1984 Bhopal toxic gas crisis in India or the 1986 Chernobyl nuclear accident in the Ukraine, but for the most part such 'accidents' were regarded as aberrant phenomena. Only recently have the complexity of their sources and the consequences of their impact resulted in what might be regarded as a fixed point on a spectrum of catastrophes and a reflection of 'normal life'. The very nature of technology, as with many crisis drivers, too often remains confined to the analysis of the technical expert.

Moving along the spectrum, more and more points reflect an increasing awareness of complexity. Pandemics are a case in point. Their cross-sectorial impacts are appreciated more and more as well as the multidimensional interventions that will be required to anticipate and address them. Similarly, the link between nuclear tailings and climate change is gaining a degree of resonance amongst crisis analysts, and here, too, the potential dynamics and dimensions of their impact are slowly beginning to be seen as a multi-dimensional problem that requires multidimensional solutions (Hobbes 2011). These sorts of complex threats and their implications are consistent with the sorts of threats that the military take into account in their longer-term planning.

Towards the extreme end of the spectrum

Multidimensional problems and solutions become even more evident as one approaches the more extreme end of the spectrum of catastrophic risks. Towards that end, a few examples might well demonstrate the range of such risks as well as their plausibility. The risks that are noted below are existential. In other words, the criteria for selection include the possibility that each of these complex interactive crisis drivers could leave in their wake death in the millions and debilitating, long-term destruction of livelihoods. In so saying, one needs to be mindful that 'existential risks' are distinct from 'global endurable risks', for the former is where humankind as a whole is dangerously imperilled, and where the latter has impacts of horrific proportions, though not necessarily globally uniform. Potential crises include solar super storms, viruses, artificial intelligence, nanotechnology, climate change, cybernetic failure, nuclear weapons and mega-tsunamis.

As noted at the outset of this chapter, if one looks at the patterns of humanitarian crises, it is evident that the types of crisis drivers, their dimensions and dynamics are increasing, in various ways, exponentially. In the words of one UN body, even now the ripple effects of recent intensive disasters have contributed to a world viewed more and more as an intersecting set of disasters where it is increasingly difficult to separate cause from consequences. Many future disasters will form part of a challenging terrain of improbable and unpredictable events (United Nations 2013: 237). None of this is to suggest that the sorts of existential risks noted above are inevitable. They are plausible, and that plausibility is reinforced by scientific opinion. The purpose of noting these, however, is not to assess the extent to which they are predictable or inevitable, but rather to see to what extent the nature of future humanitarian threats and solutions can be better addressed through closer partnerships between traditional and non-traditional actors, in particular the role of the military.

In the case of Western militaries, as operational demands diminish post-Afghanistan, increasingly complex changes in the strategic and operational environment and the subsequent interaction and spillover of crises and crisis drivers are likely to see the military redefining its role in humanitarian action – with that in mind, the timing is now essential to ensure that cross-sector interaction to support more effective humanitarian action is much more systematic. Such systemisation will be needed to ensure that the military with its attention to standard operating procedures is able to ensure that there are methods in place not only to respond to crises, but also to engage with other potential collaborators in ways that are predictable and consistent. Similarly, those who have not engaged in any consistent way with the military – be they, for example, international or non-governmental organisations or those from the private sector – will also wish to understand in more predictable ways the strategic and operational resources that the military can bring to humanitarian activities.

When it comes to most militaries in the West, there is growing evidence that efforts to promote greater systematic interaction are increasing. That said, the stimulus for exploring ways to promote greater systematic interaction stems paradoxically from the number of recent incidents in which 'both sides' – military and non-military – find serendipitously that they need to work together. Be it the 2014 Ebola crisis or the 2010 floods in Pakistan, there is an emerging 'habit of cooperation' between the two. In all likelihood, this trend will lead to a greater inclination to seek more systematic and coherent ways to collaborate. This will in part stem from the new and expanding types of crises that both sides will have to face, and by the fact that the military in the West might need to seek a range of different roles to survive, and that the traditional humanitarian sector might need to work with the military to have any chance of fulfilling its own functions in an increasingly complex humanitarian world.

Structural and systemic challenges

One of the challenges for those dealing with the complexities and uncertainties that mark the catastrophic risk spectrum is that the sorts of perceptions and processes required to deal with such risks are all too often regarded as 'impractical' and 'academic'. Yet, for even hard-headed practitioners in the private sector, it is less the abstract nature of catastrophic risks that blinds them to such threats, and more the institutional realities that lead them to 'remain largely reactive, fragmented and self-interested rather than strategic, integrated and public spirited' (World Economic Forum 2010).

The sorts of institutional realities or, in other words, the structural and systemic challenges that emerge when dealing with catastrophic risks are varied but very familiar. They all too often hamper initiatives to collaborate, limit efforts to understand the value-added of potential partners, hinder innovation and innovative practices, and frequently result in disjointed and uncoordinated responses at the expense of the crisis affected.

From the perspective of structural and systemic challenges, there is, for example, a persistent concern about the nature and utility of speculating about future threats and opportunities. Practitioners – be they private sector, humanitarian or from the military – are reluctant in some very fundamental ways to venture into the 'unknown'. While some private-sector organisations specialise in longer-term speculation, as do various military establishments, the application of 'speculation' is normally more consistent with what is already known and with deeply entrenched standard operating procedures and repertoires. To that extent, the military, like the private sector, is more readily prone to 'upgrade' their equipment as well as operations based upon a longer-term timeframe than the vast majority of organisations in the humanitarian sector. In this context, it is not by happenstance that this chapter began with a demonstration of AFRICOM's role in strategic planning for SADC.

In the humanitarian sector, however, there appears to be an inherent reluctance to look beyond the immediate. In no small part the art of speculation, an attempt to be sensitive to the *what might be*'s, is too often confused with the perceived need to predict, and if one cannot predict, then speculation, per se, is a poor use of organisational time. In bureaucratic contexts where evidence-based criteria dominate so much of the thinking and subsequent action, anticipation is all too often intentionally short term in order to avoid the risk of being wrong. There, too, is the concern that by suggesting plausible, longer-term risks and the need to prepare, the public will panic and overreact. While a growing body of evidence suggests the contrary, the norm is to avoid creating possible anxieties.

The role of experts, essential for dealing with highly technical problems, can paradoxically limit understanding by interpreting events and solutions through unnecessarily narrow lenses. Such views are in various ways sustained by the screening devices inherent in most organisational systems that limit the flow of information perceived as discrepant or inconsistent. In a related vein, there is also a tendency towards collaboration that is self-referential. The adage about 'the like mind', while positive in some instances, also suggests a tendency to engage with those who share similar perspectives, methodologies and 'language'. These self-evident truths inhibit organisational responsiveness in various ways. Nevertheless, they reflect barriers that can be reduced. Without embarking on that process, the full potential of effective engagement for dealing with future risks will inevitably suffer. Even worse, effective engagement of the sort that will be required to meet future risks may never come adequately into play.

Embedding a culture of anticipation

This chapter assumes that greater cross-sector engagement will be essential to deal with the sorts of threats suggested in the proposed spectrum of risks, in particular cross-sector engagement related to the relationship between the military and humanitarian sector. Ways to move towards such engagement could include measures to help organisations be more adept at dealing with the *what might be*'s. Towards that end, there are five measures that could support organisations in becoming more 'fit for the future' and, in so doing, make them more willing to go beyond conventional institutional boundaries. Indeed, of these measures, the majority are inherently characteristic of the military and its institutional DNA: (i) anticipation; (ii) adaptation; (iii) collaboration; (iv) innovation; and (v) promoting strategic leadership.

There is a growing acceptance across the humanitarian sector that much greater time and effort must be devoted to longer-term strategic thinking and becoming more inherently anticipatory. The starting point begins with a change in *mindset* through strategic leadership to foster an organisational ethos of speculation. Mindset change can be enhanced by devoting time, for example, to horizon scanning, scenario development and simulation exercises. Such techniques can provide the conceptual space that is needed not only to identify future risks, but also to underscore the importance of such thinking for the organisation.

'There is a drawer that is marked strategies', remarked an official from a major US-based NGO; 'It is the lowest drawer in the filing cabinet, and rarely gets opened'. It is generally accepted that strategies, per se, are often regarded as fodder for periodic executive board meetings or an institutional requirement that needs to be fulfilled at least every five years. The results of such strategies are seen all too rarely as 'living documents', let alone statements about objectives and benchmarks that directly impact upon operations – the programmes and projects of humanitarian organisations.

Enhancing the adaptive capacities of an organisation can be approached from a variety of perspectives. There are, however, three essential starting points. The first has to do with an organisational commitment to regular reviews of longer-term strategic objectives, focusing upon anticipated changes in the operating environment. A second characteristic of the adaptive organisation

involves regular reviews of operational or programmatic activities against strategic objectives and related benchmarks. Third, the adaptive organisation is intensely interactive.

Dealing with crises will increasingly require expertise that reflects multi-sector perspectives. The self-referential nature of many within the humanitarian sector often results in very narrow networks, and profoundly hampers the ability to identify future risks and potential solutions to reduce such risks. Successful collaboration is based upon a number of factors, including: the need for a clear understanding of the respective and often complicated motives and objectives; and the need for complementary rather than duplication of comparative advantages or 'value-added'.

One of the critical challenges for the humanitarian community is to find the capacity to identify risks and seek ways to mitigate or eliminate them. 'Currently, humanitarian organizations – responsible for implementing projects over a relatively short time frame [usually 12 to 18 months] – have little time to observe and reflect on the profile and changing needs of their customers and on the efficacy of their implementation of goods and services' (Kent and Crabtree 2013). To prepare for future crises, new innovations and innovative practices will be of vital importance.

Key to the effectiveness of each of the factors detailed above is the issue of strategic leadership. Indeed, essential to strategic leadership is the ability to promote a collaborative rather than an authoritarian structure. In light of what is needed to be a more anticipatory organisation, sensitive to the *what might be*'s, strategic leadership is ultimately about promoting a collaborative rather than an authoritarian structure. Strategic leadership, therefore, is not about having answers, but instead about the ability to release collective creativity and capacity, or 'the capacity to release the collective intelligence and insight of a group of organisations' (Binney et al. 2005). While many current models of successful leadership are based on projecting certainty and confidence, real strategic leadership involves a more experimental process in which a leader does not provide categorical answers. In various ways, this attitude from a military perspective is beginning to seep into Western military thinking, as reflected in the North Atlantic Treaty Organization's (NATO) 2013 CIVAID Action Plan. That plan acknowledges the need to be more collaborative than has been the case to date, and accepts the importance of a 'comprehensive approach' that is underpinned by a commitment to acknowledge 'other actors' interests' (NATO 2013).

The five competencies that are likely to enhance organisational capacities for exploring potential risks, risk reduction and preparedness approaches are in and of themselves no guarantee that the complexities of the future can be adequately anticipated, let alone addressed. Yet, organisations that fail to take the implications of such competencies into account would appear to be too stuck in the past to be able to deal with the uncertainties and complexities of the future. Here, the related skills and capacities of the military might provide a logical case in point from which lessons can be drawn.

The military-humanitarian dimension

When attempting to describe the perceived motives and intentions of two large and diffuse institutions such as the military and humanitarian sectors, one cannot emphasise too strongly that each in various ways encompasses an enormous range of differences, not only in terms of size, objectives and needs, but also geographically, experientially, culturally and politically. Nevertheless, there are certain elements in both of these sectors that allow for general propositions to be explored about potential capabilities in a humanitarian context.

This chapter suggests that the military, amongst other 'non-traditional' humanitarian actors, has a considerable amount to offer when it comes to preventing, preparing for and responding to humanitarian threats and crises. In that sense, there has been considerable work looking at the ways that the military and humanitarian sectors do and should interact and collaborate more effectively in dealing with humanitarian issues. It is generally recognised that the military has a range of capacities that might offer potential support for dealing with humanitarian threats and crises, and it is also recognised that there are serious limitations when it comes to effective engagement. In seeking to move beyond recent debate, this chapter seeks to propose preliminary steps for meeting what is a humanitarian capacities challenge, through more systematic interaction across the military and humanitarian sectors.

The relationship between military and humanitarian organisations has traditionally been marked by a set of stereotypes that remain difficult to overcome for many within the respective sectors, and indeed beyond. Many of these reflect Western attitudes about the traditional roles of the military, the inherent conflict between the roles of the military and humanitarian principles, and a perceived difference in objectives and institutional styles. Yet, these stereotypes all too often are insensitive to different situational contexts, fail to take into account cultural and geopolitical differences and all too often ignore the evolution occurring in both sectors not only in the Western world, but more globally as well.

In this context, it is worth bearing in mind that it is only relatively recently that the perceptible decline of Western hegemonic influence in the humanitarian aid sector has begun to reveal the fact that the militaries of a large number of crisis-prone countries regard the military as 'first providers'. The regions of South and South-East Asia as well as China generally assume that the military will be the first in to provide aid. There is no doubt that humanitarian organisations are confronted with extremely complex operations, often under trying conditions. The military also face complexity in their operations, but their approaches to programme management often result in more focused action. It is in that context that a former US Agency for International Development (USAID) administrator remarked in 2008 that he was tired of calls for greater coordination and simply wished that humanitarian organisations could be more effective at programme management.

Poor programme management partially reflects the lack of strategic vision that should guide humanitarian operational activities, but it also reflects poor information management and ineffective operation integration. In a relief operation that should be managed as a single programme, for example, it is not unusual to find food and health inputs being administered separately, with little recognition of their inherent relationship to one another. This extends to the issue of incompatible assessment tools and numerous layers of administration for what should be treated as a simple task (Kent and Ratcliffe 2008: 36).

From a humanitarian perspective these sorts of criticisms underscore what many in the humanitarian sector perceive as the military's insensitivity when dealing with humanitarian crises – particularly in the context of engaging with local communities. This criticism is compounded by what also is perceived as an inherent contradiction between the roles of the military as part of government's pursuit of national self-interest and the humanitarian's abiding concern with principles that seek to promote assistance in a neutral, impartial and independent manner. While few would deny that the latter is all too often aspirational and frequently thwarted by operational realities, the humanitarian argument is that the aspiration is in and of itself essential to pursue as a value, and also provides basic protection for the aid worker by disassociating him or her from the security objectives of the military.

Yet, there, too, are other issues that separate the two sectors. One is the sheer size of most militaries when compared with the humanitarian sector. When the military does provide support for humanitarian endeavours, there is a sense on the part of many humanitarians that they are being swamped by the comparative enormity of the human and material resources of the military as well as its infrastructure. Since crises in Rwanda in 1995 through to Kosovo four years later, and subsequently in Haiti, Iraq and Afghanistan, there has been an abiding concern amongst a large proportion of the humanitarian sector that they will be seen as secondary players in comparison with military weight and the attention that this can generate from local and national leaders in affected states. The issue of infrastructure opens up another array of negative comparisons. The humanitarian sector, for example, finds its own machinery of decision making and operational prioritisation relatively slow and cumbersome when compared with the military.

At the same time, there is a degree of resentment – certainly among Western NGOs – that in all too many instances when the military suggests or agrees to collaboration, it does so with an air of condescension and a presumption that 'getting together' means meeting at a place that more often than not is military headquarters and not a mutually acceptable neutral ground. This issue was introduced in a NATO Allied Command Transformation programme in May 2013 by a senior representative of a participating NGO. This reality was acknowledged by a majority of those NATO military participants attending the meeting, and was recognised as an issue that had to be resolved.

That said, the military is nevertheless regarded as having a limited, though acceptable, place in humanitarian action in various ways. Often the military, when compared with other authorities such as local police, find themselves 'a preferred option', a more respected provider of assistance than many local authorities[1] (Kent and Crabtree 2013). In situations of conflict, UN Peace-keepers' roles in protecting civilians in armed conflict are deemed essential, and a role that falls well outside the competencies of the humanitarians. There are conditions, too, in which that role extends to national militaries where access to the crisis affected can only be gained through military intervention. So, too, do most humanitarians accept the military's logistics capacities as an asset in certain circumstances, though even here there are serious differences within the humanitarian sector.

There are also instances, principally when it comes to crises created by natural hazards, that the role of the military is deemed more acceptable. The military's relatively rapid response to the 2013 Typhoon Yolanda (international name Haiyan) in the Philippines, including US and British naval involvement, the 2010 Haitian earthquake, foreign as well as domestic militaries' involvement in the 2005 Pakistan earthquake and subsequent floods five years later are indicative examples. Yet, for many in the humanitarian sector (certainly when it comes to those representing Western institutions), these are the exceptions that prove a more general rule – namely, the inherent incompatibility between the military and humanitarian sectors.

From a Western military perspective, this incompatibility has until relatively recently cohered with the military's own view of its role. Humanitarian action is not the military's 'primary function', and certainly at the outset of this project it was apparent that at least at senior levels there was considerable reluctance to institutionalise humanitarian response within the military's mission. It was seen as diluting the Western military's traditional focus. Current definitions of military objectives had until recently been built around a rather narrow conception of national security, resulting in a relatively limited interest in taking on humanitarian issues. The end result remains to date that there are pockets of effective programmes, but there is little that is standardised beyond very limited areas. Asian militaries, on the other hand, are expected to be prepared to engage in humanitarian response when crises strike.

Those *limited areas* since HFP's[2] initial efforts to capture the relationship between military and humanitarian sectors have expanded in various ways. In the first place, it has become increasingly evident that military roles from non-Western perspectives have taken on a more integrated approach in terms of national and regional humanitarian policies. In countries such as India the military has traditionally been involved in emergency response. Now, however, more and more countries are using their military as actors of first rather than last resort (Fischer 2015). This takes various forms and covers aspects of crisis prevention, preparedness and emergency response. These are deemed core activities alongside conventional military obligations, and are not activities undertaken in isolation.

Of equal significance is the growing number of arrangements in which the military can support the humanitarian requirements of another country. The

ASEAN Treaty amply demonstrates this sort of arrangement where in principle, member states can call upon the military forces of others in the region to assist in humanitarian response. To date, there appears to be only one instance when a request was made, but it is very evident that ASEAN member states' training programmes suggest a clear cross-border approach to humanitarian support. Regional arrangements such as that of ASEAN are not new, and there are variations of such arrangements in Europe, Latin America and Africa.

Beyond such regional arrangements there is an emerging reality that the very concept of national security, too, is changing. The disruptive impact of a pandemic can, if taken to its logical conclusion, see large segments of societies descend into riots and disorder, across borders and across regions and continents. In this sense, the military – though by no means immune to the impact of such crisis drivers – is the ultimate safety net for humanitarian action.

In the context of an agenda for future military-humanitarian interaction, this chapter proposes six key considerations. In the first place it is important to recognise that the roles of many militaries around the world are changing due in no small part to a changing perception of national security, including the relationship between natural hazards across borders and regional and national security. Second, there is a growing awareness that militaries from different nations, principally within regional contexts, will have to collaborate to ensure enhanced response capacities in dealing with severe crisis situations. This growing military awareness does not seem, however, to have enhanced communications between militaries and local and international humanitarian actors to a level where collaboration and cooperation are automatic responses when it comes to planning or operations.

Following from this point, a third issue is that institutional differences within the humanitarian sector have to be taken into account. There are, on the whole, considerable differences when it comes to perceptions of the military between those humanitarians that are in the UN system, those in the Red Cross movement, principally the International Committee of the Red Cross, traditional Western NGOs and non-Western humanitarian organisations. These differences will have to be better understood when trying to promote mutual understanding. Traditional humanitarian actors and the military in various ways will have to have a better appreciation of what can be called each other's 'language', or, in other words, a greater appreciation of the 'motives', driving forces, terms and processes that distinguish different organisations and types of organisation.

In a related vein is a fourth and essential point – namely, that there has to be a far greater understanding and appreciation of the value-added that different types of organisation can bring to the humanitarian table. Despite forums to share information in operational contexts and those intended to discuss overall policy commonalities and differences, there too little focus on respective value-added beyond immediate operational needs. Issues such as approaches to strategic planning, innovations and innovative practices, surge capacities and ways of engaging local communities are not considered in any systematic and consistent manner by either side.

Yet, despite poor understanding between the two sectors about issues defined as 'language' and 'value-added', there are a variety of positive initiatives that humanitarian practitioners are undertaking with the military and private sector that suggest a growing awareness of the importance of engagement, particularly when it comes to issues such as pandemics and major environmental catastrophes. Hence, a fifth point is for both sectors to acknowledge such developments and find ways to build upon them.

One route for greater collaboration that both sides might wish to explore concerns cross-border plans and planning mechanisms. Although it is increasingly evident that major crisis drivers such as pandemics, floods, hurricanes and cyclones are not constrained by borders, there is a dearth of relevant plans and planning mechanisms that bring the military and humanitarian sectors into systematic and consistent contact. A sixth point, therefore, is that in light of ever more complex crisis threats and crises, an increasingly important setting for testing collaboration could be in that relatively underdeveloped realm of regional planning and response.

Conclusion

In various ways many parts of the humanitarian sector and the military find themselves in a shared, though not necessarily recognised, space. For those with humanitarian roles and responsibilities, that space might well be reflected in the term 'resilience', and for a growing number of the military, preventative action as reflected in stabilisation activities or what had been described as the US Phase Zero approach. It is a potentially common space that could be the basis for providing greater attention to anticipating risks and their potential consequences, and a space in which the military might increasingly find itself.

To date, that space has not led to any systematic means for sharing sector perspectives, let alone for looking for strategic synergies. Nevertheless, there are signs that increasingly the time might be right to explore ways to foster more coherent dialogue across the military (and other 'non-traditional' actors) and humanitarian sectors, and that there is a growing awareness that their respective contributions together might serve to provide more effective anticipatory, adaptive and innovative approaches for dealing with an ever growing spectrum of humanitarian risks.

The range of catastrophic risks is growing, with the types, dimensions and dynamics of humanitarian threats increasing, in some instances, exponentially. While this is recognised across the military and humanitarian sectors, there is very little evidence that adequate attention is being given to such threats in consistent and systematic ways. Both sectors are increasingly aware of the complexities and uncertainties that face the international community when it comes to crisis threats. That awareness focuses upon how such trends may spill over into their respective areas of interest and responsibility. At the same time, there are few indications that the individual sectors are focusing on such complex threats consistently and in ways that reflect adjustments in their strategic objectives or procedures. Those engaged in preparation for longer-term crisis threats is limited though slowly expanding, as is the appetite and knowledge for such preparedness thinking. Nevertheless, unless this spectrum is further widened and deepened, the sorts of anticipatory and adaptive capacities that are needed will remain sporadic and incoherent.

The sorts of capacities that the military, amongst other actors, have could enhance the abilities of those with humanitarian roles and responsibilities to be more anticipatory, innovative and strategic in their humanitarian approaches, and ways to bring together such capacities increasingly will have to become a global priority consistent with the status given to the 2016 World Humanitarian Summit and the revised Millennium Development Goals and Hyogo Framework for Action.

Organisational constraints continue to block greater attention to the potential consequences of an ever widening spectrum of catastrophic risks, and these constraints are generally reflected in most organisations by a lack of a speculative ethos, poor partnering, limited attention to transformative innovations and a lack of strategic vision and objectives.

'Language' is a major barrier to effective interaction and collaboration across the military and humanitarian sectors. The issue of language includes the cultural norms, institutional objectives, procedures and processes that are unique to each. There is little understanding about the 'value-added' that each sector could bring to crisis prevention, preparedness and response. For the most part, perspectives by each sector about the others remain mired in stereotypes that take little account of contextual transitions and the full range of potential capacities. As increasing efforts are made by governments around the world to be more effective when it comes to humanitarian action, there is a substantial difference emerging between the attitudes of those non-Western humanitarian actors to their national militaries when compared with the attitudes of Western humanitarian actors. In the former case, there appears to be a more natural relationship between humanitarian actors and the military, though here, too, there is not a full appreciation of the military's value-added.

There are a growing number of events and initiatives that bring together the military and the humanitarian sectors, amongst other sectors at country and regional levels, to simulate ways in which they might collaborate when it comes to dealing with more complex risks such as pandemics. Though increasing, such events are isolated and often sporadic, and are not supported in ways that appear consistent or systematic.

Indeed, there are also a variety of institutions that appear willing to consider longer-term, more complex and uncertain risks, such as the World Economic Forum, the UNOCHA, ECOWAS and the NGO Start Network. Yet, few have looked at such potential threats in any consistent way or have the necessary capacity to do so.

New incentives have to be put in place to erode some of the persistent organisational constraints that inhibit anticipatory and adaptive behaviours. This applies to both sectors when it comes to looking to the sorts of crisis drivers that will inevitably affect their institutional survival and organisational objectives. Efforts to enhance cross-sector collaboration and interaction across the military and humanitarian sectors will continue to be piecemeal and will falter as long as there are not means and measures in place to provide a better understanding about the sectors' respective 'language' and value-added. There are a growing number of organisations and networks that could potentially promote understanding about 'language' and comparative value-added within and across the three sectors, and in pursuing measures to promote greater understanding of these, initiatives have to be sensitive to the types of cultural norms and perceptions that make attitudes about the military, humanitarian and private sectors geographically different.

Notes

1 Based upon interviews with military contingents in West Africa and in South-East Asia, this appears to be the case. In a very frank interview with representatives of the Economic Community of West African States (ECOWAS) Standby Force, it was stated that 'the perceptions of affected populations was that soldiers were "rough men", and yet the police were even less well regarded than the military. At least one of the advantages of the military is that when it comes to humanitarian operations, they spend more time and had a clearer idea about the terrain of an operation than their humanitarian counterparts. Soldiers inevitably have to understand operating environments, and when it comes to disasters, they not only have a better idea of the terrain, but also of the people who live in those areas' (Kent and Crabtree 2013: 25).

2 The Humanitarian Futures Programme (HFP) was an independent policy research programme based at King's College London, which strives to act as a catalyst within the humanitarian sector to stimulate greater interest in more strategic approaches to the changing types, dimensions and dynamics of future humanitarian crises. Through a wide-ranging programme of research, policy engagement and technical assistance, HFP promotes new ways of planning, collaborating and innovating so that organisations with humanitarian roles and responsibilities can deal with future humanitarian threats more effectively.

Bibliography

Binney, G., Wilke, G. and Williams, C. (2005) *Living Leadership: A Practical Guide for Ordinary Heroes*, London: Prentice Hall.

Fischer, E. (2015) *Disaster Response: The Role of a Humanitarian Military*, http://www.army-technology.com (accessed 20 March 2015).

Hobbes, C. (2011) 'Current and Future Risks Posed by Unprotected Radioactive Waste Sites in Central Asia', Contributing paper to Chapter 2 of the 2011*Global Assessment Report on Disaster Risk Reduction*, http://www.preventionweb.net/english/hyogo/gar/2011/en/bgdocs/Hobbs_%202010%20TS.pdf (accessed 8 January 2015).

Kent, R. and Crabtree, C. (2013) *The Virtuous Triangle and the Fourth Dimension: The Humanitarian, Private and Military Sectors in a Fragile World*, Humanitarian Futures Programme.

Kent, R. and Ratcliffe, J. (2008) *Responding to Catastrophes: US Innovation in a Vulnerable World*, Washington: Centre for Strategic and International Studies.

Metcalfe, V. (2011) 'Friend or Foe? Military Intervention in Libya', HPG Briefing Note, London: Overseas Development Institute.

Ministry of Defence (2008) *Disaster Relief Operations*, Joint Doctrine Publication 3-52, http://www.gov.uk/government/uploads/system/uploads/attachment_data/file/43340/jdp3522nded.pdf (accessed 8 January 2015).

n.a. (2013) *Interviews with representatives of the ECOWAS Standby Force, Randolph Kent and Charlotte Crabtree*, Abuja, Nigeria, 18 April.

NATO (2013) (Unclassified), *CIVAID Action Plan*.

Ramalingam, B. (2013) *Aid on the Edge of Chaos*, Oxford: Oxford University Press.

United Nations (2013) *United Nations International Strategy for Disaster Risk Re-education, Global Assessment Report on Disaster Risk Reduction – 2013*, New York.

Whiting, M. (2012) 'Military and Humanitarian Cooperation in Air Operations in Haiti', *Humanitarian Exchange*, No. 53, London: Overseas Development Institute.

World Bank (2013) *World Development Report*, http://siteresources.worldbank.org/EXTNWDR2013/Resources/8258024-1320950747192/8260293-1322665883147/WDR_2013_Report.pdf (accessed 8 January 2015).

World Economic Forum (2010) *Global Agenda Council on Catastrophic Risks (GAC), Creating a Better Architecture for Global Risk Management of Catastrophic Risks*.

3 Post-conflict reconstruction

Concepts, issues and challenges

Alpaslan Özerdem

Introduction

In the context of war-torn areas the term post-conflict reconstruction is often used interchangeably to indicate three major realms of post-conflict activity, namely the rebuilding of the physical infrastructure and essential government functions and services; capacity building to improve the efficiency and effectiveness of existing institutions; and structural reform within the political, economic, social and security sectors. When conceptualising reconstruction it is important to bear in mind that it is fundamentally a developmental challenge, taking place in special 'post-conflict' circumstances, which involves the full range of integrated socio-economic and political activities and processes (Barakat 2005). However, it is also important to bear in mind that 'post-conflict' is itself a misnomer, as in contemporary contexts it is increasingly difficult to assume that there would be a total cessation of political violence and armed conflict. For the purposes of this chapter, though, the term 'post-conflict reconstruction' will be considered as a process initiated by a peace accord, agreement or ceasefire, despite full acknowledgement that the term 'post-conflict' is unfortunately often only in the minds of donors and politicians.

In common with other key terms such as 'relief', 'development' and 'peace building', the definition of post-conflict reconstruction is imprecise and often driven by its source. Principally, this is because what is considered to be reconstruction will depend on the agenda of the particular 'agencies' concerned – that is, the interaction of the institutions and actors involved. There has been an ever increasing involvement of the military in post-conflict reconstruction over the last two decades. The impact of civil-military relations on programme planning and implementation has become a significant characteristic of peace-building environments. This has been apparent particularly in post-9/11 reconstruction environments such as Afghanistan and Iraq. An analysis of the agencies involved would therefore provide a better understanding of how ideas are marshalled into objectives and how objectives are translated into the practice of reconstruction. In addition to the questions around who sets the post-conflict reconstruction agenda and what it entails, the debate over the divide between relief and reconstruction also tends to focus on the timing of those activities, though experience in conflict-affected countries shows that relief and recon-struction are not sequential phases and need to be undertaken simultaneously.

There is a need for a review of how reconstruction is considered by different agencies, including the World Bank and United Nations (UN). This forms the starting point for discussion in the first section of this chapter. The chapter will then set out the theoretical conceptualisation of the reconstruction process by exploring what it is and what it is not, in relation to other key processes of relief, development and peace building. In the second section, the focus will be on key post-conflict reconstruction challenges, including preventing the resumption of violence, avoiding a solely goal-based approach, prioritising and setting objectives according to the needs of conflict-affected societies, appro-priately timing reconstruction, linking relief and reconstruction activities, enabling a participatory environment, 'winning hearts and minds' of conflict-affected communities, and the coordination and mobilisation of adequate resources.

The analysis of post-conflict reconstruction will be undertaken through a critique of what the liberal peace agenda claims to be its primary values, qualities and principles, and how they can be translated into practice. The scope and characteristics of 'post-conflict reconstruction' differ considerably according to whether this process is led by national or international actors. However, the chapter is primarily concerned with what the international community does in the name of post-conflict reconstruction. The way that Western militaries have become agents of the liberal peace agenda will be investigated with reference to 'social' military transformation. In the conclusion, future trajectories of post-conflict reconstruction and emerging challenges and opportunities will be addressed.

Post-conflict reconstruction and peace building

The history of the use of post-conflict reconstruction as a major international peace-supporting process is relatively short. During the Cold War period, the UN and the broader international community paid most attention to humani-tarian relief, peacemaking and peacekeeping activities. The term 'post-conflict reconstruction' rarely appeared in international security debates, except with reference to a few programmes implemented in the post-colonial, post-World War II and post-communism eras, such as the Marshall Plan for Western Europe after World War II. It was only at the end of the 1990s that the concept of post-conflict reconstruction emerged as a distinct activity. As the need for a more comprehensive understanding of the peace-rehabilitation-development nexus in post-conflict societies was recognised, this triggered active discussions on the theoretical and practical aspects of post-conflict reconstruction. In particular, the World Bank's publication *Framework for World Bank Involvement in Post-Conflict Reconstruction* and its launch of the Post-Conflict Fund in 1997 provided significant momentum for the emergence of post-conflict reconstruction as a core aspect of international peace building. In the 2000s, post-conflict reconstruction became one of the central concepts in international intervention, and the UN created its Peacebuilding Commission, which proposes integrated strategies for post-conflict peace building and recovery.

The Western military interventions in Bosnia and Herzegovina in the mid-1990s and Kosovo at the end of the decade were highly significant in the transformation of the post-conflict reconstruction agenda. For example, such North Atlantic Treaty Organization (NATO)-led military missions as Implementation Force (IFOR) and Stabilisation Force (SFOR) in Bosnia and Kosovo Force (KFOR) were closely concerned with creating a security environment in which post-conflict reconstruction could take place. Western militaries and non-governmental organisations (NGOs) explored innovative ways of cooperating. In these environments, the provision of relief and development assistance was important for the continuation of constructive relationships between local populations and international military deployments. This symbiotic relationship continues to form one of the key features of contemporary post-conflict reconstruction efforts.

Peace building was first defined in *An Agenda for Peace* as 'action to identify and support structures which will tend to solidify peace in order to avoid a relapse into conflict' (UNSG 1992: 21). During the last two decades, the scope of peace building has been widened to include the political, economic, social and psychological aspects of such activities in order to 'shift centres of gravity' away from violent protagonists. It is important that peace building is considered a process, rather than a goal, and not from the perspective of merely achieving a 'negative' peace, which would only indicate the ending of armed conflict (Dayton and Kriesberg 2009). Rather, it should be understood from the perspective of a 'positive' and sustainable peace, able to ensure security as well as socio-economic, structural, political and cultural stability, and reduce the likelihood of relapse into or the continuation of violence. As a note, the chapter follows Galtung's (1990) definition of positive peace – the removal of structural and cultural violence – and acknowledges that the concept has played a significant role in evolving the context of peace building and broadly includes any activity designed to prevent and help resolve violent conflict.

In order to achieve this, it is important to bear in mind that peace building is a multi-faceted and multi-agency process accompanied by a wide range of challenges, from the creation of a positive security environment and functional governance structures, to responding to the basic needs of war-affected communities. The inter-linkages between peace building and the security environment are important. Without a secure environment it would be almost impossible to undertake comprehensive peace-building efforts, but at the same time, peace-building efforts in general are likely to play a pivotal role in sustaining that security environment. Peace building also encompasses processes ranging from micro-level changes in the opinions and behaviour of communities affected by conflict to macro-level institutional changes that address the structural causes of conflict (Chimni 2003; Lilly 2004; Luckham 2004; Paris 2004). However, the liberal peace doctrine, with its two main elements of 'democracy' and 'market economy', has come to define the main contour of peace-building work by the international community – regardless of the extent to which 'post-conflict' environments around the world differ from each other (Ginty and Richmond 2009).

With a liberal peace agenda in mind, the overall objectives of post-conflict reconstruction by the World Bank are set as the facilitation of the transition to sustainable peace after hostilities have ceased and to support economic and social development. To achieve these objectives a successful reconstruction strategy must focus on: investment in key productive sectors, good governance, repairing physical infrastructure, rebuilding key social frameworks and normalising financial borrowing arrangements (World Bank 1998: 14). The UN, on the other hand, considers post-conflict peace building to be a process in which the following would form the main undertakings: 'disarming the previously warring parties and the restoration of order, the custody and possible destruction of weapons, repatriating refugees, advisory and training support for security personnel, monitoring of elections, advancing efforts to protect human rights, reforming or strengthening governmental institutions and promoting formal and informal processes of political participation' (Boutros-Ghali 1995: 11). This definition is structured around sectors rather than focusing on what reconstruction would mean as an overall goal. It proposes key undertakings in a post-conflict environment as signposts for planning and implementation. It is a manual of what possible areas would need to be covered in order to lay the foundations for sustainable peace building. It is also important to note that this definition is redolent of those structures proposed for nation-state building. This is unsurprising, since reconstruction has become the new post-Cold War tool of nation-state building interventions from a liberal peace perspective (Bachler 2004).

For example, the cases of Iraq and Afghanistan have shown that without a secure environment, reconstruction becomes practically impossible. In fact, the US military has learnt a hard lesson that the first phases of an intervention can be relatively straightforward, but the post-conflict (phase IV) stages can turn into a quagmire. There are a number of reasons why the experience of post-conflict reconstruction has resulted in drastic failure for Western powers. The most significant of these reasons is the manner in which the liberal peace agenda is enforced externally in a top-down manner on such environments.

Overall, as the preceding definitions show, the World Bank and UN channel their reconstruction efforts through a range of different directions and activities. While the World Bank places emphasis on assisting economic recovery and normalisation, the UN emphasises the importance of political reform. More importantly, what post-conflict reconstruction needs to avoid is a return to the status quo of the pre-war society. It is important to recognise that post-conflict reconstruction encompasses a range of activities in an integrated process designed not only to reactivate economic and social development, but also to create a peaceful environment that will prevent a relapse into violence (Mason and Meernik 2009). Accordingly, many aspects of post-conflict reconstruction overlap with issues related to conflict resolution and conflict transformation

(Barakat and Zych 2009) and post-conflict reconstruction is sometimes referred to as 'post-conflict peace building'.

The preceding discussion on post-conflict reconstruction and peace building indicates that the processes identified as critical to both endeavours are similar in each case, and it is possible to categorise them under four main areas. First is the *security-sector reform*, which includes disarmament, demobilisation and reintegration of former combatants, dealing with the availability of small arms and light weapons, and creating a new police force and army. Second, *governance*, which incorporates undertakings such as the establishment of a transitional government, constitutional reform, organisation of elections and respect for democracy, human rights, and the rule of law. Third, *socio-economic recovery*, which deals with the challenges of providing relief aid to vulnerable groups, reintegration of displaced populations, rebuilding of infrastructure and services, and economic revitalisation. Finally, *justice and reconciliation*, which seek to deal with the distrust and psychological trauma prevalent among communities affected by conflict (Miall et al. 1999: 203).

Post-conflict reconstruction experience shows that the military is the lead actor in the context of security-related activities. The military works with a number of civilian actors closely in the implementation of security reform programmes such as the demobilisation and reintegration of former combatants. In fact, the effectiveness of the military-civilian partnership in such programmes becomes an important litmus test for ensuring successful outcomes. Cooperation between these actors is also demanded in other aspects of post-conflict reconstruction. In contemporary contexts, the military is often involved in the facilitation of humanitarian protection, economic recovery and the rebuilding of the physical environment. The military might even take the lead, as was the case in Afghanistan and Iraq, in areas where the security environment does not permit civilian agencies to operate.

The four phases of post-conflict reconstruction

Implementing reconstruction programmes to revitalise the four broad areas outlined above is a huge task, especially given that contemporary post-conflict reconstruction aims not only to provide short-term aid in war-affected countries but also to promote a more durable peace. The reconstruction process has thus become an increasingly long-term venture. The Centre for Strategic and International Studies (CSIS) identifies three main phases in transitions from war to peace: the initial response phase (relief), the transformation and transition phase (reconstruction), and the phase of fostering sustainability (CSIS 2002). However, by considering the entire duration of war-to-peace transition within the context of reconstruction, this chapter identifies four periodical phases for post-conflict reconstruction: the emergency relief phase, the rehabilitation phase, the reform and modernisation phase, and the peace consolidation phase.

Emergency relief

Immediately after the end of hostilities, many peace-building programmes concentrate on the need for emergency aid. The focus of emergency relief is to discourage the resumption of hostilities by providing the basic security necessary for the survival of people. In cases where there is a high degree of violent instability, external actors may intervene militarily by dispatching peacekeeping forces or establishing an international interim authority. From Kosovo (UNMIK), Haiti (MINUSTAH) and Timor-Leste (UNMIT) to Sierra Leone (UNAMSIL), the UN-led interim authorities were tasked with a wide range of security, relief and development activities. Both Western and Asian militaries have been involved in such activities under the umbrella of UN peacekeeping deployments and peace operations. At the same time, international humanitarian agencies implement emergency relief programmes to provide water, food, shelter and essential amenities. Once the emergency relief programmes are in operation, the preparation for mid-term rehabilitation and recovery begins. Internal actors in war-torn societies are generally occupied with the issue of basic survival, they often lack capacity or experience to undertake programmes effectively and sometimes they are highly politicised. Consequently, emergency relief is normally provided by external agencies such as the military or foreign NGOs (Beristain 2006).

Rehabilitation

The recovery and rehabilitation process for post-conflict society usually runs simultaneously with emergency relief or immediately after such programmes. The physical reconstruction of social infrastructure such as health care facilities, roads and schools and the efforts to restore basic public services such as governmental administration, policing and restructuring of other security apparatuses are implemented in this phase. External interveners would need to begin to support local initiatives aimed at restarting the economy and the recovery of broken social relations and institutions. It can be difficult for peace builders to establish a comprehensive long-term plan for rehabilitation due to the unstable and highly changeable social environment, and many of the previous programmes conducted during this phase have been adversely affected by the problems of inefficiency and lack of coordination. Moreover, since much of the state infrastructure is likely to have been completely destroyed, including public administration systems, private-sector mechanisms and public transportation, and there is limited internal drive to take on new initiatives, reconstruction projects frequently require proactive assistance from external sources to meet the technical, financial, logistical and social needs. Experience across the world shows militaries tend to undertake a number of essential activities in this phase, such as helping civilian actors with the rehabilitation of infrastructure, housing and providing services. This may be essential in the early days of rehabilitation interventions while civilian actors take time to accumulate resources and capacities. For example, for the civilian actors to initiate their programmes in the hinterland of countries affected by conflict, physical access via roads is critical. The heavy equipment and trained manpower of militaries can undertake the initial rehabilitation of roads and the provision of temporary bridges.

Reform and modernisation

The third phase of post-conflict reconstruction aims to restore local people's capability to rebuild their society. Programmes focus primarily on reforming all aspects of existing governance institutions – their procedures, structures and information management, and the capabilities of actors and the relations between them. The major programmes attempted in this phase may typically include the election of a new legitimate authority, security-sector reform, the restructuring of public administration, demilitarisation of the police force and reorganisation of the judicial system (Boas 2009). Programmes for social reconciliation such as truth-finding projects and education for reconciliation are also usually initiated. With the gradual empowerment of the local community, the relationship between external peace supporters and local people gradually transforms into a more equal partnership and towards the handing over of responsibilities. For example, in Timor-Leste the United Nations Mission in East Timor (UNAMET), the International Force in East Timor (INTERFET) and the UN Transitional Administration in East Timor (UNTAET) represent three distinct phases of the military's involvement. While the former was to ascertain whether the East Timorese people accepted or rejected autonomy from Indonesia by registering voters and holding a referendum, the second was tasked to restore peace and security, facilitation of elections and securing the provision of humanitarian assistance, while the latter was fully responsible for the administration of East Timor during its transition to independence. Western and Asian militaries were actively involved in these activities under the UNTAET mandate: the military pillar for security, the Humanitarian Assistance and Emergency Rehabilitation pillar (HAER) and the Governance and Public Administration (GPA) pillar. The peacekeeping force was formed by contributions from 30 different countries comprising around 8,000 troops.

Peace consolidation

The final phase is concerned with consolidating the transitional initiatives with a view to ensuring sustainability. The initiatives are normally applied in the final phase of peace building and are likely to take place over a considerable length of time. In many cases, the intention is that enhanced collaboration between local communities and international peace-supporting organisations would be expected to lead to the empowerment of local institutions and pave the way for the roles and responsibilities of external actors to be transferred to indigenous people. At the same time, the provisional security and social measures that had been applied in the earlier phases, such as deployment of UN peacekeeping forces, emergency humanitarian aid and interim governmental organisations, are withdrawn (Colletta and Muggah 2009). The facilitation of social reconciliation and further development of socio-economic reconstruction are also considered important in this phase. In the course of conducting these projects, local people relearn how to balance their conflicting interests and opinions by contributing to and participating in social development programmes.

In Timor-Leste, the activities of UNTAET set about laying the foundation for the reconciliation process which needed to address two imperatives: facilitating the reintegration of anti-independence leaders within East Timorese society and allowing those who had fled to return home from West Timor; and settling differences within the wider East Timorese population. The country's national leaders and their UN partners instituted a formal process of reconciliation by establishing a Commission for Reception, Truth and Reconciliation (CRTR). At its point of closure in 2005, the commission had conducted eight national hearings, collected 7,927 victim statements and facilitated 206 community reconciliation events. The commission was certainly an innovation, building in a substantial local component with teams at regional and district levels. These were mandated to facilitate community reconciliation hearings to allow for the reconciling of lesser crimes in line with local culture and customs.

Challenges faced by contemporary post-conflict reconstruction

The extent and the degree of post-conflict reconstruction may vary depending on the particular contexts of the war-torn societies. For instance, the progress of social reform in countries where severe violence and destruction have occurred (such as Rwanda in 1994) is generally slower than in countries in which relatively strong community structures remain (such as in Kosovo in 1999). In post-conflict societies, a range of factors affects the progress of reconstruction: devastated economies, destroyed physical infrastructure, ineffective governance, and corrupt legal and judicial systems. When these factors are combined, the following barriers to reconstruction are very likely to emerge.

Resumption of hostilities

Economic, social and political issues have often been cited as important factors in fomenting conflicts. Unless these underlying issues are addressed and survivors perceive a change in their situation, the likelihood of hostilities resuming is high. The signing of peace accords and the period following it are in most cases characterised by tension and insecurity. In countries with protracted political conflicts, negotiated settlements and plans for reconstruction are often frustrated by the resumption of fresh hostilities. In fact, historical evidence reveals that there has been a recurrence of war in one-quarter to one-half of post-conflict countries. Examples include Sierra Leone, Liberia and Ivory

Coast where several peace-building and recovery plans were abandoned due to ceasefire violations (Kurz 2010; Maclay and Özerdem 2010). In all three cases the engagement of outside military forces played a significant role in the provision of security. For example, the British Army intervened in Sierra Leone in May 2000 (Operation Palliser) and assisted with the evacuation of besieged international peacekeepers and assisted UNAMSIL and the Sierra Leone Army (SLA). By September 2000, the main belligerent group, the Revolutionary United Front (RUF), signed a ceasefire and entered the disarmament, demobilisation and reintegration (DDR) process. The British military continued to be involved in Sierra Leone by training and advising on a restructuring of Sierra Leone's armed forces. When there were a number of indictments and arrests made by the Special Court for Sierra Leone in 2003, a small British force was deployed once again to provide stability. Overall, the British military intervention in Sierra Leone was not only successful in responding to security challenges in a timely manner, but also provided effective assistance in a number of other post-conflict reconstruction activities.

The term 'spoilers' denotes those actors who do not want an end to armed conflict through peace negotiation and actively frustrate such efforts. Even where peace deals are agreed, the presence of peace spoilers continues to be a paramount risk. To avoid a resumption of hostilities, the way that the vision of reconstruction is designed and implemented is critical, as it offers possibilities for 'taming' warring factions and tying them to the reconstruction process. Inducement, coercion and socialisation strategies can be applied, but considering that they often fail to elicit the expected behaviour from disputing groups, a better strategy would likely be to break down the power relationships between such groups and ordinary people affected by conflict. A successful post-conflict reconstruction strategy with direct and tangible peace dividends is integral to this (McRae 2010; Menkhaus 2006/07). Military actors have engaged in various counterinsurgency programmes in contemporary contexts as Afghanistan and Iraq with this objective in mind. Some of the inducements were provided by the DDR programmes through the delivery of reintegration assistance or the efforts under the umbrella of the provincial reconstruction teams (PRTs) in those two countries were also trying to deal with the challenges posed by peace spoilers.

The politics of aid, political primacy and legitimacy

Post-conflict reconstruction is greatly influenced by the attitude of donors and the resources they provide to address the aftermath of conflict. The allocation of resources for recovery interventions can have implications for the balance of power at national, regional and local levels. Although aid is meant to address inequalities and the legacies of conflict, the distribution of aid can actually cause or exacerbate inequality, and improper use can undermine peace and recovery efforts. The allocation of aid is frequently determined by the partial interests of donor agencies, the stance of the media, or rivalry between the donors (Boyce and O'Donnell 2007). When agencies concentrate development efforts in one region while excluding others this can create imbalances, and if not handled properly can breed resentment and lay the foundations of future conflict (Brown 2009; Dobbins 2006). Afghanistan would be a good example for this, where large levels of Western aid were siphoned off through corruption. The inability to deliver better living standards has weakened the role and legitimacy of Western forces.

Furthermore, as everything done during post-conflict reconstruction is political, effective intervention in this area is essential if the performance of the state authority and local government agencies is to improve. At the local level, the politics of local communities and regional municipalities can be a considerable barrier to the implementation of reconstruction programmes. Bearing in mind their potential impact on the political dynamics of conflict, reconstruction programmes need to take such power structures and relationships into consideration, and take each step carefully. This is particularly important in post-conflict societies, as reconstruction projects should be conducted not under conditions of enforcement but rather legitimacy (Donini 2007). A number of strategies to gain legitimacy have been suggested, including a social contract between citizens and the government, transparent planning and implementation, management of expectations and communication, and proactive engagement by the international community (Özerdem 2012). Various senior military officers have made this point in different contexts. For example, US General David Petraeus in Afghanistan argued that the military are only a small part of the solution and the rest is very much socio-political (see the chapter by Rees). Therefore, cross-sectorial engagement in the peace-building process and ensuring that the peace dividends are tangible and substantial means that the negative peace achieved by military means has a chance to become sustainable. In other words, the post-conflict reconstruction efforts need to be guided by an effective socio-political strategy. Such strategies, which relate to positive peace building, have resulted in the social transformation of military activity.

The PRTs in Afghanistan which included combat forces, military personnel (up to 95 per cent of 50 – 300 staff) and civilian expertise for various assessments, relief assistance delivery and reconstruction works, were to some extent meant to be serving this purpose. However, the key point with PRTs is that they also represented a reversal of the structure of the relationship between the military and civilian actors of the early 1990s. The delivery of assistance with PRTs had the key objective of 'winning the hearts and minds' of local Afghans so that they would not become a threat to the international military presence. PRTs often prioritised the creation of an enabling environment for stabilisation and the continuation of military operations as part of the 'war on terror'. As a result, the effectiveness and relevance of relief and reconstruction undertakings were often questionable (Adams 2009). The involvement of the military in relief and reconstruction programmes also blurred the separation between the military and civilian responses in the eyes of local Afghans and spoilers. Subsequently, civilian actors have become a target of attacks from the belligerent groups. It was also argued that PRTs created a parallel governance structure competing against local and national authorities. In turn, this undermined the local ownership of the reconstruction process, and to some extent their presence did more harm than good (Eronen 2008).

Reconstruction: goal-based vs. process-based

In the reconstruction process, the critical issue is less to do with *what* reconstruction is able to deliver, and much more about *how* it is able to deliver it and *when*. Despite being one of the most important aspects of reconstruction, it is often neglected as the process is structured as a goal-based rather than process-based framework. However, when reconstruction is considered from a transformation perspective there is an opportunity to address the root causes of the conflict, such that the process itself can be a key factor in the hope, healing and reconciliation of conflict-affected communities (Barakat and Hoffman 1995). Such a goal-based approach could also be applied in social military transformation as this would need to involve both cross-sectorial understanding and community-level trust building. Comprehensive community engagement in reconstruction programmes is more likely to bring a strong sense of ownership towards peace building.

It is critical that the reconstruction process provides peace dividends as early as possible. A lack of tangible dividends would make it difficult to ensure the continuation of war-torn societies' support for peace building. However, this requirement brings with it its own dilemmas, since the rush for peace dividends in a post-conflict environment can also result in ill-advised planning decisions and the waste of resources. It is essential that the process manages to strike the right balance between the time needed for effective planning and coming up with peace dividends as early as possible. This is particularly the case when dealing with the legacy of war economies. It is clear that not all lose out from armed conflicts – indeed, some elite groups and communities may frequently profit from the continuation of the conflict. In some cases the 'war economy' that emerges means that some communities make a living out of the production of crops like poppy seeds or marijuana, or the smuggling of a wide range of goods from oil and weapons to domestic goods. If it is envisaged that the end of the conflict will bring an end to such sources of revenue without replacing them by peace dividends such as employment, then it will prove extremely difficult to convince such communities to support peace (Cramer 2006; Duffield 2010; Felbab-Brown 2009).

The reconstruction process can also be a means for healing societal wounds caused by armed conflicts. This could be achieved in a variety of ways, by using the reconstruction of key lifelines such as water supply systems, education and health services as opportunities for those conflicting communities to work towards an improved infrastructure or service beneficial to all. It is also essential that there are adequate human and financial resources for such an approach, which is likely to have a high level of resource consumption, and to

involve painstaking negotiations and appropriate skills of conflict management. Those involved in the process would also be able to say 'no' to donor
funding that would only be sufficient to meet the needs of certain groups in
the community, as this would be likely to exacerbate distrust and reignite
animosities created by the conflict. Failures in such objectives can undermine
security. For example, the inability of the US military to restore critical
infrastructure such as water, sanitation and electricity in Iraq after the 2003
invasion fundamentally weakened the security situation.

Setting and prioritising post-conflict reconstruction objectives

It is crucial that the process of post-conflict reconstruction establishes a vision
that can be shared by the majority of stakeholders. This can only be achieved
by involving as many stakeholders as possible in the process through an action
planning methodology. Post-conflict reconstruction should not be planned
remote from the locale of that conflict-affected environment. Stakeholders
need to perceive and experience that their concerns, priorities and objectives are
being consulted, considered, negotiated and incorporated in the reconstruction
planning as much as possible. Unfortunately, in too many post-conflict environments the prioritisation and setting of reconstruction objectives is carried
out from a largely utilitarian, external and technical perspective.

There are a number of reasons for this. First, it should be accepted that it is
not an easy challenge and it is often impossible to secure the full support of all
'stakeholders'. It is necessary to be realistic in regards to what can be achieved in
ensuring comprehensive support for reconstruction. Nevertheless, the handling
of this challenge by both international and national actors has been far from
exemplary in recent times, as demonstrated in Afghanistan and Iraq. Second,
the way this challenge tends to be tackled is often based on a Darwinian
approach of the 'survival of the fittest'. Whoever manages to get their voice
heard tends to get an upper hand in the building up of this vision. For example,
when the international community intervenes and acts as a third party in a
post-conflict environment, the local politicians they work with tend to be those
who waged the conflict. In the 'peace-building market place' peace is often
'traded' for political opportunity or economic advantage, or to put it another
way, there may be no option but to work with the belligerents of a conflict,
but this does not mean that this should be the only way ahead (Miall et al. 1999).

It is also important to build up a range of methodologies so that the
reconstruction agenda is not completely dominated by a few internal actors,
and in order that civil society can contribute to the process on an equal basis.
All too often the way in which the international community tackles this
challenge has a significant negative impact. For example, by rushing to organise
the first post-conflict elections before the society and socio-political environment is actually ready for it, the result is that those belligerents or politicians
involved in the conflict will turn themselves into the legally elected representatives of the people. Not surprisingly, the vision set for reconstruction

comes to reflect only the views, opinions and agendas of those involved in waging the conflict (Englebert and Tull 2008). This phenomenon has been repeated in many environments affected by conflict, from Bosnia and Herzegovina and Kosovo to Afghanistan and Iraq.

Contemporary practices of reconstruction establish a vision where external actors tend to play a central role. This marginalises the views of internal actors and how they envisage the reconstruction process. Such a view of reconstruction also tries to set quantifiable goals and objectives for all activities, some of which are largely in the socio-political and cultural realms of life and not easily quantifiable in numbers and statistics. They are also naturally value-based, and therefore those objectives set by the international community would not necessarily reflect the preferences of war-affected communities. Although it is not easy to generalise, the internal and external agendas concerning what constitutes effective reconstruction, how it can be achieved, and the expected outcomes from this process could be quite different. For example, it is often the case that external actors would like to see a sectorial process or, in other words, a compartmentalisation of the process due to funding policies and structures, while internal actors would prefer a process in which inter-linkages between different areas and priorities are well recognised. At the same time, internal actors may be more prepared to make sacrifices in short-term gains in order to establish stronger long-term prospects, while the agenda of external actors tends to dictate the contrary since they would often prefer quick, uncomplicated and cheap solutions to long-term involvement with complex structures and mechanisms based on local socio-political and cultural frameworks.

Timing of reconstruction

There are two schools of thought relating to the timing of reconstruction and development activities. The first is that peace is a precondition for reconstruction and development. The second is that through well-timed initiation of reconstruction and development activities during the conflict the seeds of long-term recovery can be sown. The former view advocates a linear progression from the end of the conflict through different phases of recovery such as relief and reconstruction. Such a view is not only misleading in relation to how such activities need to take place in a post-conflict environment but also represents a lost opportunity since it considers peace as an end product instead of a dynamic process. On the other hand, this does not mean that all forms of reconstruction activity can take place in the midst of a high level of conflict. It is clear that a certain level of security is needed to ensure the implementation of reconstruction projects, with the well-being of staff and logistics – in terms of procurement, transport and storage needs – two critical factors to consider. Most reconstruction activities are necessarily comprehensive and long-term undertakings. Therefore it is critical that the security environment allows for the implementation of such activity. However, security on its own should not be the only deciding factor (Barakat 2005).

The critical issue here is whether or not a conflict-affected country is seen as a homogenous or heterogeneous unit. If response strategies are based on media reporting then it may seem appropriate to assume that countries are affected by the *same* conflict in an *equal* way *throughout* their territory. However, experience shows that this is never the case. In many protracted armed conflicts certain parts of a country may be engulfed by a high-intensity conflict, while other parts may be experiencing only a low-intensity conflict or even minimal stability. For example, reviewing different phases of the conflict of 30 years in Afghanistan shows that the high-intensity conflict was prevalent in certain parts of the country at different times. This is not only the case for large countries but even for small conflict-affected countries such as Sierra Leone and Liberia. It can be argued that the way the conflict was waged and its impacts on these countries are certainly not uniform throughout.

The first step in undertaking any post-conflict activity, relief or reconstruction, would be to ensure a comprehensive and in-depth understanding of the conflict with its root causes and dynamics. Through such an analysis of the conflict it would be possible to identify which parts of the country are affected by what type of conflict, what the *real* needs of war-affected populations are and to decide what type of undertakings – relief or reconstruction – would be the most effective. It is only through such a perspective that reconstruction programmes would be likely to achieve sustainability, and it would become clear that reconstruction activities should not actually wait for a ceasefire or the signing of a peace agreement.

Ensuring that reconstruction activities are planned and, if possible, implemented before the ending of hostilities would mean that in the aftermath of an accord, there would be a limited preparedness for the reconstruction process. This would mean that there would be existing operational mechanisms capable of providing a suitable framework for the planning and implementation of a new phase of reconstruction programmes. Having carried out reconstruction activities before the signing of a peace accord could also help identify a number of lessons, including: how to form an effective coordination system, how to work with local communities, what resources are available for local partnership, and what the key areas of socio-political and economic concerns would be for the post-conflict reconstruction environment. More importantly, the chances of creating a relief-dependency culture would be considerably reduced.

Linking relief and reconstruction

One of the most difficult reconstruction challenges is how to reverse economic trends and social attitudes that may have developed during the years of conflict. Wars distort economies, including patterns of production, trade and employment. With the arrival of the international community those patterns are further diverted from their original structures. With time, external relief efforts run the risk of being misinterpreted as a substitute for local authority and governmental budgetary allocations. The same applies to rebel groups who see themselves as fighting on behalf of the people but who do not carry the responsibility for their welfare (Anderson 1999). Amidst a conflict humanitarian aid can also unintentionally weaken the relationship between state and citizen, since the provision of relief assistance can be perceived as the state no longer being able to fulfil its role. The result is that external agencies become overly dominant. The relief sector provides work for locals on aid programmes, mostly in supporting positions within the aid infrastructure including in logistics, protection and translation. Locals may also be recruited into a revived service sector, working in shops, restaurants, bars and other facilities that serve aid workers (Walker 1994).

One of the most effective ways of linking relief and reconstruction is to create opportunities for employment and securing livelihoods within populations affected by conflict. The rebuilding of an individual's life should be their own responsibility, and it can only be fully assumed if they are independent economically. A common assumption is that by rebuilding infrastructure and housing, economic regeneration will occur automatically. However, this assumption neglects the fact that although physical rebuilding is essential for economic revitalisation, on its own it is inadequate for the task. A clear focus on livelihoods and employment opportunities for people affected by conflict is imperative for a sustainable recovery.

A top-down response centred on physical reconstruction often strips away the dignity of people who have already lost so much in armed conflict. The very survival and coping mechanisms of people affected by conflict are themselves indicative of just how much they can offer to the reconstruction process. Too frequently they are treated as 'victims', lacking any useful capacities. They are given no means of involvement in the rebuilding of their own future and their situation is compounded by the lack of any meaningful employment opportunities to enable them to feed their families. Consequently, one of the areas policymakers and others involved in the conflict response need to acknowledge is that by not putting enough emphasis on the regeneration of livelihoods and the ownership of reconstruction programmes, they can diminish all possibilities of linking relief and reconstruction phases.

A crucial determinant of success in the recovery of areas affected by conflict is the reconstruction approach to be adopted by policymakers. The provision of relief assistance, particularly in the early days of crises, might require a top-down and centralised decision-making process in order to decide on the assistance to be provided and to ensure that it is distributed in a timely manner. Delays in the provision of relief assistance can mean the difference between life and death. For example, the moment at which NATO forces received the initial waves of Kosovars expelled by Serb paramilitaries from Kosovo in 1999 would have been an inappropriate moment for relief agencies to try to foster participatory approaches. A top-down approach can be excusable in the immediate relief phase, yet it should give way to more bottom-up approaches as reconstruction efforts progress. Without a gradual change in the way decision making is carried out from relief to reconstruction, the recovery response may waste resources or generate inappropriate outputs. Militaries, with their hierarchical decision making and focus on getting a task completed can be insensitive to some of these considerations. It is the role of NGOs to exhibit more cultural sensitivity and bridge the divide with the local communities.

Another critical way of linking relief to reconstruction would be to recognise the need for reconstruction programmes to be tailor-made to the specific socio-economic, cultural and physical characteristics of war-affected environments. In response to basic needs, standardised methods can be effective. For example, the provision of water by using Oxfam water purification and distribution systems would be the same in different war-affected countries. However, to seek blueprints and templates for reconstruction that can be used as ready-made solutions would be futile. No matter how similar two war-affected countries are, a method of reconstruction that worked well in one would have no guarantee of providing similar positive outcomes in another. This was strongly argued in the case of Kosovo, as it was thought that reconstruction strategies used in Bosnia could be applied as possible templates for this war-torn province. However, it soon became clear that Kosovo was a completely different context to Bosnia. The same rule can apply to different regions or localities within the same country. In moving from relief to reconstruction it is essential to bear in mind that there needs to be a corresponding move from standardised to tailor-made responses. Finally, the way in which relationships with conflict-affected populations and local authorities are structured will play a significant role in facilitating an effective progression from relief to reconstruction – something which will be explored in the next section.

Enabling a participatory environment

To enable a participatory environment in post-conflict reconstruction is a major task. More importantly, it is an area in which the international community frequently fails. However, there are some key entry points in seeking to address this challenge. First, the programming strategies need to include many representatives in decision making, which has the advantages of legitimising the decisions taken by the local community itself. This is particularly important, as being open and transparent with people affected by conflict in the local community often results in them being more open to cooperation with international actors. It also provides an opportunity for bringing in respected representatives from excluded groups within the society. In establishing an inclusive strategy in decision making, reconstruction strategies also need to build economic interdependence between different ethnic and religious groups, which can help to lessen tension and so enforce peace.

Second, hiring local staff can also help in creating a participatory environment. It is easier to reach local beneficiaries by using the local language and having a good understanding of local culture and traditions. The costs of hiring local staff are also almost always much lower than employing expatriates, and so this may allow the agency to increase the outreach. Providing employment evenly to different groups within the community is critical, however, as this plays a significant role in determining local perceptions around whether or not international agencies are impartial in their approach.

The way reconstruction programmes are implemented is also significant in creating a participatory environment. Reconstruction programmes are likely to be much more beneficial if they focus on community-owned assets rather than individually owned assets. For example, the reconstruction of an irrigation system can play a significant role in the reassertion of inter-group relations and interdependence, whereas the reconstruction of individual family housing may cause populations to compete and compare with each other. The rebuilding of community services such as schools and health clinics is likely to transcend divisions among groups and promotes sharing resources, leading to a more participatory environment and peaceful coexistence. The military may be well placed to facilitate such reconstruction projects due to their superior manpower and technical knowhow. The involvement of the military in such processes, preferably working in tandem with local civilian organisations, can help to consolidate socio-economic stability and shift 'the centre of gravity' away from violent alternatives to local grievances. The last critical factor in this challenge revolves around whether or not international actors work with local partners in a constructive way.

There are a number of benefits to working with local partners, including enhancing programme sustainability and community participation; providing an accurate understanding of local communities (since indigenous organisations have their roots in these communities); laying a foundation for transitional and development programming; providing opportunities for working with existing local structures that cross lines among groups; and finally, providing space, through partnering, for local communities to get involved in non-conflict activities such as the provision of community services noted above. It is through such an approach that the international community can begin to recognise a number of issues. To start with, it is necessary not to regard local authorities as monolithic structures. Even in the most repressive of places it is often possible to find people with different opinions and motivations, and to work with them in the pursuit of their objectives. Trust building between local and international actors is also critical, since local authorities often tend to perceive internationals, particularly military personnel, as suspicious entities working for the interest of foreign governments. In order to enable a participatory environment, it is important to identify such barriers as early as possible and address them through confidence-building measures, transparency and partnership approaches. A joint identification of potential areas of cooperation and the creation of common objectives to serve the local population could be an effective entry point in this quest. Finally, it is invaluable to take every opportunity to strengthen civilian structures and encourage authorities to be more responsive to the public.

Mobilising adequate resources

One of the most critical challenges to be overcome for the sustainability of reconstruction strategies is the mobilisation of adequate resources. Post-conflict reconstruction experiences around the world show that there are often two major problems. The first concerns the type of resources that are given priority, which tend to be more financial and physical than human and organisational. The second shortcoming relates to the timing and amount of resources provided in the progression from relief to reconstruction.

The scale of the challenge of rebuilding war-torn communities requires the development of collaborative structures of governance with the participation of actors from national and local authorities, local NGOs and grassroots-level organisations, the international aid community (donors and NGOs), and the private sector. The absence of any of these actors, particularly local ones, could result in programme failure, long delays in responding to urgent needs, the waste of scarce resources and, most significantly, renewed conflict (Bray 2009). However, the critical question in resource mobilisation concerns what kind of resources should be given priority and who should coordinate the process. The current practice often focuses on those financial resources that are provided from external to internal actors, and invariably the process is led and coordinated by external actors, forcing internal actors to assume a 'support' role in 'helping' the work of the international community. For example, the military could provide a wide range of non-financial resources which could play an essential role in the reconstruction process, such as the collaboration between foreign militaries and local security forces through the provision of training and transfer of know-how.

The transfer of financial resources for reconstruction comes with a package of conditionality that may incorporate economic, social and political requirements. It is in the process of this 'power' transfer that the agendas, aspirations and values of the international community are made clear and sometimes even imposed on the local context. The prioritisation of financial resources creates a multi-layered hierarchical system of decision making in which the quantity of funds to be provided, and to whom, forms the main element of relationships between different agencies. Such a structure usually creates its own dynamics, altering power relations between donors and governments, donors and international NGOs, international and local NGOs, local NGOs and community-based organisations, and military and civilian actors. Instead of adopting such a financial-centric focus in resource mobilisation, priority should be given to empowering and enabling local human resources. This kind of a perspective can place local agencies in the driving seat of the process, supported by external actors, as and when needed (Goodhand 2006). The reconstruction strategy adopted by the international community would have to entail more than simply working with local actors, and it would need to ascertain what would be the most empowering means of transferring know-how, experiences and financial resources to local actors.

Timing also presents a challenge to the deployment of financial resources as policymakers in conflict-affected environments frequently assume that external resources will remain consistent throughout the period needed for the reconstruction and development of war-torn areas. In reality, international experience has shown that donor interest reaches its peak in the aftermath of establishing peace and declines sharply thereafter. This is in direct contrast to the needs of war-affected areas (Boyce 2007). It is often the case that with increasing media attention during peace negotiations, the international community tends to be much more willing to make generous pledges for reconstruction. To a large extent this generosity may be for the cameras, and pledges made may be conveniently forgotten or reduced once the country in question starts to enjoy a certain level of security and stability (Berdal and Ucko 2010).

There are a number of reasons for this. First, the international community seems to focus on 'signing a peace agreement' much more than actually implementing it. There is often a lack of interest among donors to continue with their commitments. For example, following the US intervention in Afghanistan, there was a high degree of interest within the international community in reconstructing the country. There were generous pledges and initially it seemed that there was a great level of commitment to provide the necessary funds for the task. However, it was not too long after the Bonn Agreement that President Karzai had to visit donor countries to remind them what they had actually promised. Second, other priorities for funding may arise elsewhere. The focus of media attention will shift to new emergencies caused by natural disasters and armed conflicts around the world, so donor attention also tends to move from one area to another. Third, poor performance in terms of reconstruction on the ground and the inability of local authorities to manage the initial influx of funding can create implementation gaps. Reports of corruption and mishandling of funds often discourage donors from committing further funds, although this particular challenge may also be used as an excuse to halt existing commitments. Finally, there may be a re-emergence of violence and funds for reconstruction tend to be moved to respond to relief needs, thereby bringing the reconstruction process to a halt.

Lack of coordination

A challenge created by the proliferation of agencies in post-conflict settings is the lack of effective coordination between agencies. In some countries, the end of hostilities attracts a large number of players with genuine intentions to contribute to reconstruction. This influx of players can create two problems. Multilateral institutions such as the UN and the World Bank emphasise shifting the focus of intervention from emergency and development programmes to peace building and conflict transformation, and their position is usually based on the assumption that interventions which focus on preventing recurrence of violent conflict could preclude the need for large investments in future development programmes. For these agencies, initiatives aimed at development assistance focus on the terms set out in peace agreements, peace-building and building capacities for conflict prevention. International NGOs, however, have different priorities – some in providing humanitarian relief, while others focus entirely on building local capacities through long-term development interventions. Another possible area of clash is likely to be between military and civilian agencies due to their respective priorities and political agendas. A clash in the priorities of peace-building actors and the subsequent lack of coordinated action is often evident in post-conflict settings, and most practitioners agree that not enough has been done to improve the situation (Junne and Verkoren 2005).

Conclusion

Since the end of the Cold War, experiences in post-conflict reconstruction have shown that the international community presents a mixed performance in its engagement in making such programmes more 'inclusive', 'nuanced', 'locally driven', 'process oriented', 'community based' and 'legitimate'. The politics of post-conflict reconstruction, particularly the liberal peace agenda that dictates the norms, principles and actions of reconstruction efforts in most peace operations, tends to create difficult paradoxes and challenges. With the increasing numbers and range of actors participating in contemporary post-conflict reconstruction, efforts undertaken based on different priorities of practice and dissimilar moral values present little or no links with each other (Bellamy and Williams 2009). The recent reconstruction experiences of Afghanistan and Iraq have been marred by the duplication and overlap of project areas, competitiveness of responses, spread of limited resources over many independent areas and an ever increasing involvement of the private sector, especially in the provision of security (Barton and Crocker 2008; Hill 2010).

Discussions in this chapter have also shown that the military has become one of the key actors in contemporary post-conflict processes, playing a crucial part both in creating a secure environment as well as in providing key functions and liaising with civilian agencies in many aspects of peace-building programmes. Such engagement has brought a number of opportunities for the specific deployment of military resources beyond their immediate area of responsibility, such as the reintegration of former combatants and reconstruction tasks in insecure contexts. Such a shift has been a result of the recognition that social military transformation is absolutely essential to deal with the challenges posed by insurgency and peace spoilers, as well as ensuring that the peace will last.

One of the main problems with the liberal peace agenda and its tool of post-conflict reconstruction has been its lack of legitimacy. The legitimacy argument was used to counter-balance the shortcomings with the legality of the international community's presence in such environments as Kosovo. However, for the post-9/11 context peace-building operations like Afghanistan and Iraq, the entire legitimacy of the international community and its post-conflict reconstruction efforts has faced serious questions (Ghani and Lockhart 2008). The liberal peace project has experienced its most significant crisis, calling into question its assumptions over what peace is, what it should look like in terms of post-conflict governance and economic structures, and how it would and should be achieved (through which approaches and modalities). It has started to face serious scrutiny and criticism. The liberal peace was clearly failing to achieve what it promised to do in terms of security, human development and post-conflict reconstruction in its new areas of operation. Post-conflict reconstruction has been carried out by those who lack the appropriate credentials in the eyes of local populations – one day they were occupiers, the next day peacekeepers, then becoming the providers of humanitarian aid and reconstruction. In such contexts, security-sector reform was no longer part of overall peace-building efforts, as was the case in the early 1990s, but has become the peace-building process itself (Brzoska 2006).

More latterly, the so-called 'Arab Spring' has inflicted another major blow to the liberal peace doctrine and the way it translates the challenge of peace building into different programmes. Within new 'post-conflict' contexts such as Libya, and possibly further down the line in Syria, there are serious question marks about the international community's claims to knowledge of peace building and post-conflict reconstruction. The experience that has been accumulated over the last two decades in a wide range of contexts seem to become rather helpless to advise how societies like Libya, emerging from dictatorial regimes, can rebuild from the ruins of civil war. The hybridity of peace building, especially for the requirement of working with non-state armed groups, in the reconstruction of these societies has been demanding new approaches and methodologies. This proves to be a particular challenge in the case of working with those non-state armed groups who are anti-Western in their ideology (Ginty 2010). Thus, post-conflict reconstruction, both as a concept and practice, is now facing another critical departure point. Although the experience of the last two decades can guide the action to some extent, it is important to recognise the fundamental problems with the way the enterprise has always envisaged what peace is and how it can be built (Richmond 2010).

The key issue to remember in post-conflict reconstruction is that the process is highly politicised and deals with complex and sensitive power dynamics of conflict-affected societies. In setting the overall vision for post-conflict reconstruction and identifying priorities, different groups often contest key principles and directions. In most contemporary conflicts peace deals do not tend to bring a complete halt to the conflict, and post-conflict reconstruction can seem to set the stage for the continuation of war politics through different means. Post-conflict reconstruction is an evolving concept and practice. It has already gone through a number of generations and reincarnations. For it to have purpose in the post-Arab Spring context to respond to the destruction and divisions caused by political violence, for example, it would need to reinvent itself.

Bibliography

Adams, N. (2009) *Policy Options for State-Building in Afghanistan: The Role of NATO PRTs in Development in Afghanistan*, Washington: SAIS.

Anderson, M. (1999) *Do No Harm: How Aid Can Support Peace or War*, London: Lynne Rienner.

Bachler, G. (2004) *Conflict Transformation through State Reform*, Berghof Research Centre for Conflict Transformation.

Barakat, S. (ed.) (2005) *After the Conflict: Reconstruction and Development in the Aftermath of War*, London: I.B. Tauris.

Barakat, S. and Hoffman, B. (1995) *Post-conflict Reconstruction: Key Concepts, Principal Components and Capabilities*, Paper presented at Post-conflict Reconstruction Strategies – An International Colloquium, UNDMSMS & UNIDO, 23–24 June, Vienna, Austria.

Barakat, S. and Zych, S.A. (2009) 'The Evolution of Post-conflict Recovery', *Third World Quarterly*, Vol. 30, No. 6, pp. 1069–1086.

Barton, F. and Crocker, B. (2008) *Progress or Peril? Measuring Iraq's Reconstruction*, Washington, DC: Center for Strategic and International Studies.

Bellamy, A.J. and Williams, P.D. (2009) 'The West and Contemporary Peace Operations', *Journal of Peace Research*, Vol. 46, No. 1, pp. 39–57.

Berdal, M. and Ucko, D.H. (2010) *Reintegrating Armed Groups After Conflict: Politics, Violence and Transition*, New York: Routledge.

Beristain, C.M. (2006) *Humanitarian Aid Work: A Critical Approach*, Philadelphia: University of Pennsylvania.

Boas, M. (2009) 'Making Plans for Liberia – A Trusteeship Approach to Good Governance?' *Third World Quarterly*, Vol. 30, No. 7, pp. 1329–1341.

Boutros-Ghali, B. (1995) *An Agenda for Peace*, Geneva: United Nations.

Boyce, J. (2007) *Post-Conflict Recovery: Resource Mobilization and Peacebuilding*, Working Paper Series, No. 159, Amherst, Mass.: Political Economy Research Institute, University of Massachusetts at Amherst.

Boyce, J. and O'Donnell, M. (2007) *Peace and the Public Purse: Economic Policies for Postwar Statebuilding*, Boulder, Col.: Lynne Rienner Publishers.

Bray, J. (2009) 'The Role of Private Sector Actors in Post-conflict Recovery', *Conflict, Security & Development*, Vol. 9, No. 1, pp. 1–26.

Brown, A.M. (2009) 'Security, Development and the Nation-building Agenda in East Timor', *Conflict, Security & Development*, Vol. 9, No. 2, pp. 141–164.

Brzoska, M. (2006) 'Introduction: Criteria for Evaluating Post-conflict Reconstruction and Security Sector Reform in Peace Support Operations', *International Peacekeeping*, Vol. 13, No. 1, pp. 1–13.

Chimni, B.S. (2003) 'Post-conflict Peace-building and the Return of Refugees: Concepts, Practices and Institutions', in Newman, E. and van Selm, J. (eds) *Refugees and Forced Displaced Persons: International Security, Human Vulnerability and the State*, New York: United Nations University Press.

Colletta, N.J. and Muggah, R. (2009) 'Context Matters: Interim Stabilisation and Second Generation Approaches to Security Promotion', *Conflict, Security & Development*, Vol. 9, No. 4, pp. 425–453.

Cramer, C. (2006) 'Labour Markets, Employment and the Transformation of War Economies', *Conflict, Security & Development*, Vol. 6, No. 3, pp. 389–410.

CSIS (2002) *Post-Conflict Reconstruction Framework*, http://csis.org/files/media/csis/pubs/framework.pdf (accessed 11 October 2012).

Dayton, B.W. and Kriesberg, L. (2009) *Conflict Transformation and Peacebuilding: Moving from Violence to Sustainable Peace*, New York: Routledge.

Dobbins, J. (2006) 'Preparing for Nation-building', *Survival: Global Politics and Strategy*, Vol. 48, No. 3, pp. 27–40.

Donini, A. (2007) 'Local Perceptions of Assistance to Afghanistan', *International Peacekeeping*, Vol. 14, No. 1, pp. 158–172.

Duffield, M. (2010) 'The Liberal Way of Development and the Developmental-Security Impasse: Exploring the Global Life-Chance Divide', *Security Dialogue*, Vol. 41, No. 1, pp. 53–76.

Englebert, P. and Tull, D.M. (2008) 'Postconflict Reconstruction in Africa: Flawed Ideas about Flawed States', *International Security*, Vol. 48, No. 2, pp. 106–139.

Eronen, O. (2008) *PRT Models in Afghanistan: Approaches to Civil-Military Integration*, Vol. 1, No. 5, Finland: Crisis Management Centre.

Felbab-Brown, V. (2009) 'Peacekeepers Among Poppies: Afghanistan, Illicit Economies and Intervention', *International Peacekeeping*, Vol. 16, No. 1, pp. 100–114.

Galtung, J. (1990) 'Cultural Violence', *Journal of Peace Research*, Vol. 27, No. 3, pp. 291–305.

Ghani, A. and Lockhart, C. (2008) *Fixing Failed States: A Framework for Rebuilding a Fractured World*, New York: Oxford University Press.

Ginty, R.M. (2010) 'Warlords and the Liberal Peace: State-building in Afghanistan', *Conflict, Security & Development*, Vol. 10, No. 4, pp. 577–598.

Ginty, R.M. and Richmond, O. (2009) *The Liberal Peace and Post-War Reconstruction: Myth or Reality?* New York: Routledge.

Goodhand, J. (2006) *Aiding Peace? The Role of NGOs in Armed Conflict*, Boulder, Col.: Lynne Rienner Publishers.

Hill, A. (2010) 'The Unavoidable Ghettoization of Security in Iraq', *Security Dialogue*, Vol. 41, No. 3, pp. 310–321.

Junne, G. and Verkoren, W. (eds) (2005) *Postconflict Development: Meeting New Challenges*, Boulder, Col.: Lynne Rienner Publishers.

Kurz, C.P. (2010) 'What You See is What You Get: Analytical Lenses and the Limitations of Post-Conflict Statebuilding in Sierra Leone', *Journal of Intervention and Statebuilding*, Vol. 4, No. 2, pp. 205–236.

Lilly, D. (2004) *The Peacebuilding Dimension of Civil-Military Relations in Complex Emergencies: A Briefing Paper*, London: International Alert.

Luckham, R. (2004) 'The International Community and State Reconstruction in War-torn Societies', *Conflict, Security & Development*, Vol. 4, No. 3, pp. 481–507.

Maclay, C. and Özerdem, A. (2010) '"Use" Them or "Lose" Them: Engaging Liberia's Disconnected Youth through Socio-Political Integration', *International Peacekeeping*, Vol. 17, No. 3, pp. 343–360.

Mason, D.T. and Meernik, J.D. (2009) *Conflict Prevention and Peace-building in Post-War Societies: Sustaining the Peace*, New York: Routledge.

McRae, D. (2010) 'Reintegrating and Localised Conflict: Security Impacts Beyond Influencing Spoilers', *Conflict, Security & Development*, Vol. 10, No. 3, pp. 403–430.

Menkhaus, K.J. (2006/07) 'Governance without Government in Somalia: Spoilers, State Building, and the Politics of Coping', *International Security*, Vol. 31, No. 3, pp. 74–106.

Miall, H. et al. (1999) *Contemporary Conflict Resolution: The Prevention, Management and Transformation of Deadly Conflicts*, Cambridge: Polity Press.

Özerdem, A. (2012) 'A Re-conceptualisation of Ex-combatant Reintegration: "Social Reintegration" Approach', *Conflict, Security & Development*, Vol. 12, No. 1, pp. 51–73.

Paris, R. (2004) *At War's End: Building Peace After Civil Conflict*, Cambridge: Cambridge University Press.

Richmond, O.P. (2010) 'Resistance and the Post-Liberal Peace', *Millennium – Journal of International Studies*, Vol. 38, No. 3, pp. 665–692.

UNSG (United Nations Secretary-General) (1992) *UNSG Report: An Agenda for Peace*, A/47/277-S/24111.

Walker, P. (1994) 'Linking Relief and Development: The Perspective of the International Federation of Red Cross and Red Crescent Societies', *IDS Bulletin*, Vol. 25, No. 4, pp. 107–111.

World Bank (1998) *Post Conflict Reconstruction: The Role of the World Bank*, Washington, DC: The World Bank.

PART II
The West

4 The United States and transformation

Wyn Rees

Introduction

The US military has been synonymous with the word 'transformation'. The USA has been the dominant military power in the post-Cold War era and the underpinning for the Western-led international order. It has been at the forefront of efforts to develop new military capabilities and, in the process, restructure its armed forces. America has been at the cutting edge of technological developments as well as the conceptual thinking that has been necessary in order to bring the ideas into reality.

Transformation has been regarded by the politico-military elite as a means to ensure the continuing supremacy of the USA. It is designed to provide the means to out-see, out-fight and thereby assert superiority over any form of adversary. Such capabilities would minimise the risk of casualties and enable the USA to partake in wars at an acceptable cost. This would ensure that decision makers would not be deterred from embarking on conflict in the first place as well as maintain domestic political support for overseas interventions.

There is considerable debate over how the term 'transformation' should be understood. It has tended to be treated as synonymous with the so-called 'Revolution in Military Affairs' (RMA) – a preceding concept which involved the fusion of modern weapons with information technology. The concept of transformation is, however, more complicated than just the development of advanced weapons. It also involves the way in which the technology is utilised and exploited by the military in order to accomplish strategic objectives. It requires the interaction of emerging technologies with both new organisational structures as well as with the concepts to use them operationally (Jasper 2009: 2–3). In the words of US Defense Secretary Donald Rumsfeld, a strong advocate of transformation, '[it] is about more than building high-tech weapons, […] it is also about new ways of thinking and new ways of fighting' (Rumsfeld 2002: 21).

The nature of the word 'transformation' excites expectations of radical change: that it should result in fundamentally different ways in which to fight wars. The concept should mean more than just modernisation. After all, military forces could be expected routinely to bring forth succeeding generations of weapons systems. The most ardent advocates of transformation have envisaged changes of magnitude in military technology or fundamentally new ways in which wars are conducted. According to these visionaries, the USA would leapfrog phases of military development in order to arrive at capabilities that would revolutionise the battlefield. Such military assets would far outstrip those of any adversary and would guarantee US superiority.

Yet it is problematic to consider military power as operating in a vacuum, divorced from its environment and the objectives to which it is directed. Armed services must not only procure new generations of weapons, iron out the problems in their development and train to use them; they must also integrate them doctrinally and adapt them to fit the range of contingencies that they may confront. Since the end of the Cold War, Western countries, including the USA, have faced a more complex and unpredictable array of security challenges. Conflicts have differed in scale as well as intensity, and protagonists have varied from states to non-state actors. It has been necessary for the USA to prepare for a broader range of conflicts. In some of these scenarios, high-intensity war-fighting capabilities have been of dubious utility. For example, in post-conflict stabilisation roles and in counterinsurgency, the sophistication of weapon platforms has been a secondary importance compared with the need for highly trained personnel capable of flexible thinking and exercising restraint in sensitive situations.

As a result, a more modest vision is also compatible with the concept of transformation, one that envisages an evolutionary pattern of change. According to this view, developments are manifest over a period of time as new technologies are brought from the design stage into the inventories of the armed services. They are then married to other forms of technological innovation before being incorporated into force structures and anticipated ways of conducting military operations. The implications of the new weapons systems need to be understood in the context of the various roles that the military might be required to perform. The resulting capability is transformational in that it facilitates military objectives to be achieved more efficiently, with greater confidence and expectations of fewer losses. In sum, the armed services become a more effective instrument of national power.

This chapter argues that this more modest vision of transformation has been the experience of the American armed forces over the last two decades. There has been no wholesale change in the mission profiles of the US armed forces; services have not disappeared or been amalgamated. Whilst the US military has improved its capacity to perform essential roles, it has not sought to fight wars in fundamentally different ways. Nevertheless, this should not detract from the sense in which there has been a transformation in America's ability to conduct and prevail in wars. The USA has striven ceaselessly to enhance the capabilities of its forces, integrating new technologies at a rapid rate and developing military doctrine that has enabled its personnel to exploit their potential. The result has been armed forces that far surpass any of their rivals, and which serve as a model for other countries to emulate (see Chapter 5).

In order to achieve such an outcome, the process of transformation has involved trade-offs between, on the one hand, spending on various types of technological capabilities and, on the other, assumptions about the roles that US forces will fulfil. Even the US military cannot afford everything and consequently it has been necessary to make choices. In the first part of this chapter is the argument that the US armed forces have pursued a transformation agenda focused primarily on their ability to fight inter-state war. As powerful bureaucratic actors, each of the armed services has sought to preserve their most high-profile and prestigious missions, and the major weapons programmes associated with them. They have configured their own transformation paths around this agenda and inter-service rivalry has been an important motivating factor. Yet the second half of the chapter argues that the resulting narrow conception of the types of tasks that the military were likely to face has served US foreign policy badly. On too many occasions the US armed forces have found themselves with the most technologically proficient fighting forces in the world but ill-adapted to the military campaigns that their enemies have imposed upon them.

A unique US model of transformation

At the heart of the US vision of force transformation has been an emphasis on three sorts of capabilities: full information awareness of the adversary and the contested environment; speed of action that undermines the enemy's capacity to resist; and lastly, the means to strike with precision and lethality anywhere in the world. The USA moved away from former concepts that extolled the importance of scale, mass and firepower. No longer was the USA seeking to defeat an adversary on the battlefield by the concentration of forces of superior size, able to deliver overwhelming destructive force. A new set of priorities became the watchwords of transformation in which political decision makers would be provided with a range of options over the type of effects that they might want to inflict upon an adversary.

Full information awareness has been sought by developing so-called 'network centric' capabilities (Mitchell 2009: 31). This is based on the ability to gain the maximum amount of intelligence on an enemy through a variety of platforms, including satellites, manned aircraft and unmanned aerial vehicles. There has been a leap in the information-processing technologies involved in information acquisition, processing and dissemination. The central principle is then to share these data across a network to enable a multiplicity of air-, sea- and land-based platforms to be the beneficiaries of, and act upon, real-time intelligence. The flow of information gives force commanders a more complete picture of the battlespace, thereby facilitating timely and informed decisions. The USA has invested in highly capable sensors and reconnaissance capabilities as well as the command and control systems to utilise information. At the same time, information is denied to the enemy so as to ensure that the US speed of decision making far outpaces that of the other side.

A second element has been speed and manoeuvrability. Transformation has envisaged lighter, more agile US forces being deployed, rather than the heavy armoured formations of the past. Their lightness would facilitate their transport to a conflict zone by long-range aircraft rather than by sea lift (Adams 2006). Once in theatre, these forces would be capable of both protecting themselves as well as being designed to engage with the enemy. They would possess the means to destroy an adversary at long range without making themselves vulnerable to attack. Allied to this has been the concept of 'jointery' between all of the US armed services so that they can operate seamlessly together. The integration of capabilities across land, sea and air has sought to develop a combined arms approach to operations.

Lastly, precision targeting is a vital component of the overall capability. Platforms able to operate in all weather, day and night would mean that a foe would never experience a pause in a US campaign, its forces would constantly be under attack. Munitions with infra-red guidance systems, terrain mapping or the capability to receive guidance from global positioning systems (GPS) would provide a very high degree of accuracy. Whether delivered by land-based missiles, cruise missiles on ships or submarines, or from aircraft, the USA has sought to perfect the ability to acquire, track and destroy targets with a high degree of certainty.

Transformation has roots that stretch back into the Cold War. It was originally conceived as a means to offset the numerical superiority of the Warsaw Pact by exploiting the West's technological sophistication and doctrinal flexibility. The ideas of the RMA and the North Atlantic Treaty Organization (NATO) strategy of 'Follow-on-Forces-Attack' (FOFA) were designed to take the fight to the Soviets rather than waiting for successive waves of their armoured formations to attack the Alliance's Central Front. Architects of FOFA, such as Supreme Allied Commander General Bernard Rogers, foresaw a battle in which Western forces would strike deep into Warsaw Pact territory from the outset of a conflict. The aim would have been to disrupt and degrade the rear echelons of Soviet and Eastern European forces before they could be brought to bear on the NATO front line. The technologies and thinking that were developed for these purposes became the kernel of the transformation agenda.

Yet transformation developed within a post-Cold War context in which the Soviet Union had collapsed. There were pressures for reduced defence spending in the West and expectations of a 'peace dividend'. Although the Soviet Union, and later Russia, remained a formidable conventional and especially nuclear power, its ability to project force against the West, following the revolutions in Central and Eastern Europe, was massively diminished. Post-Cold War, the strategic landscape changed dramatically for the USA as the threat had all but evaporated. Spending on defence at the tempo undertaken during the previous era became unsustainable. What resulted was the 'Base Force' concept in which cuts were imposed on all of the armed services. It was considered too politically sensitive to determine which service should be cut the most, so equal pain was inflicted on all of them. From 18 divisions, the US Army was reduced to eight (it later increased to ten), and the size of the surface fleet was reduced to 400 vessels. The number of aircraft carriers was reduced from 15 to 11 and the Air Force was reduced from 15 to 11 tactical wings (Sapolsky et al. 2012: 3).

At the same time as cuts were being exacted on all of the services, the USA was reassessing its most likely threats. In the absence of the overriding threat from Soviet power, the USA switched to a capabilities-based approach. In the 'Bottom up Review' of 1993, conducted by Secretary of Defense Les Aspin, the military were requested to plan on the assumption of fighting two major conflicts simultaneously. Inter-state war was considered to be the most likely scenario in which US forces would be confronted by a state such as Iraq, Iran or North Korea with a full complement of land, sea and air forces. It was considered imperative that the USA should have no peer competitor. In the light of these requirements transformation became the means to reduce defence spending whilst leveraging America's technological prowess. Although the armed forces would be smaller in size, the aim was to make them more mobile and capable. Their capacity to be deployed around the world was improved and their increased lethality was designed to guarantee that they would be able to deliver a bigger punch against whichever enemy they faced.

The 1990–91 Gulf War was the first test of the US approach. It was ironic that military forces conceived of to fight against the Soviets were first tested against a second-order adversary like Iraq. This is not to belittle the size or experience of Iraqi forces, which after all had fought an eight-year conflict against Iran in the 1980s. Yet Iraqi forces were much less technologically sophisticated than the Soviet military and they proved no match for the coalition headed by the USA. Essential, albeit nascent, elements of military transformation were employed to eject Iraqi forces from Kuwait. The conflict began with an aerial bombardment that devastated Iraqi air defences as well as the leadership's command and control over its forces. Cruise missiles targeted command bunkers and waves of combat aircraft, some almost invisible to radar, knocked out airfields. The second phase of the conflict was a period of sustained attack on Saddam Hussein's ground forces, including with precision guided weapons, and the severing of supply lines back to Iraq. Airpower was used to cripple the Iraqi occupation forces in Kuwait and render them incapable of offering sustained resistance. The land campaign, when it was eventually launched, lasted for only 100 hours. It still demonstrated the superiority of US ground forces in terms of both their long-range artillery and their ability to manoeuvre on the battlefield and catch their adversary unawares. The resulting Iraqi losses were horrendous whilst Western losses were comparatively negligible.

This set the framework in which the transformation of US armed forces was subsequently pursued. It was harnessed to an expeditionary orientation for rapid overseas deployment. Under the leadership of figures such as Admiral William Owens, who was vice-chairman of the Joint Chiefs of Staff (JCS) between 1994–96, the Pentagon became the focal point for steering the

transformation process. Owens believed that the key to achieving US dominance lay in the application of information technology and in the ability of
all branches of the armed services to operate smoothly together (Shimko
2010: 109). These became the priorities for change during the period.

With the inauguration of the Administration of George W. Bush in 2001,
a renewed impetus was given to transformation efforts. Bush appointed
Donald Rumsfeld as his secretary of defense, someone who had enormous
experience as both a previous office holder as well as the former chairman of
two military commissions. Rumsfeld was a fervent supporter of the concept of
transformation, believing that it was necessary for the USA to strive to
develop the next generation of military power in order to keep ahead of its
rivals. He created the 'Office of Force Transformation' in the Pentagon and
put in charge Vice Admiral Arthur Cebrowski, one of the leading exponents
of network-centric warfare.

In the 2001 Quadrennial Defense Review (QDR), transformation was
declared to be 'at the heart' of the new approach (Brake 2001). US military
forces were configured to be smaller in overall size but more capable and with
a smaller logistical tail. The assumptions underpinning defence policy were
also changed, from the capacity to fight two major conflicts simultaneously,
to one where America had to be capable of fighting one major conflict whilst
being able to deal with lower levels of conflict or deterrence missions in other
theatres.

The conflicts in Afghanistan in 2001 and Iraq 2003 proved the high-water
marks of transformation. Under Rumsfeld there was pressure on General
Tommy Franks, at Central Command (CENTCOM), to plan the campaigns
in a manner that accorded with the tenets of transformation. In spite of the
recommendations from the US Army for a large ground force invasion,
Operation Enduring Freedom involved a force of only token size. President
Bush stated that 'this revolution in our military is just beginning, [...] this
combination – real time intelligence, local allied forces, Special Forces, and
precision air power – has really never been used before' (Bush 2001: para. 22).
US Forward Air Controllers, Central Intelligence Agency (CIA) representatives
and Special Forces called in devastating aerial strikes whenever the Taliban
forces massed for battle. The aerial bombardment was precise and the Taliban
were unable to provide an effective resistance. The strategic objectives of
Mazar-i-Sharif, Kabul and subsequently Kandahar were wrested from their
control, with the resultant self-congratulation within the defence establishment. Leading military commentator Max Boot declared that the USA had
pioneered a 'new way of war' (Boot 2003).

In the case of Iraq, a similar campaign plan was executed, albeit on a
larger scale. Around 150,000 US troops invaded the country – a much smaller
force than had been mobilised in the first Gulf War and far below the levels
recommended by the JCS. Two armoured columns advanced quickly up the
Euphrates River towards the nerve centre of the regime in Baghdad. At the
same time, whenever the Iraqis massed for an engagement with US forces,

they were struck by devastating aerial attacks which kept them permanently off-balance. Mastery of the air proved a major force multiplier for the Americans and ensured that their losses were kept to a minimum. Three weeks of ground and air operations were a textbook demonstration of the concepts behind transformation. However, the success of the invasion was subsequently over-shadowed by the failure to plan for the post-war phase. The inability to restore order, to begin large-scale reconstruction efforts and the start of a lethal insurgency came to preoccupy US attention.

The impact of 9/11 changed the financial context in which transformation had been pursued since the Cold War. The sense of renewed threat to the USA from international terrorism and its alleged state sponsors resulted in the ballooning of defence spending. In the period after the fall of the Berlin Wall, transformation had offered a panacea for pressures to constrain military budgets, whilst preserving and enhancing capabilities. After 9/11 the massive injection of resources made it possible for all branches of the military to enjoy a period of expansion. This diminished pressures to pursue the organisational change that might have accompanied the adoption of new technologies. The Office of Force Transformation within the Department of Defense lost its zeal to cull some of the major weapons programmes being pursued by the armed services. Major legacy programmes, such as the F-22 Raptor and the F-35 Joint Strike Fighter, were continued amidst the new focus on fighting the 'global war on terror'.

Service interests and transformation

Sapolsky et al. (2012) argue that innovation derives from competition between rival organisations for a greater share of available funds and for the prestige that comes from being the leader in their field. Large organisations such as the US armed services find change difficult. Whilst not impervious to change, the momentum behind the pre-existing direction of travel renders it difficult for them to alter course. Each branch of the armed services represents a powerful vested interest and embodies a strong sense of internal identity. This bureau-cratic identity is tied up with how they see their futures and the weapons programmes that they have considered to be integral to fulfilling their roles.

As noted earlier, the US Army, Navy, Air Force and Marine Corps all emerged from the Cold War fearful of the impact of resource constraint upon their personnel and their missions. The new environment in which they found themselves was uncertain and threats were ill defined. The armed services were forced to justify their continued existence and this promoted competition between them. With its focus upon inter-state warfare, transformation offered the services a rationale for remaining committed to large and expensive weapons programmes. These programmes preserved missions on which the services had constructed their own identities and doctrine.

The US Air Force was in the best position to benefit from the transformation debate after 1989. It had been at the forefront of efforts to generate an RMA in relation to Soviet power in the latter stages of the Cold War. It had also developed concepts such as 'effects-based operations' in which emphasis was placed on the role of military power in achieving strategic objectives (Hallion 2011: 109). It had adopted many of the technologies that made such an impact when they were first employed in conflict. Stealth technology made manned aircraft practically invisible to radar; synthetic aperture radar enabled aerial platforms to see deep into enemy territory and monitor the movement of land forces and precision guided munitions (PGM) made it possible to attack targets with a high degree of accuracy. These were amongst many developments that led the Air Force to argue that the military power it could deliver could be decisive. It even led some to contend that air power was the only instrument that needed to be deployed, that the other services were of strictly secondary importance.

On the one hand it could be argued that the US Air Force has made possible a transformational way in which America can fight. In the first Gulf War and then in Afghanistan, airpower played a decisive role. It enabled ground forces to win victories over more numerous opponents without suffering more than token numbers of casualties. On the other hand, those victories occurred within a context that was uniquely favourable for airpower. Conventional conflict in desert environments provided the opportunity for the US Air Force to use its strength to maximum effect. The availability of identifiable targets in open spaces with little fear of causing collateral damage were circumstances likely to prove rare in contemporary conflicts.

The Air Force remained committed to major weapons programmes such as the F-22 Raptor air superiority fighter, the F-35 combat aircraft and a long-range heavy bomber. Although these systems could be employed against a relatively low-technology opponent, their rationale lay in combat against a high-technology adversary. These are cutting-edge, fourth-generation systems designed to operate in the most demanding operational environments. They are symbolic of the desire of the Air Force to preserve its focus on challenges emanating from countries like China and Russia, rather than second-order military powers.

The US Marine Corps has fared well in the post-Cold War environment because it has been able to involve itself in all the major military tasks. The versatility of the Corps has enabled it to participate in conventional land force operations as well as more specialised amphibious roles. Marine Corps units, for example, led the assault into Kuwait in 1991 whilst a Marine Amphibious Unit was the first to come ashore in Somalia in 1993 to deliver humanitarian relief. US Marines were centrally involved in the defeat of Saddam Hussein's regime and also replaced British forces in Sangin in Afghanistan in 2011.

If events have been relatively favourable to the US Air Force and Marine Corps, the same cannot be said for the US Navy. The post-Cold War period has proven difficult because the enemies of the USA have lacked naval power. In the two wars against Iraq, the US Navy played only a peripheral role: in the case of the first Gulf War, tying down Iraqi forces by pretending to prepare for a seaborne assault. It was only in the early stages of Operation Enduring Freedom that a significant role existed for carrier-borne airpower to be used against Taliban targets. Similarly, the US submariner community has suffered from the lack of a significant enemy. With Soviet submarines no longer presenting a threat to transatlantic resupply, the requirement for hunter-killer submarines has diminished. Few countries possess a submarine force capable of threatening US interests. One answer from the US Navy was to stress the role that submarines could play in projecting force against the shore: in launching Tomahawk cruise missiles and in serving as platforms for the infiltration of Special Forces.

This limited role for traditional naval power in the last two decades has not deterred the US Navy from embracing the concept of transformation. The networking of platforms has enabled surface vessels, submarines and aircraft to be able to share data in real time so that maximum control can be exerted over the battlespace. 'Link 16' has been at the heart of the ability to connect together computers on different platforms to facilitate a Cooperative Engagement Concept in which the best-placed ship can fire upon the enemy (Osinga 2010: 24). Another significant development has been the Secret Internet Protocol Router Network (SIPRN) which has made possible secure e-mail contact between ships and National Command Authorities (Mitchell 2009: 57–58).

Although the Navy has been forced to reduce in size, it no longer needs to mass its naval platforms against an enemy; it can now bring devastating firepower to bear from a single ship or aircraft carrier. Nevertheless, the absence of a serious maritime challenge has made it harder for the US Navy to justify its share of resources. The Navy has sought to preserve its sea control mission built around aircraft carriers, major surface combatants and hunter-killer submarines. Yet these major weapons systems are hugely expensive and presuppose a peer competitor. The US Navy has been eager to refocus US defence policy around such threats.

In contrast to the Navy, the US Army has witnessed the greatest demands over the last two decades. It has been called upon to fight in a variety of theatres around the world, often in lengthy campaigns. Paradoxically, it has been the service that has experienced the most troubled relationship with the concept of transformation. Land forces have traditionally been the least technologically focused branch of the armed forces. They are less dependent than the other services on large weapons platforms because their principal technologies focus around armoured vehicles, artillery, helicopters and battlefield communications. In essence, the US Army requires its soldiers to engage with and kill the enemy. Thus, the technologically orientated approach to transformation adopted by the Air Force and Navy is perceived to carry more risks for the US Army.

This is not to suggest that the Army has neglected the concept of transformation. It actually offered significant potential advantages to a service heavily dependent upon manpower, because it made possible cuts in the size of the Army whilst concurrently increasing combat power. After the Gulf

War of 1991, Army Chief of Staff General Gordon Sullivan championed transformation as part of an effort to configure America's land forces for dealing with regional crises (Farrell et al. 2013: 18). This led to the 'Force 21' programme which sought to exploit the digital information revolution to provide greater battlefield awareness to the Army (Lovelace 1997: 48). Force 21 envisaged that the Army would develop a proof of concept digitised brigade by 1996 and a digitised division two years later (Kagan 2006: 203). General Carl Reimer took this forward in the adoption of 'The Army After Next' concept. He believed that structuring the Army around divisions was unnecessarily cumbersome and argued for a lighter and more versatile formation of modular brigade combat teams with high levels of firepower (Osinga 2010: 17). Whilst the Army was reducing its heavy armoured forces, it was designed to become more capable by concentrating on situational awareness and the ability to strike at targets with great accuracy.

Under General Eric Shinseki, this became the foundation for the Stryker Interim Brigade concept and the Future Combat System (FCS). These was a new generation of light and medium-weight vehicles that would fulfil a range of battlefield roles, along with the operational thinking that would facilitate their integration into the force structure. It was envisaged that both Stryker and FCS would be airlifted quickly to a theatre of operations. However, the concept experienced problems when the weight of the new generation of vehicles began to exceed the payloads of the aircraft that were designed to transport them. The early optimism of transformation was never fully realised in the case of the US Army.

All three services regarded transformation, to varying extents, as a means to protect themselves from cuts and preserve their state-centric war-fighting missions. The result has been US forces unchallengeable in conventional warfare, capable of defeating opponents with low levels of casualties. However, the focus on inter-state warfare obscured the need to prepare for other types of lower-intensity conflict.

Transformation and low-intensity conflict

By focusing on high-intensity, inter-state conflict, the US military neglected other types of less kinetic operations. It took up the challenge of contributing to disaster relief and humanitarian operations on a case by case basis, as evidenced by assistance rendered to the Philippines (see Chapter 10). Yet, the US military has been opposed to diluting its war-fighting capabilities to undertake operations other than war. This reluctance to embrace a broader range of military roles came to haunt the USA in the counterinsurgency campaigns in both Iraq and Afghanistan.

Focusing on inter-state conflict proved to be a mistake because the USA has found itself frequently in conflicts resulting from civil strife and state failure. Even those inter-state wars in which it has become embroiled have usually been followed by a conflictual and complex phase of military operations. In parts of the world, the Cold War bequeathed an international environment characterised by instability and conflict. US politico-military authorities were nevertheless reluctant to become involved on the grounds that its own national interests were not at stake. They remained wedded to the lessons that had been drawn from the experience of Vietnam that forces should only be engaged when US vital interests were at stake and should be used to guarantee a rapid victory followed by a speedy withdrawal. It became a totem of American foreign policy that there needed to be a clear mission and exit strategy before troops were committed. As a consequence, there was little incentive for the armed services to train and equip themselves for low-intensity conflict.

The US military did not lack the doctrinal thinking for so-called 'military operations other than war' (MOOTW); it had appropriate military doctrine to hand since 1995 in the form of *Field Manual 3-07* (US Army 1995). This document envisaged four types of stability operations, from peace operations and counterinsurgency through to foreign humanitarian assistance and national assistance. Yet preparations for these types of complex and unglamorous tasks received inadequate priority. This was due to both the prejudices of the armed forces and to the political masters to whom they answered. Political leaders were reluctant to dissipate military strength on humanitarian and state-building tasks that were considered a distraction from the military's proper focus of winning wars. On coming to office, the Administration of George W. Bush criticised the previous presidency of Bill Clinton for running down US military strength. In echoes of the criticisms of Mandelbaum (1996), the previous incumbents were seen as guilty of treating 'foreign policy as social work', such as in operations in Haiti or post-conflict roles in the Balkans. The Republicans were of the view that the military should be used only for war-fighting tasks.

Yet the USA came to find that war-fighting was rarely enough – that failure to address the post-conflict period (phase IV) of an operation often robbed its forces of the fruits of victory. Policing, peace enforcement and providing a safe environment for civilian agencies to undertake reconstruction were vital in order to allow conflict zones to transition to functioning societies. If the USA chose not to prepare for these eventualities, it risked handing the initiative to insurgents. Such opponents have the capacity to blend into the civilian population and can fight the USA asymmetrically, offsetting its technological sophistication, and refusing to engage American forces in conventional battles.

The roles played by the three services would change amidst these prolonged counterinsurgency (COIN) struggles. In early campaigns such as the first Gulf War, the US Air Force played the dominant role, but in other campaigns, such as in Kosovo in 1999, the ability of airpower to combat elusive paramilitary forces conducting ethnic cleansing had been circumscribed. For all America's technological prowess, it had been unable to employ the full weight of its aerial assets due to the lack of appropriate targets. Similarly in Afghanistan, once the insurgency became mobilised after 2005, airpower was of limited utility. The Air Force continued to provide tactical air support to troops on the ground, vital intelligence and the ferrying of supplies, but its combat role diminished in importance.

In the case of the US Navy, the rise of COIN operations led it to try to prove its relevance. The Navy Expeditionary Combat Command was established in January 2006 to enable contributions to post-conflict reconstruction and force-protection roles in combat theatres (Friedman 2012: 89). This was a tacit acknowledgement that concentrating on expensive weapons platforms had made the Navy appear out of touch. In reality there has been only a marginal role it can play in such circumstances due to the fact that COIN operations require large numbers of personnel to be based on the ground.

COIN has presented real challenges even to the Army. Although it was the branch of the armed forces best suited to this type of operation, the nature of COIN challenged many traditional assumptions. Advocates of transformation have traditionally argued that the sorts of capabilities offered by technology would make the US military capable of responding to the full spectrum of challenges. A military force equipped with the latest weapon systems would, by definition, need to be highly trained and therefore flexible and able to adapt to conflicts of varying intensities. Yet COIN operations did not offer decisive battles in which the Army would be able to destroy many of the enemy's military assets. Transformational concepts, such as information superiority and battlefield awareness, were only of limited relevance against a dispersed and non-hierarchical enemy (Serena 2011: 52). Low-intensity operations prevented the Army from exploiting its technological expertise and its skills in manoeuvre warfare.

COIN campaigns are notorious for being principally political campaigns in which the military effort represents a subordinate part. Other agencies concerned with law and order, communication with the populace and economic reconstruction have a more important role to play. Where the military is engaged, the emphasis is upon traditional infantry skills as well as strong command and control. Such tasks are much more political than kinetic in nature and more akin to policing functions. They require a high concentration of troops to the civilian population in order to create a tranquil security environment. They also require more attention to be paid to the adversary's political will to sustain the struggle, rather than calibrating the physical losses that have been incurred (Kagan 2006: 217).

In the post-invasion phases in both the wars in Afghanistan and Iraq, it was US ground forces that fought the critical counterinsurgency campaigns. In Iraq this entailed fighting Sunni insurgents, foreign *jihadists* and members of the Shia militias, whilst in Afghanistan it meant fighting the Taliban and foreign fighters who crossed the eastern border from Pakistan. In 2007 the Army responded to its recent experiences by increasing its manpower by 65,000. These conflicts also caused the Army to rethink some of its recent transformational efforts in relation to modular brigades and lightweight armoured vehicles (Farrell et al. 2013: 79–80). The Stryker Combat Brigades were found to suffer from inadequate force protection in Iraq. Rocket-propelled grenades and especially improvised explosive devices (IEDs) came to be the largest cause of fatalities and injuries amongst US personnel serving in Iraq and later Afghanistan. Robert Gates made purchase of the mine-resistant, ambush-protected vehicle (MRAP) a priority of his tenure as secretary of defense, whilst noting that they were, 'contrary to Secretary Rumsfeld's goal of lighter, more agile forces' (Gates 2014: 121).

Recognition that configuring the Army for high-intensity operations had left it ill-prepared for counterinsurgency operations was reflected in the decision in the Pentagon to rewrite US COIN doctrine. General David Petraeus was tasked to undertake a wholesale review and he authored *Field Manual 3-24: Counterinsurgency* in December 2006 (US Army 2006). This approach shifted the centre of gravity of American operations away from combating insurgents to protecting the general population. It was recognised that an insurgency depended on the acquiescence of the population, and that if you could insulate the people from the insurgents whilst guaranteeing their security, then you had the prospect of defeating the enemy. This was accompanied by a 'surge' in personnel on the ground, living and working within the localities in which the insurgency was operating. This reversed the earlier emphasis upon maintaining a small footprint of forces in the theatre. When President Barack Obama came to office he argued that Afghanistan should be prioritised and that the deteriorating security situation be turned around. He dispatched an additional 17,000 US troops to Afghanistan and then, in December 2009, authorised a further deployment of 30,000 troops (Woodward 2010).

Based upon those experiences, the US Army has come to the view that it cannot afford to focus narrowly on war-fighting capabilities. In 2004, Andrew Krepinevich, a highly experienced analyst, warned against configuring the Army for only one eventuality – namely, 'conventional warfare and the open battle' (quoted in Farrell et al. 2013: 94). The lessons from Afghanistan and Iraq have been that the Army must be prepared and trained for conflict at all points in the spectrum: from high-intensity war-fighting to counterinsurgency operations (Korb 2009).

Post-2010 developments

Since the US withdrawal from Iraq in 2010 there have been three major drivers of change impacting on the size and orientation of US armed forces. The first is the hangover from over a decade of fighting insurgencies. Despite General Petraeus's (2013) warning that 'the insurgency era is not over', there is a desire to shift the focus from low-intensity conflict. The armed forces want to switch attention to the risk from major conflicts that could present an existential threat to America (Scott Taylor 2012: 6). Even the Army has advocated the need to relearn how to conduct armoured warfare. It is unsurprising that there is an aversion in Washington to protracted military engagements for its ground forces (Gates 2011). The USA is wary of commitments that could result in long-term counterinsurgency campaigns.

The Obama Administration's predilection for the use of remotely piloted aerial systems (RPAS) is a reflection of this reluctance to be drawn into combat on foreign soil. There has been a marked increase in the use of RPAS for both intelligence gathering and targeted killing. The advantage of these systems is that they enable the USA to conduct surveillance and then strike at targets in inaccessible locations, without putting the lives of its service men and women at risk. America's wariness of overseas conflicts was illustrated by its reluctance to be drawn into both the Libyan and Syrian conflicts.

A second driver, closely related to the first, are the reductions in the size of the US defence budget. Exhausted by seemingly endless wars, the USA has exacted deep cuts to its military. This was initiated in 2010 by Defense Secretary Robert Gates's decision to impose cuts of US$300 billion and was followed by the Budget Control Act that ordered a further $487 billion in cuts over a ten-year period (Khimm 2012). It was then compounded by the process of sequestration that has resulted from the failure of the Executive and Congress to agree on budget cuts, and could lead to an additional $500 billion of cuts over the same period (Odierno 2013). This has echoes of the situation after the Cold War when the military was subject to reductions across the board. The only differences now are that the military are starting from a higher funding base as well as from a decade of being at war.

The third driver is the US military 'pivot to Asia'. In January 2012, the Pentagon's Strategic Guidance announced that the USA would 'rebalance toward the Asia-Pacific region' (US Department of Defense 2012). The move has been symbolised by plans to base US Marines at Darwin in Australia, thereby complementing their other bases in Japan, Guam and Hawaii (Donilon 2012). The USA has undertaken to move up to four ships to Singapore and between one and two additional attack submarines to its base in Guam. By 2020 this will result in 60 per cent of US naval power being deployed in the Pacific theatre (Donilon 2013). It reflects a sense that the Asia-Pacific region is the source of the leading challenges to US policy. The rise of China and its hostility towards Taiwan, the tensions between China and Japan over the Diaoyu/Sankaku Islands, China's dispute with its South-East Asian neighbours over ownership of the South China Sea, and the longstanding confrontation between North and South Korea, are all sources of concern to American policymakers. The US priorities have been to reassure allies such as Japan and the Philippines (see Chapters 8 and 10), put pressure on China by threatening its trade routes, and deterring North Korea from threatening South Korea.

In order to be capable of exerting 'Full Spectrum Dominance' (the ability to overcome an adversary in any operational environment) in the Asia-Pacific region, America would need to be able to project force and to damage an enemy with precision strikes (Cordesman and Hess 2013). It would be neither realistic nor desirable to engage in a manpower-intensive land war in Asia because of the probability of facing numerically superior forces. Reliance would have to be placed on long-range airpower as well as the use of US naval power, both to control the seas and to undertake strikes and amphibious operations against selected targets ashore. The development of Chinese forces is indicative that they seek to offset America's strength in asymmetric ways. They are developing attack submarines, ballistic missiles and cruise missiles to be able to target US carrier battle groups rather than attempting to challenge America's dominance with their own surface vessels. The challenge for the USA is to be confident that its offensive surface fleet could overcome these area-denial capabilities. They would need to be able to survive in an intensely hostile environment, within the so-called 'first island chain' extending from Taiwan and Japan through to the Philippines and the South China Sea (Ross 2012). The American strategy has been designated 'Air-Sea Battle' and was outlined in the Quadrennial Defense Review of 2010 (Greenert and Schwartz 2012). A similar sort of challenge confronts US naval forces seeking to operate within the Persian Gulf against Iran.

The 'Air-Sea Battle' strategy represents a swing of the pendulum towards a strategic posture that is consistent with the interests of the US Navy and Air Force. With its emphasis on agility and long-range strike, a more muscular forward presence in the eastern Pacific satisfies naval and airpower interests (Kwast 2013). It plays to America's technological edge and mollifies those critics who argue that the USA should be an external balancer of threats rather than an expender of blood and treasure in ground wars. The role for the US Army in such a scenario is less clear. Although considerable ground forces remain on the Korean peninsula, the US Marine Corps is seeking to fill the role for naval infantry in the Pacific. With much of the Army now stationed in the continental USA rather than in bases overseas, the challenge of deploying it over long distances is even greater. As a result, the Army is still trying to carve out a role for itself in the Pacific theatre.

Even in the midst of the campaigns in Iraq and Afghanistan, there was a strong sense that the debates within the Pentagon remained focused on future conflicts. With the end of those campaigns, there was a shift in the transformation debate back to inter-state war. The roles of major weapons platforms, such as surface ships and strike aircraft, were once more at the top of the agenda. Emphasis returned the role of air and naval power in deterring major state rivals, rather than focusing on conflicts of lower intensity but greater likelihood.

Conclusion

The term 'transformation' excited expectations that technology would fundamentally change the nature of warfare. Whilst America has been in the vanguard of developments in transformation, it has not delivered such dramatic results. Even an advocate of transformation within the US Army, General Gordon Sullivan, acknowledged that Army efforts had fallen short of a 'bold step into the next century' (quoted in Farrell et al. 2013: 36). Nevertheless, the USA has successfully incorporated a range of new technologies into the inventories of its armed services with the result that they have become unchallengeable on the battlefield. Its mastery of conventional warfare has been evident in all the major post-Cold War conflicts, enabling them to defeat state rivals with relatively negligible losses. When surveying the success of US military power this fact should not be underestimated.

Yet this chapter has argued that transformation was used by America's armed services to continue force postures and weapons programmes that were designed for large-scale, conventional conflicts. They remained wedded to major weapons programmes that would afford them dominance in high-intensity conflict. This was driven by military cultures that regarded preparations for inter-state war as the *raison d'être* of their services. The Army, Air Force, Navy and Marine Corps competed for roles amongst themselves in the midst of a post-Cold War environment that experienced both highs and lows in the provision of defence resources. Although jointery was practised to varying extents on the battlefield, within the Beltway in Washington there was inter-service rivalry.

In doing so, the armed services neglected to prepare for a broader range of conflicts. These included post-conflict, stability and counterinsurgency operations where transformational military capabilities were less relevant. This served America badly in conflicts such as Afghanistan and Iraq when, following the downfall of the regime, large-scale irregular warfare continued. US forces found themselves fighting protracted low-intensity conflicts for which they had been inadequately trained, equipped and prepared. This was apparent from the fact that an extremely capable and technologically advanced force was unable to assert its will over insurgent forces in both theatres.

The reluctance of the armed services to re-orientate their thinking in the midst of the Afghan and Iraqi conflicts was surprising. The adherence to traditional modes of warfare was deeply ingrained. Even before these conflicts ended, the armed services had refocused their energies around the prospect of future conventional conflicts, particularly those in Asia. For the Air Force and the Navy this has enabled them to plan for operations that will reassert their central role in national security planning.

Bibliography

Adams, K. (2006) *The Army after Next: The First Post-industrial Army*, Westport: Praeger Security International.

Boot, M. (2003) 'The New American Way of War', *Foreign Affairs*, Vol. 82, No. 4, pp.41–58.

Brake, J. (2001) *Quadrennial Defense Review (QDR): Background, Process and Issues*, Washington, DC: Library of Congress, Congressional Research Service.

Bush, G.W. (2001, 12 December) *Speech of the US President to the Corps of Cadets*, South Carolina: The Citadel.

Cordesman, A. and Hess, A. (2013) 'The Evolving Military Balance on the Korean Peninsula and Northeast Asia', *Report of the CSIS Burke Chair in Strategy*, Lanham: Rowman & Littlefield.

Donilon, T. (2012, 15 November) 'President Obama's Asia Policy and Upcoming Visit to Asia', Speech of the National Security Adviser to the CSIS. http://www.white house.gov (accessed 15 February 2015).

Donilon, T. (2013, 11 March) 'The US and the Asia Pacific in 2013', Speech of the National Security Adviser to the Asia Society. http://www.whitehouse.gov (accessed 15 February 2015).

Farrell, T., Rynning, S. and Terriff, T. (2013) *Transforming Military Power since the Cold War. Britain, France, and the United States 1991–2012*, Cambridge: Cambridge University Press.

Friedman, B. (2012) 'The Navy after the Cold War', in Sapolsky, H., Green, B. and Friedman, B. (eds) *US Military Innovation since the Cold War: Creation without Destruction*, London: Routledge.

Gates, R. (2011, 25 February) *Speech of the Secretary of Defense to the West Point Military Academy*.

Gates, R. (2014) *Duty: Memoirs of a Secretary at War*, London: W.H. Allen.

Greenert, J. and Schwartz, N. (2012) 'Air-Sea Battle Doctrine', Presentations by the Chief of Naval Operations and the Chief of Staff of the Air Force, Washington, DC: Brookings Institution.

Hallion, R. (2011) 'US Air Power', in Olsen, J.A. (ed.) *Global Air Power*, Washington, DC: Potomac.

Jasper, S. (2009) 'The Capabilities-Based Approach', in Jasper, S. (ed.) *Transforming Defense Capabilities: New Approaches for International Security*, pp. 1–22, London: Lynne Rienner.

Kagan, F. (2006) *Finding the Target: The Transformation of American Military Policy*, New York: Encounter Books.

Khimm, S. (2012, 14 September) 'The Sequester, explained', *The Washington Post*. http://www.washingtonpost.com/blogs/wonkblog/wp/2012/09/14/the-sequester-expla ined/ (accessed 8 January 2015).

Korb, L. (2009) 'Defence Transformation', in Wheeler, W. and Korb, L. (eds) *Military Reform: An Uneven History and an Uncertain Future*, Stanford: Stanford Security Studies.

Krepinevich, A. (2013) 'Transforming the Legions: The Army and the Future of Land Warfare' Washington, DC: Center for Strategic and Budgetary Assessment.

Kwast, S. (2013) 'Military Strategy with Major-General Steven Kwast, Director of the United States Air Force Quadrennial Defense Review', Washington, DC: CSIS.

Lovelace, D. (1997) *Shaping the Future US Armed Forces*, Pennsylvania: US Army War College.

Mandelbaum, M. (1996) 'Foreign Policy as Social Work', *Foreign Affairs*, Vol. 75, pp. 16–32.

Mitchell, P. (2009) *Network Centric Warfare and Coalition Operations: The New Military Operating System*, London: Routledge.

Odierno, R. (2013, 15 February) 'Sequestration is a "Bermuda Triangle" of Uncertainty', Speech by the Army Chief of Staff, Brookings Institution.

Osinga, F. (2010) 'The Rise of Military Transformation', in Terriff, T., Osinga, F. and Farrell, T. (eds) *A Transformation Gap? American Innovations and European Military Change*, Stanford: Stanford University Press.

Petraeus, D. (2013, June) *Speech by General David Petraeus to the Royal United Services Institute*, London.

Ross, R. (2012) 'The Problem with the Pivot. Obama's New Asia Policy is Unnecessary and Counter-productive', *Foreign Affairs*, Vol. 91, No. 6.

Rumsfeld, D. (2002) 'Transforming the Military', *Foreign Affairs*, Vol. 81, No. 3.

Sapolsky, H., Green, B. and Friedman, B. (2012) 'The Missing Transformation', in Sapolsky, H., Green, B. and Friedman, B. (eds) *US Military Innovation since the Cold War: Creation without Destruction*, London: Routledge.

Scott Taylor, G. (2012) *Beyond the Battlefield: Institutional Army Transformation Following Victory in Iraq*, Letort Paper, Pennsylvania: US Army War College, Carlisle Barracks.

Serena, C. (2011) *A Revolution in Military Adaptation: The US Army in the Iraq War*, Washington, DC: Georgetown University Press.

Shimko, K. (2010) *The Iraq Wars and America's Military Revolution*, Cambridge: Cambridge University Press.

US Department of Defense (2012) *Sustaining US Global Leadership: Priorities for the 21st Century*, Washington, DC.

US Army (1995) *US Army Field Manual 3-07 – US Stability Operations Joint Publication*. http://usacac.army.mil/cac2/repository/FM307/FM3-07.pdf (accessed 3 February 2014).

US Army (2006) *Counterinsurgency, FM 3-24*. http://armypubs.army.mil/docs/pdf/fm 3_24.pdf (accessed 31 January 2014).

Woodward, R. (2010) *Obama's Wars*, London: Simon and Schuster.

5 Western European armed forces and the modernisation agenda

Following or falling behind?[1]

David J. Galbreath

Introduction

The US armed forces are unrivalled in their ability to deliver military power persistently around the world. The future of armed warfare as we know it will be greatly dependent on what the USA and its rivals bring to the table in terms of emerging technologies and the concepts, strategies and tactical operations that follow and use them. From the Revolution in Military Affairs (RMA) to network-centric warfare (NCW), the US armed forces have steadily evolved towards reconceptualising high-intensity warfare, not to mention advances in low-intensity warfare (counterinsurgency, or COIN). RMA, NCW and COIN, along with the geo-political shift towards Asia, Africa and the Middle East, leaving Europe without a definable role in US grand strategy.

At the same time, the role of Europe in the USA's vision of its own national security and the way it conceptualises the world has changed. The USA made a clear signal under the Barack Obama Administration that its sense of security and power projection did not encapsulate the transatlantic relationship that had developed since the end of World War II. If we scratch the surface of the George W. Bush Administration, we can also see that the USA was unwilling to be constrained by Western Europe (or 'old Europe') for the sake of maintaining a good security relationship. Indeed, without the Yugoslav wars, one could argue that the US withdrawal and refocus away from Europe would have occurred earlier, as suggested by John Mearsheimer (1990). Indeed, from Casper Weinberger – US secretary of defense during the Ronald Reagan Administration from 1981 to 1989 – onwards, the USA was evolving away from Europe and the so-called 'third generation' of military developments that came with it. In as much as Europe remains important strategically, it is as a Rumsfeldian 'lily pad' for American power projection to Africa and the Middle East.

The key research question here is how Western European armed forces have responded to the US transformation agenda. Are they following or falling behind? 'Following' entails a role for European forces projecting military power outside Europe while at the same time maintaining a stable and secure Europe. 'Following' requires smart militaries, innovative war technologies and changes in how the battlespace is conceptualised and engaged. 'Falling behind' suggests a Europe unwilling to engage in the wider world, at first militarily and eventually politically. 'Falling behind' leaves Western Europe unable to project outwards or to ensure European security independently. Europe's response has the potential to shape global security in the twenty-first century, and thus the consequences of following or falling behind matter for Europe, the USA and the world.

This chapter examines Western European armed forces, particularly in relation to the transformation agenda. The first section looks at how Western European militaries have changed since the Cold War. Particular attention is paid to the key drivers of US and European military relations. The second section examines how the transformation agenda has impacted on UK, French and German forces. Attention is devoted to network centricity, expeditionary forces and effects-based operations, and transformation is assessed in terms of operations, organisations and personnel. The final section concludes by arguing that European forces are more likely to follow than fall behind the USA.

Changes in European defence

The role of armed forces in Western Europe has changed greatly since the Cold War – or at least, one would expect so. Despite the nature of risks and threats to European national security, many of the militaries we have today do much the same thing as they did some two decades ago: remain ready to deploy conventional forces to defend or attack a territorial position. Yet, despite much of what European forces saw in Yugoslavia, not to mention Afghanistan and (for some) Iraq, many European states remain unsuited for anything other than territorial defence. At the same time, European societies are increasingly unsure of what to make of their militaries. European societies want to see their militaries as a force for 'good'. European governments want to see their armed forces as stabilisers. Militaries themselves, on the other hand, are concerned with high-intensity kinetic warfare. All of these roles are about force projection, but each requires different sorts of militaries. Finally, and in many ways most importantly, European militaries exist in a larger security community where the USA plays an important role in shaping national interests and arguably even security identities. As the USA has repositioned itself towards Asia, European militaries have been asked by the Americans to 'pick up the slack', 'get on board' and 'be ready to play ball'.

While we see changes in armed engagement, public expectations and the geo-political projection of power, we have to ask to what degree Western European armed forces are able to cope with the post-territorial warfare of the future. Why should we assume that warfare would be post-territorial? First, proximity is becoming less important as power and technology change the way we think about space and time. For instance, the ability to project power has the potential to decrease costs as human-controlled and autonomous systems become more efficient and less resource heavy. Second, and most importantly, is the decline of defence in favour of security. We can see that in Europe, especially, there is a decline in what we consider a matter of martial defence, though we can agree that some security issues, such as environmental crises, may lead to martial responses.

In other words, for good or ill, national and regional security is no longer a factor of the scale of military response, but rather something broader and more encompassing including environmental, economic, social and political challenges. For both of these reasons, the need for European militaries is more likely to be implementing security beyond the border rather than the defence of it. For this reason, we can see why Western European states put a premium on force transformation. As a result, Europeans understand that there is an impetus for their militaries to change, not only because of budget pressures, but also because what Europeans want and expect from their militaries is changing. When European militaries think of modernisation and force transformation, the transatlantic relationship, the North Atlantic Treaty Organization (NATO) and the US military all play a role as socialisers and ordering from the menu (Jacoby 2004).

European militaries have deployed in joint operations with the USA in and out of NATO in the former Yugoslavia, Iraq, Afghanistan, Libya and elsewhere. The future of joint operations depends on these allies being able to continue to work together and, as discussed, this relationship is both empowered and threatened by transformation. This section looks specifically at how the USA and NATO have tried to influence European militaries through the transformation and modernisation agendas. Following this, we will be in a better position to analyse specific instances of impact amongst Western European forces.

Contemporary force transformation is a result of changes in US thinking on how to plan and execute swift military operations on the 'digitalised battlefield' (Boyer 2004: 75). Transformation is not only about how militaries evolve to fight wars but is also aimed at changing the nature of war itself. As a consequence, as Yves Boyer has shown, European states must understand and in some cases even meet the challenges of transformation (Boyer 2004). The natural interface between the USA and European states is NATO, and the transformation agenda has been a part of the NATO agenda since the 1990s but particularly after the Bush Administration in 2001. Yet, questions about post-Cold War interoperability were first addressed in the establishment of the Multinational Interoperability Council (MIC) in 1996. Among the USA and its Anglophone allies, naval interoperability was also addressed in AUSCANNZUKUS, otherwise known as 'Five Eyes'. While the MIC and 'Five Eyes' agreement have been important for interoperability, NATO became the vehicle of choice for US attempts to bring RMA to its European allies.

The ability of Western European military powers to respond to US calls for transformation relies on two functions. The first is the product of transformation as it has emanated from the USA. The *Joint Vision 2010* established both a view of technological change in the American military and the scope for implementation throughout the services. Importantly, the document established a joint strategy for implementing transformation. US transformation relies on 'Full Spectrum Dominance' – readiness to engage with everything from peacekeeping and crisis management to 'fight to win' scenarios. The document also calls on the greater communication and manoeuvrability between services as personnel, expertise and equipment are shared and distributed across the US military. In 34 pages, *Joint Vision 2010* attempts to formulate a template for force transformation. We can see that the RMA would evolve the US military to deal with full-spectrum operations, greater organisational communication and increased training of personnel towards the use and deployment of ever increasingly sophisticated technology. As Boyer illustrates, the RMA was 'made in America'.

The second function of force transformation is the ability and willingness of European forces to adapt to this American vision of modern and future warfare. Boyer argues that European allies were 'first intrigued and then "requested" to adjust their force posture to the shift in military affairs apparently being made by the US' (Boyer 2004: 77). The launch of the NATO Defence Capabilities Initiative (DCI) at the Washington NATO Summit in 1999 also emphasised for US allies that change in line with RMA was encouraged. Boyer (2004: 77) states: 'the ambitions rapidly faded away, however, and the goals set by the DCI were, for the most part, never met by the Europeans'.

Was NATO the wrong vehicle for transformation in Europe? Boyer points to several constraints. The first is that the USA pushed transformation at a moment when both NATO and the European Security and Defence Identity (ESDI) were changing. Following the Washington Summit, NATO was being altered further away from its Cold War roots of collective defence. Questions were being asked about what role it had to play in Europe, allowing some to say that NATO's existence started and ended with enlargement. At the same time, the St Malo agreement between the UK and France and the subsequent Helsinki and Cologne European Councils allowed for the establishment of a European Security and Defence Policy (ESDP), though its operationalisation would not be sanctioned until the 2001 Nice Treaty.

Second, 'transformation' itself was pushed by the USA in NATO as more than simply changes in how the alliance prepared and deployed for war. Rather, the transformation agenda appeared to go far beyond this to represent the future of Europe's continued military alliance with the USA: keep up or give up. Much has been written on the so-called capabilities gap between the USA and Europe (Coonen 2006; Yost 2007). Not only was Europe being told to keep up, but it was also being told that the rules of the game had changed. The US transformation agenda was taken in military circles in Europe much as it had been taken in much of the American military: as a passing fad. Christopher Schnaubelt (2007) argues that many in the US military were sceptical of why one should transform areas in which one was already dominant.

The final reason why NATO was not fit for the transformation agenda was the breakdown in trust between European governments and the Bush Administration, especially in the first term (2000–04). The unreciprocated European response to the USA after the terrorist attacks of 11 September 2001 and the subsequent fallout over Iraq are well documented. As Boyer states, 'the problem is that these efforts at change and "Alliance transformation" no longer coincide with an automatically agreed vision of the international scene between the US and many of its European allies' (Boyer 2004: 81). He goes on to say: '[NATO's] eminent task is so vague that indeed it authorises every type of action and opens the possibility that the Alliance address every type of problem that could be seen as threatening [its] values' (Boyer 2004: 82).

NATO's ability to be a transformer of sorts was curtailed in the first instance by changes in the alliance, changes in ESDP and changes in the transatlantic relationship. Yet, the wars in Iraq and Afghanistan have had a much larger impact on the way that militaries think about transformation as modernisation. In the next section, we look at the impact of the US transformation agenda on Europe within new martial and technological environments.

Transformation agenda in Western Europe

What exactly are we asking our militaries to do? Transformation can be defined as 'a continuous process that shapes the nature of military competition and cooperation through new combinations of emerging technologies, streamlined organisational structures, innovative processes, and adapted personnel developments that exploit national advantages and protect against asymmetric vulnerabilities' (Jasper 2009: 2–3). For Jasper, thus, this transformation meant a move from a 'threat-based model' of defence planning to that of the 'capabilities-based' model. On this scale, we should be able to see transformation along the lines of operational, organisational and personnel changes that exploit technological innovation (Jasper 2009: 4). Jasper argues that transformation is fundamental given the rise in diversity in the sorts of insecurities that states face today, in the form of non-state actors, rogue states, piracy and failed states. Christopher Dandeker (1994) argued that the West is facing constant shifts in the international system: shifts in power, threat, decision making, sovereignty and public opinion. All of these shifts impact in some way on the way that militaries respond to events. The diversity of challenges brings us back to a 'capabilities-based model'. With this, we should be able to see the impact of the transformation agenda through operational, organisational and personnel changes.

In addition to this framework, we need to be able to identify transformation when we see it in Western European militaries. This is possible through the 2001 US Quadrennial Defense Review (QDR), which laid out transformation in the following way:

1   *Strengthening joint operations*: Transformation prioritises speed and flexibility in operations. Speed refers to the start-up resources to respond to immediate deployment. Flexibility, on the other hand, refers to the 'scalable' and 'modular' nature of forces 'to allow combatant commanders to draw

on the appropriate forces to deter or defeat an adversary' (US Department of Defense 2001: 32). Further on, the QDR refers to the practical applications of this: 'US forces require the ability to communicate not only with one another, but also with other government agencies and allies and friends' (US Department of Defense 2001: 33).

2   *Experimentation on the ways of war*: The QDR set out ways in which transformation could be tested in the battlespace. The document has a heavy focus on the role of exercises, war games and simulations in addition to experiments. Iraq and Afghanistan acted as live experimentation spaces. For the US military, command, control, communication, computers, intelligence, surveillance, targeting acquisition and reconnaissance (C4ISTAR) was of particular interest as it enabled experimentation with ways to control space (US Department of Defense 2001: 37).

3   *Exploiting intelligence advantages*: Transformation included rethinking the way data would be used in intelligence and engagement. Of particular interest here is the US military tasking, processing, exploiting and dissemination (TPED) system (US Department of Defense 2001, 40). The system is a combination of human intelligence (HUMINT) and Signals intelligence (SIGINT) used to inform and enhance integrated command infrastructures (themselves part of the transformation agenda). The effects of maximising intelligence advantages can be seen also on the ground in the battlespace with the increased use of situational awareness displays.

4   *Developing transformational capabilities* (US Department of Defense 2001: 40): Herein lies the clearest sense of a military in transformation. These new transformational capabilities are about how to collect and process data faster, cover space faster, and be flexible and respond more quickly. These transformational capabilities are directed towards defending bases as well as maintaining a presence in anti-access and area-denial environments.

For the purposes of this chapter, we will look at the following as indications of this transformation, as laid out above: 1 network centricity; 2 expeditionary forces; and 3 effects-based operations. These transformative capabilities have had considerable impact on the US military as dictated by the literature and tactical operations in Iraq and Afghanistan.

An important part of this revolution are the technological advances and edge that the USA has enjoyed over potential enemies. It is unclear whether this technological transformation is changing the nature and character of the battlespace itself. Nevertheless, this provides a guide to how transformation might look if it were adopted by European militaries. It would not be expected that an American version of transformation would transfer directly to European forces. However, privy to much of the same doctrine and technology, not to mention having fought one, and in some cases two, wars with their American ally, we should expect some degree of transformation in Western European militaries.

The American approach to RMA has been discussed often in the literature (Morgan 2000; Cohen 2004; Hamilton 2004; Hoffman 2006; Farrell and Rynning 2010). The changes in the US military around operations, organisations and personnel, and how these have been affected by changes in strategic doctrine generally and advances in science and technology more specifically, are a point of interest and concern for European forces, particularly because of the disparity in resources and posturing between the USA and its transatlantic partners in and out of NATO. Our goal is to see how the USA has shaped Western European forces. Our analytical framework looks at the UK, France and Germany across operations, organisation and personnel, to see how they have changed in relation to network centricity, expeditionary forces and effects-based operations. The result of this study can be seen in Table 5.1.

While taking part in numerous military operations since the end of the Cold War, European militaries have been configured for fighting Cold War operations. Whether in terms of large-scale mechanised infantry or submarine hunters, European militaries were orientated towards engaging the Soviet Union and its allies in a regional, if not global war. The ability of European militaries to evolve away from this has been discussed in the literature in detail. If we look, for example, at the level of military spending by the UK, France and Germany over time, we can see that Germany dramatically reduced its defence budget and number of personnel. The UK and France did see some reduction in defence budgets, though these were temporary until around 2010 when they began to decline again. The ability of European militaries to make a discernible shift in how they engage with asymmetric warfare, which has become most common in the post-Cold War period, has been slow.

Network centricity

The transformation agenda in the USA started, as Colin Gray (1981) contended, with a focus on technological advances. The nature of how technology could make militaries more flexible and responsive was especially appealing to early strategic thinkers such as Admiral William Owens, Vice Admiral Arthur Cebrowski and others. Network centricity became an important part of the US transformation agenda and subsequently a cornerstone for NATO transformation efforts. The notion of NCW is one of networks over platforms. Where platforms are preformed WYSIWYG ('what you see is what you get') units that serve specific operational functions, networks are intended to inform operations in real time to allow for greater responsiveness and aptitude. Networks have become a part of transformation of European militaries in strategic and operational terms.

The three militaries under observation came to network centricity at different times, though all taking the concept from the USA. Network centricity was a product of the US transformation agenda in and around NATO. The UK, France and Germany were affected by the US concept of NCW through

Table 5.1 Snapshot analysis of force transformation in Europe

	Network centricity	Expeditionary forces	Effects-based approach
Operations	UK: Iraq, Afghanistan, NATO joint exercises, close US support	UK: Iraq, Afghanistan, Army 2020 programme, FRES (delayed), resource poor	UK: Iraq, Afghanistan, NATO joint exercises, diverging from US approach
	France: Afghanistan, Operation Nemausus, NATO exercises	France: Afghanistan, Francophone Africa	France: Afghanistan, Stabilisation operations, Kapisa mission
	Germany: AMN, Thales system	Germany: limited application in Afghanistan	Germany: 'three-block warfare' focus
Organisations	UK: NEC, Joint Doctrine and Concepts Centre, Bowman combat infrastructure platform (CIP), Skynet 5	UK: TRACER and MREV programmes ended, MRAP replacement	UK: JDCC/DCDC, Permanent Joint Headquarters, Comprehensive Approach, Tactical Conflict Assessment Framework
	France: NEB (digitisation), SICAT, SIC21 (a new-generation command information system), 'C4ISR On-the-Move'	France: Model 2014, consistent Army budget (joint services) Scorpion, système de contact de futur (SCF), bulle opérationnelle aéroterrestre (BOA)	France: Emergency First Response (EFR), DGA/Army split
	Germany: NetOpF, NEC, Transformation Coordination Group, SATCOMBw2, MobKommSysBw	Germany: Konzeption der Bundeswehr (2004), Eingreifskraefte, modularisation	Germany: Bundeswehr Transformation Centre
Personnel	UK: DII training and refit, 12 Mechanised Brigade (Iraq)	UK: Strategic doctrine development via Lessons Exploitation Centre (LXC), filtered into COIN	UK: refitted for a commander-led culture, 52 Brigade-Musa Qala
	France: limited	France: ground manoeuvre brigades, Félin, HOBOT	France: PP30, Commission Départementale d'Equipement
	Germany: limited	Germany: ISAF high/low-intensity mix, skill set change	Germany: limited

bilateral coordination, institutionally in NATO and also by socialisation. Later, combat experience would play a major role in bringing networks to the fore for those operating in Iraq and Afghanistan. Being the most closely aligned with the USA, there was considerable openness to military ideas from across the Atlantic (Farrell et al. 2013: 184–85). As the USA and UK went to war together in Iraq in 2003, the UK defence establishment was consolidating its approach to NCW. Where NCW amounted to thinking of war and operations differently, the UK was more constrained in its approach. The concept of 'network-enabled capabilities' (NEC) was the British approach to network centricity. That change from NCW to NEC can be seen as the result of brakes being put on transformation, particularly in the British Army. 'Two core British Army interests – organisational autonomy and size – were under assault during this period' (Farrell et al. 2013: 184). At the same time, concerned with their relationship with the US military, the UK military maintained an emphasis on network centricity even as the Army was being scaled back: 'it is to their tempo of deployment that the UK must aspire.' As we shall see, the status of the British Army in Europe, as it was in the USA, would be a major factor in the take-up of transformation concepts.

The UK Ministry of Defence took NEC as an important feature that characterised the development of the military (and in particular the British Army). The creation of the Joint Doctrine and Concepts Centre (JDCC, later the Development, Concepts and Doctrine Centre – DCDC), following the 1998 Strategic Defence Review (SDR), is an illustration of how a shared programme of NEC would influence the implementation of network centricity in operations. The JDCC was an important organisational shift for the progress of NEC to take hold. The centre also reflected its US equivalent. The application of NEC in the field was also related to effects-based approaches to operations. NEC shaped personnel through the Defence Information Infrastructure (DII) training and the related equipment refit. This change in operations can be seen in the deployment of the 12 Mechanised Brigade in 2005 as the first brigade in the Army to bring the Bowman system into service. British forces have been at the forefront in Europe of introducing network centricity, though France has not been far behind.

France came to the concept of network centricity more slowly, though they diverge on what has been accomplished. The French approach to transformation came about in the mid-1990s with a change in government and the introduction of the 'Model 2015' military. With a model in hand, there were still considerable problems of professionalisation and strategic thinking that needed to be done before transformation could take hold. In the late 1990s, though, NATO began running Multinational Digitised Interoperability Exercises (MDIEs) aimed at testing networks in combined and joint environments. According to Farrell et al. (2013: 220), 'these exercises … sparked new thinking in France'. The result was the French Army's *numerisation de l'espace de bataille* (NEB). 'NEB was new because it went beyond – below – the level of strategy and envisaged the operational and tactical integration of forces in one overarching information system' (Farrell et al. 2013: 220). The French defence armaments procurement agency (DGA) established the PP30 programme for modernising the military. The French Army came away from the modernisation experience with a need to create NCW within and developed SICAT (*Systéme informatique de communication de l'armée de terre*). SICAT was 'quite reasonably [...] suited to the Army's operation needs as opposed to technological or industrial imperatives, [...] the problem was that SICAT did not communicate outside the Army' (Farrell et al. 2013: 222). In other words, the French Army network was smaller than operationally necessary. For France, a major brake was the tension that existed between the DGA and the Army, where the former wanted to design and build out of what the latter thought best to fight.

Unlike the UK, there was no direct pressure from either side for Germany to follow the US lead in NCW. The German Bundeswehr was aware of the introduction and use of information technologies in the USA for the same reason as the French – through NATO programmes and exercises. However, the German response was quite different. The first major mention of network centricity was in the 2006 Defence White Paper. From this introduction, there was the establishment of the NetOpF protocol which, relying on the US characterisation of network centricity, lays out a future unveiling of NEC throughout the Bundeswehr. Ina Wiesner highlights how network centrality was introduced in Germany as based on the US notion of NCW, but was 'holistic and intellectual in nature' (Wiesner 2013: 114). The German approach to network centricity is NEC. The German military linked NEC specifically to effects. In other words, where the USA sought to change the way specific functional operations looked and were used in the battlespace, NEC was a way to enable 'jointness and combinedness' (Wiesner 2013: 116).

The lofty role of NEC itself says something about the lack of implementation of network centricity in the Bundeswehr. Integration in the Bundeswehr is relatively poor in comparison with our other countries studied. Where the USA, UK and France have all established joint command structures, the German Ministry of Defence has a long history without core competencies in this area (Young 1996). As a result, coordination and even vital delegation of the NEC programme was lacking, though the Bundeswehr Transformation Coordination Group would wish it otherwise. Wiesner (2013: 117) states: 'between 2000 and 2005 the Bundeswehr Chief of the Armed Forces Staff and the Armed Forces Staff did not have the necessary authority over the other services, let alone the civilian directorates in the Ministry to direct NEC conceptualisation.' Most importantly, many of the drivers that we see in the UK and French cases, such as a 'special relationship' with the USA, global position or vested interests in defence industries, are not present in the German case.

While the US concept of network centricity had taken different tones in the UK, France and Germany, combat operations would have a crystallising effect on the implementation of network centricity on the battlefield. The UK worked with American soldiers both as special and conventional forces in

Helmand province. Interoperability with the USA was a vital function of that combat relationship. The UK has been able to use its NEC systems, such as Bowman and Skynet 5, in operations. The French have also used Afghanistan as a way to deliver NEB through the use of SICAT and 'C4ISR-on-the-move'. The French military were already showing their use of network centricity in 2004 in Operation Nemausus as part of a peace enforcement exercise (Rynning 2010: 66). In Ivory Coast and later in Afghanistan, the French military used fully networked deployments to their advantage in the battlespace. Though slower to start, Germany too has implemented some degree of network centricity in combat operations. Two programmes that have made this easier are worth mentioning (Wiesner 2013: 121). The first is SATCOMBw2, which saw the launch of two military community satellites in 2009 and 2010. This programme meant that the German military was less reliant on commercial satellites for broadband. MobKommSysBw, initiated around the same time, offers tactical data transfer across the network. The British, French and German militaries were all impacted by the launch of the Afghan Mission Network (AMN), established by the USA, to improve communications within the International Security Assistance Force (ISAF). In 2010 when the German Ministry of Defence could not provide a ready interoperable communication and information system (CIS) solution, they responded by leasing the 'off-the-shelf' FOC+ system developed by the Thales Group. Wiesner (2013: 114) explains: 'this decision was spurred by the announcement of NATO headquarters to deploy two US brigades to the Regional Command North, which was under German command'. The lesson is that when the Americans come to join you, interoperability is a necessity.

Network centricity has been an important development for nearly every major military in the world. The Western European militaries discussed here have used it as a way to augment the way they collect and share information in the battlespace, as well as how they cooperate and coordinate with others. One of the major features of this development is the impact that it has had on equipment.

Expeditionary forces

As US secretary of defense, Donald Rumsfeld had said that he wanted a 'leaner, faster, meaner' military. Yet, the move to make the US military 'meaner' and 'faster' started before Rumsfeld took office. The move to be faster and more responsive was an important element in the US transformation agenda. As US forces began to question how to master time and space in warfare, the role of expeditionary forces as rapid-reaction, full-spectrum forces rose again in interest that it had not seen since before World War II. The US focus on expeditionary forces built on a common martial heritage with European militaries. This shared history, as well as a similar realisation of the changing character of the operations in which European states would take part, gives us reason to look at how the US transformation agenda influenced the UK,

French and German forces. The key features of expeditionary forces are weight, resources and modularity as we look across operational, organisational and personnel effects.

The 1998 SDR in the UK set in motion a rethinking of how UK forces could respond to national and global security crises. Coming out of the wars in the former Yugoslavia, the focus was how to get forces in and out quickly. The focus in the USA was rethinking firepower: in other words, 'meaner' forces. In the UK, the focus was less on lethality and more on deployability on a faster timescale.[2] Following the SDR, the Ministry of Defence focused on the idea of a medium-weight force that could be quickly deployed to a Yugoslav-type conflict. The programme was the Future Rapid Effects System (FRES), a suite of vehicles for various purposes. The US military had equipped their forces with Stryker vehicles which could be deployed quickly and could withstand the risks in Iraq and Afghanistan. The British Army was fighting primarily a budgetary battle while undergoing the greatest downsizing it had ever seen. The conundrum became finding a vehicle that could suit forces while at the same time being generic enough to be used in a greater range of operations. The FRES programme was designed to do just that. Furthermore, the selected vehicle would need to be 'Bowmanised' (equipped with computerised information technology systems) to support NEC in the field. The move to equip expeditionary forces properly has continually been thwarted, with the end of the TRACER and MREV programmes, the hunt for the mine-resistant, ambush-protected (MRAP) vehicle replacements and further delay of the FRES programme. The hunt for a medium-weight, quick-response force remains ongoing, though COIN operations have dampened the demand for one. Even strategic doctrine development from the Lessons Exploitation Centre formerly aimed at expeditionary forces has become much more engaged with COIN. More recently, the 'Army 2020' initiative set out a new, smaller, more responsive British Army that would be able to provide the type of forces required for expeditionary missions. The key question is whether budgets will trump strategic necessity in the future.

The French Army has a long history of expeditionary forces, owing to their colonial and post-colonial military operations in Africa. As the Cold War needs of heavy artillery and mechanised infantry decreased, the French Army saw a new role in expeditionary forces. The US transformation agenda and its focus on rapid-reaction, responsive forces was an important driver in this thinking. At the same time, France did not take part in the NATO Military Committee but nonetheless followed the Strategy Review Group. Ministers even joined NATO ministerial meetings from 1995. A year prior, the 1994 Defence White Paper 'Model 2015' called for a greater emphasis on expeditionary forces, responding to French participation in the crisis management operations in the former Yugoslavia (Farrell et al. 2013: 209). Rather than 'leaner and meaner', the French military saw expeditionary forces as being a broader platform of engagement that could deal with anything from kinetic operations to 'military operations other than war' (MOOTW).

The development of expeditionary forces, as elsewhere, was partly determined by strategic objectives and economics. Unlike its British counterpart, the French Army was doing well in terms of budgets in relation to the other services. If transformation were to happen in the Army, it would have to pay for it. The result was the iteration of the NEB, as discussed earlier, as well as new programmes. Concentrating on the need to be fast and flexible, the French Army established new ground manoeuvre brigades, capitalising on medium- to light-weight equipment and modularity, whereby specific functions 'plug' and 'unplug' depending on the nature of the operation. Furthermore, the *Félin* combat system sets to remake the French Army soldier through the kit that s/he carries. Félin is a set of networked equipment 'enhancing his information level, vision, protection and ability to shoot without exposing his body' (Farrell et al. 2013: 260). In this sense, the system represents an exoskeleton which can be cumbersome for conventional combat infantry to withstand on a prolonged basis. The Félin system is also being used in other militaries, such as Australia. The science and technological advances of materials may make the unit less cumbersome over time. Nevertheless, the important point is that this system, along with the HOBOT (homme robot) programme, exemplifies the converging nature of transformation in the French and US cases where firepower, flexibility and intelligence are being maximised at the cost of more traditional tactics.

Unlike the UK and France, Germany has borrowed less from the US transformation agenda around the case of expedition warfare. Beyond German Special Forces, expeditionary concepts and approaches have been lacking on the ground. Where Iraq and Afghanistan have been important for experimentation of transformative concepts and technologies, Germany has been restrained for reasons to do with domestic politics, military culture and the perspective on future conflicts (Dyson 2005: 2011). Some degree of expeditionary thinking has occurred at least in the conceptual phase. For instance, the Konzeption der Bundeswehr in 2004 set out the need for the Bundeswehr to be responsive to a 'third block strategy', building on the US military notion of multiple operational needs in theatre. Furthermore, through the Eingriefskraefte units have been established to act as fast-response intervening troops that could be defined as proto-expeditionary units. Beyond this, modularisation remains a priority for the Bundeswehr as it perceives being responsive for various forms of operation, not all being kinetic. The framework for expeditionary forces is coming into place for Germany. The key difference, as Tom Dyson illustrates in his work, is the lack of will and structure for making such strategic decisions.

While the nature and implementation of expeditionary forces varies, we can see an impact from the US transformation agenda. Many of the US conceptual programmes of the 1990s have made their way through to the UK, France and Germany, especially as part of modernisation as well as combat experience, particularly in Afghanistan. 'If Europe emerges with smaller border-defence forces but far better expeditionary strike forces, it will have gained hugely in the bargain' (Binnendijk and Kugler 2007: 129). Importantly, discussing network centricity and expeditionary forces requires us to engage with how these militaries have attempted to internalise effects-based approaches to operations.

Effects-based approach

The notion of effects-based operations (EBO) was a way to ask the question: What do you want out of a military operation? From this broad perspective, EBO in the American sense came to be used for a variety of approaches. In the USA, EBO challenged the US Army to think and deliver differently. Originally a US Air Force concept, EBO was applied in the military as a way to transition away from large regimental platforms fit for defending Western Europe against a Soviet invasion, towards a 'leaner' and more flexible response to full-spectrum operations. With the wars in Afghanistan and Iraq, EBO encapsulated the wide spectrum of duties that came with military intervention in these states. For the USA, this meant tailoring ground operations to match the ends, ranging from state building to COIN to open kinetic warfare. The crux of the US approach to EBO has been the joint and combined nature of operations. European militaries also used it, especially in their armies, and applied it to their own combat experiences.

The UK sought to use EBO as a way of revising a holistic approach to military operations. While beginning with the US approach to EBO, the UK JDCC/DCDC led the way in fashioning a British approach to EBO (Farrell et al. 2013: 145). When it came time to test the concept in a joint exercise in 2005 (Joint Venture 5), the coming together of services resulted in an overly complex command structure. In a 'British culture of mission command', the JDCC quickly replaced EBO with a more British 'effects-based approach to operations' (EBAO). 'The EBAO was recast as a way of thinking about planning and operations, rather than a hard and fast science as suggested in US doctrine on EBO' (Farrell et al. 2013: 145). Furthermore, EBAO was recast as a way to improve the relationship between the military and other government agencies. The now DCDC put EBAO in place as a philosophy of operations rather than a rule book. From this point, the 'comprehensive approach' was in evidence and it found echoes in France and Germany as well. The comprehensive approach set out to encompass the multitude of political, economic, social and military objectives in the battlespace. For the UK military, network centricity and expeditionary forces were key to EBAO in as much as they were the tools that the military would use in the field to engage with this more complex, comprehensive approach. The tensions within the way the UK approached EBAO in Iraq and Afghanistan are many, but are outside the scope of this chapter. The key issue is that the US concept of EBO was worth adopting in the first instance, but quickly needed to be nationalised in the face of politics and resources in the military and government.

The French relationship with the USA, poor as it was, impacted on the nature of transformation in that socialisation and coercion did not influence France in the same way they might have done other full NATO countries.

The French Army saw in the US transformation agenda an opportunity to remake themselves following the end of the Cold War, much in the same entrepreneurial spirit as the British and German armies. The key difference, however, is that the French Air Force and Navy had less communication with the USA and less reason to seek joint operations with one another or with the Army. As a result, French EBO thinking began with a lack of 'jointness'. While France continued to reach out to NATO, and eventually re-joined, French transformation was about rethinking the use of force and not simply importing US ideas about modern warfare. Where the USA had EBO and the UK EBAO, France has a 'synergy of effects' which can be found rooted in the French martial thought from Antoine-Henri Jomini onwards. With the connection between NEB and expeditionary forces with EBAO confirmed in the UK case, it is little surprise perhaps that the 'energy of effects is an outgrowth of the information technology inherent in NCW and the mobility inherent in expeditionary warfare' (Farrell et al. 2013: 24). When we note the divisive relationship around NEB between the DGA and the Army, as well as between the Army and other services, we can see a challenge to the implementation of EBO in France. More recently, the needs for joint command operations (or coherence) have been more fully recognised, such as in the PP30 transformation process, perhaps under the return to NATO and experience in Afghanistan and in Common Security and Defence Policy missions in Africa.

Finally, Germany's relationship with EBO was perhaps the most limited. Tom Dyson (2011) illustrates the internal, structural reasons why the US concept of EBO had less traction in Germany. The key reason for its articulation in the military is the lack of a joint command responsibility within the Bundeswehr which could have made the process. Referring to what they label 'effects-based thinking', the previously introduced concept of 'three-block warfare' represents the limitations of EBO in the Bundeswehr. German doctrine, such as that coming out of the Bundeswehr Transformation Centre, has not taken EBO further despite NATO influence and the experience of Afghanistan. In as much as EBO has influenced German military doctrine, we can see a casual assumption that the Bundeswehr has been doing effects-based thinking all along. The result is a limited impact on operations, organisations and personnel.

Conclusion: transformation or adaptation?

We began with the question of whether Western European forces were following or falling behind. The previous analysis suggests that in as much as the US transformation agenda is an important driver of force transformation in Europe, there are many impediments to internalising American military concepts into domestic military contexts. Taken together, network centricity, expeditionary warfare and effects-based approaches make for an understanding of transformation as befitting the US agenda. While we have talked about them separately here, and they have different champions and constraints in reality, they are in fact very closely connected, as illustrated in the US QDR. American influence has been active through NATO as well as through combat experience in Afghanistan and (for the UK) Iraq. Currently, the role of transformation in Europe is as much hemmed in by budgets and political willingness as it is by strategic narratives of transformation coming from the USA (Strachan 2013). Based on this and the study here, the conclusion is one of following rather than falling behind.

Notes

1 This chapter is based on research produced by a grant funded by the Economic and Social Research Council, entitled 'The Drivers of Military Strategic Reform in the Face of Economic Crisis and Changing Warfare', ES/K010190/1. This chapter was first published in *Defence Studies* Vol. 23, No. 4 (2014): 394–413 (Taylor & Francis Ltd, www.tandfonline.com), reprinted by permission of the publisher.
2 Incidentally, the value of expeditionary forces comes to the fore if one reads on the conditions of the British response to the Argentine invasion of the Falklands.

Bibliography

Alberts, D.S., Gartska, J.J. and Stein, F.P. (1999) *Network Centric Warfare: Developing and Leveraging Information Superiority*, Washington, DC: US Department of Defense.
Barnett, T.P.M. (1999) 'The Seven Deadly Sins of Network-Centric Warfare', *Proceedings Magazine*, Vol. 125, No. 1, pp. 36–39.
Binnendijk, H. and Kugler, R. (2007) 'Transforming European Forces', *Survival*, Vol. 44, pp. 117–132.
Boyer, Y. (2004) 'The Consequences of U.S. and NATO Transformation for the European Union' in Hamilton, D.S. (ed.) *Transatlantic Transformations: Equipping NATO for the 21st Century*, Washington, DC: Center for Transatlantic Relations, pp. 75–90.
Cohen, E. (2004) 'Change and Transformation in Military Affairs', *Journal of Strategic Studies* Vol. 27, No. 3, pp. 395–407.
Coonen, S.J. (2006) 'The Widening Military Capabilities Gap between the United States and Europe: Does It Matter?' *Parameters* Vol. 36, pp. 67–84.
Dahl, E.J. (2002) 'Network Centric Warfare and the Death of Operational Art', *Defense Studies* Vol. 2, No. 1, pp. 1–24.
Dandeker, C. (1994) 'New Times for the Military: Some Sociological Remarks on the Changing Role and Structure of the Armed Forces of the Advanced Societies', *The British Journal of Sociology*, Vol. 45, pp. 637–654.
Dyson, T. (2005) 'German Military Reform 1998–2004: Leadership and the Triumph of Domestic Constraint over International Opportunity', *European Security*, Vol. 14, No. 3, pp. 361–386.
Dyson, T. (2011) 'Managing Convergence: German Military Doctrine and Capabilities in the 21st Century', *Defense Studies*, Vol. 11, No. 2, pp. 244–270.
Farrell, T. (2008) 'The Dynamics of British Military Transformation', *International Affairs*, Vol. 84, pp. 777–807.
Farrell, T. and Rynning, S. (2010) 'NATO's Transformation Gaps: Transatlantic Differences and the War in Afghanistan', *Journal of Strategic Studies*, Vol. 33, No. 5, pp. 673–699.

Farrell, T., Rynning, S. and Terriff, T. (2013) *Transforming Military Power since the Cold War: Britain, France, and the United States, 1991–2012*, Cambridge: Cambridge University Press.

Gray, C.S. (1981) 'National Style in Strategy: The American Example', *International Security*, Vol. 6, No. 2, pp. 21–47.

Hamilton, D.S. (ed.) (2004) *Transatlantic Transformations: Equipping NATO for the 21st Century*, Washington, DC: Center for Transatlantic Relations.

Hoffman, F.G. (2006) 'Complex Irregular Warfare: The Next Revolution in Military Affairs', *Orbis*, Vol. 50, No. 3, pp. 395–411.

Jacoby, W. (2004) *The Enlargement of the European Union and NATO: Ordering from the Menu in Central Europe*, Cambridge: Cambridge University Press.

Jasper, S. (2009) 'The Capabilities-Based Approach', in Jasper, S. (ed.) *Transforming Defense Capabilities: New Approaches for International Security*, London: Lynne Rienner, pp. 1–22.

Mearsheimer, J.J. (1990) 'Back to the Future: Instability in Europe after the Cold War', *International Security*, Vol. 15, No. 1, pp. 5–56.

Morgan, P.M. (2000) 'The Impact of the Revolution in Military Affairs', *Journal of Strategic Studies*, Vol. 23, No. 1, pp. 132–162.

RAND (1997) *In Athena's Camp – Preparing for Conflict in the Information Age*, Santa Monica, CA: RAND Publications.

Rynning, S. (2010) 'From Bottom-Up to Top-Down Transformation: Military Change in France', in Farrell, T., Terry, T. and Frans, O. (eds) *A Transformation Gap? American Innovations and European Military Change*, Stanford, CA: Stanford University Press.

Schnaubelt, C.M. (2007) 'Whither the RMA?', *Parameters*, Vol. 37, pp. 95–107.

Strachan, H. (2013) 'British National Strategy: Who Does It?', *Parameters*, Vol. 43, No. 2, pp. 43–52.

US Department of Defense (2001) *Quadriennial Defense Review*, Washington, DC, http://www.defense.gov/pubs/qdr2001.pdf (accessed 12 May 2015).

Wiesner, I. (2013) *Importing the American Way of War?: Network -Centric Warfare in the UK and Germany*, Baden-Baden: Nomos Publishers.

Yost, D. (2007) 'The NATO Capabilities Gap and the European Union', *Survival*, Vol. 42, No. 4, pp. 97–128.

Young, T.D. (1996) 'German National Command Structures after Unification: A New German General Staff?', *Armed Forces & Society*, Vol. 22, No. 3, pp. 379–400.

6 Military transformation in Russia

Keir Giles

Introduction

Operations in Crimea and eastern Ukraine in 2014 served both to illuminate and to obscure the achievements of a radical transformation programme that had been under way in the Russian Armed Forces for the previous six years. The 'little green men' who briskly and efficiently seized Crimea were so unlike the previous image of Russian servicemen as to be almost unrecognisable; however, at the same time, these well-trained, well-disciplined and well-equipped troops were not representative of the bulk of the Russian military, which is still undergoing an intensive process of reorganisation, retraining, re-equipping and rearming (Lavrov 2010). In effect, Crimea provided a snapshot of how the leading edge of Russia's special operations forces had progressed, but diverted attention from what transformation meant for the remainder of the armed forces, and where that process was heading.

Since the armed conflict in Georgia in 2008, the Russian armed forces have been undergoing their most fundamental reform programme in decades, and arguably since pre-Soviet times. However, the objectives of reform, and the desired end state for the military, are substantially different from those that inform North American and Western European efforts at force transformation. Indeed, even the word 'transformation' in a Russian context is contentious. Senior Russian military officers tend to favour the word 'reform' to describe the current overhaul process, reserving 'transformation' for describing foreign efforts at technological and social development of their militaries, as described in Chapter 1 of this volume, but elsewhere the word 'transformation' is widely used among the expert community observing the Russian armed forces. This is primarily to distinguish the current process from previous reform efforts, which, as described below, have been nothing like as transformative. After all, 'reform' of the Russian military had more than once been declared 'completed' before 2008 (Ministry of Defence 2003).

This chapter will examine the distinctly Russian appreciation of the security challenges that a modern military is expected to resolve, and how Russia seeks to address them. In common with other nations, Russia faces tension between the need to prepare its military for counterinsurgency, asymmetric warfare and operations in human terrain, as symbolised by the Russian Special Forces deployed in Crimea, and for high-technology, high-tempo, high-precision, highly destructive non-contact warfare, as exemplified by the Russian main force arrayed for much of 2014 along the Ukrainian border. The distinctive Russian hierarchy of threats described below, and the transformation and funding priorities that continue to be set to address them, suggest that despite appearances in Crimea, the latter is still treated as the highest priority.

The discussion of the required response to 'next-generation warfare' and the Revolution in Military Affairs (RMA), which began within Russian military science after observation of the Gulf War in 1991, continued thereafter with little influence from Russian and Soviet experience of counterinsurgency operations in Afghanistan and Chechnya (Slipchenko and Gareyev 2005; Thomas 2011). Meanwhile, in both of those conflicts, Russia committed a military entirely unsuited to counterinsurgency, and ignored previous domestic and foreign experience of this type of operation (Grau 1996; Finch n.d.) – a trend that was finally broken in Ukraine.

While some of Russia's aspirations for the overhaul of its military have been consistent since the Russian armed forces came into being as the rump of the Soviet forces in 1992, for most of this period little serious reform has been possible: financial constraints meant that references to 'reform' primarily denoted continued downsizing (Renz 2014). It is only since 2005 that serious efforts to achieve these aspirations have been possible, with the rise in energy prices at that time providing a sudden flood of revenue for Russia and enabling manifold increases in military spending (Giles 2007). The budget increases allowed some longstanding problems to be addressed by means of current expenditure, including raising servicemen's pay and increasing the number of flying hours for pilots, and the beginning of experimentation in new command and control structures aimed at facilitating joint operations (Giles 2006). However, serious structural reform of the military had to wait until after August 2008, when Russian performance in the armed conflict in Georgia highlighted undeniable deficiencies in equipment and organisation, and technical capability in areas such as use of unmanned aerial vehicles (UAVs), specifically drones, and electronic warfare (Cohen and Hamilton 2011) – deficiencies which, as operations in eastern Ukraine show, Russia has worked hard to address (Chatham House 2015). This chapter will not recount in detail the history of this transformation effort, since a number of excellent studies are available in both Russian and English (Frolov and Barabanov 2012). Instead, it will highlight those Russian security concerns that led to very distinct priorities being set for the outcome of transformation.

Hierarchy of threats

Russia's military transformation is intended to meet threats as they are perceived from Moscow, not from any other capital. In some cases, threat assessments that seem unfathomably remote from a Euro-Atlantic perspective are taken as read by Russian military planners and analysts. Ukraine provides a case in point: the Russian interpretation of events in Kiev in January 2014 presenting a risk that the port of Sevastopol would be handed to the North Atlantic Treaty Organization (NATO) (TASS 2015) would be likely to be dismissed out of hand by all but the most farsighted of Western planners.

Even before the crisis over Ukraine, Russia's politically stated threat assessments – including bold public statements by leadership figures as well as the more nuanced versions in published doctrine and strategy documents – consistently overstated the likelihood of armed attack from the United States and its allies, and as a result, spending and organisational priorities have been skewed and fail to address more realistic security threats to Russia. According to prominent scholar of the Russian military Stephen Cimbala (2013), 'Russian military reform is endangered by continuing threat perceptions that exaggerate Russian military weakness and by domestic forces that play against a rational assessment of Russia's geostrategic requirements'. Over 20 years after the end of the Soviet Union, there remains a widespread failure to grasp that aggression against Russia in one form or another is not a key aim of NATO or US policy. As put by leading British commentator James Sherr:

> Russia ascribes intentions to its 'partners' that they do not hold. Neither in Kosovo, nor Iraq, nor Libya was Western policy 'about' Russia [...] The result is a misdiagnosis of threat and danger, a misallocation of resources and an 'aggravation of contradictions' on Russia's periphery that, by now, might have been settled. The connection, axiomatic to Moscow and unfathomable to Brussels, between NATO policy in the Balkans and the Caucasus primed the fuse for armed conflict in 2008, and one must hope (but dare not assume) that other spurious connections will not do so in future.
>
> (Sherr 2013)

Further:

> The factors that frequently offset one another in a judicious threat assessment – capability, interest and intention – are invariably compounded in Russian threat assessments on the basis of worst-case assumptions.
>
> (Sherr 2013)

The current transformation of the Russian armed forces marks the final demise of the Soviet military, with a decisive step away from the cadre unit and mass mobilisation structure inherited from the USSR. It was clear to former Defence Minister Anatoliy Serdyukov, Chief of General Staff Nikolay Makarov and their supporters before the outset of these reforms what the new Russian military was *not* needed for: namely, countering a massive land incursion by means of mobilised mass. While the idea of vulnerability to US and NATO hostile intentions remains strong, this vulnerability is finally no longer seen in Cold War-era conventional military terms.

Instead, and again despite the impression created by high-profile operations in Ukraine, in terms of funding prioritisation it is aerospace defence that has come to the fore. The most immediate purely military threat currently described by the Russian leadership arises from the capability gap with the USA – in particular, in terms of long-range precision weapons and the aerospace threat they pose.

There is a persistent argument, voiced by senior military commentators wielding prodigious authority in Russia, that foreign powers are planning to seize Russia's natural resources, including by means of a paralysing first strike by precision munitions against which Russia's air and space defences will be entirely insufficient (Gareyev 2013). At the same time, lingering suspicions over a limited Libya-style intervention still provide a driving force for military modernisation (Giles 2011), deriving from the Russian perception of the USA as an irresponsible actor which has not learned strategic lessons from intervention in Afghanistan, Iraq and Libya, and may in future be tempted to meddle in Russia, with an air and missile campaign as the first stage of hostilities. This provides the backdrop for repeated statements by Vladimir Putin emphasising defence against this eventuality. For instance, speaking at a meeting on implementing the 2011–20 state arms procurement programme, focusing on development of the technology base for air and space defence:

> We see that work is active around the world on developing high-precision conventional weapons systems that in their strike capabilities come close to strategic nuclear weapons. Countries that have such weapons substantially increase their offensive capability [...] Furthermore, there has been increasing talk among military analysts about the theoretical possibility of a first disarming, disabling strike, even against nuclear powers. This is something that we also need to take into account in our plans for developing the armed forces.
>
> (Putin 2013)

Independent commentators like Sergey Karaganov dismiss these as a 'phantas-magoric threat' which have 'no bearing on reality and are nothing but caricature replicas of Soviet-era fantasies' (Karaganov 2012). This includes: 'horror stories about the United States acquiring a capability for a massive attack on Russia with smart conventional missiles. Even if such missiles are ever created, the threat of a strike against Russian territory looks ridiculous as the retaliatory blow can be only a nuclear one' (Karaganov 2012). Nevertheless it is this threat perception which continues to guide Russia's funding priorities. According to Putin, 'in accordance with the state arms procurement programme through to 2020, we will invest around 3.4 trillion roubles in developing our air and space defences. This is around 20 percent – around 17 percent to be more exact – of the total money earmarked for re-equipping the armed forces' (Putin 2013).

A similar hierarchy of threats, highlighting Russia's vulnerability to the USA's Prompt Global Strike, and downplaying scenarios involving the use of ground forces, was outlined by Deputy Defence Minister Yuriy Borisov (2013) and by Deputy Prime Minister Dmitriy Rogozin in a newspaper interview in July 2013. Both Borisov and Rogozin argued for procurement decisions to continue to be guided by this threat assessment (*Rossiyskaya Gazeta* 2013). Russia's new aerospace defence command (*Voyenno-kosmicheskaya oborona* – VKO) is prioritised for funding precisely due to this perception of vulnerability to US conventional precision-strike capabilities (LarouchePAC 2013).

Of particular concern is the potential for a first strike to eliminate Russia's strategic deterrent forces. According to Professor Leonid Orlenko, 'reliably protecting the strategic nuclear forces against surprise attack is the single most important mission, inasmuch as with destruction of the strategic nuclear forces Russia cannot avoid disastrous defeat and loss of state sovereignty' (Orlenko 2013). As put by President Putin, 'we must take into account the realities of the day[. W]e cannot allow the strategic deterrence system to be upset or the effectiveness of our nuclear forces to be decreased. For this reason the creation of the aerospace defence system will continue to be one of the key priorities in military development' (CCTV.com 2013).

Assessments such as these, with an emphasis on Russia maintaining a strong nuclear deterrent, refer consistently to threats to strategic stability. The shared understanding of this term as applied to deterrence during the Cold War is no longer in force: to Western policymakers it now has entirely different implications, whereas in Russia, as with so much else, the definition of the term has not moved on – leading to yet more misunderstanding in bilateral discussion.[1] One direct result of this consideration is that development of offensive strategic weapons is also prioritised. According to the head of the Russian General Staff's Centre for Military-Strategic Research (*Tsentr Voyenno-Strategicheskikh Issledovaniy* – TsVSI), Sergey Chekinov, 'parity in offensive weapons with the USA while USA develops ballistic missile defence (BMD) is fundamental for strategic stability' (Chekinov 2012). This reflects the particular role that offensive nuclear weapons play in the Russian defence psyche, as both a symbol of great power status and a last-ditch guarantee of sovereignty, which will be discussed further below (Giles n.d., forthcoming). As a result, arms of service not related to strategic deterrence correspondingly receive less urgent attention in relative terms.

In summary, a major consideration driving Russia's transformation agenda is the need to counter a threat that at present simply does not exist. As described by leading military commentators Aleksey Arbatov and Vladimir Dvorkin, 'it seems that once again, as is not rare throughout history, Russia is unprepared either militarily or politically for the real threat [and instead is] prioritising preparations for war with NATO on land, at sea and in air and space' (Arbatov and Dvorkin 2013: 29).

Threat analysis

As always, and not only in the case of Russia, there are significant differences between public rhetoric and more sober assessments by informed experts and the military themselves. Among this community, it was until 2014 accepted that aggression against Russia in one form or another was not an aim of NATO or US policy. However, in the febrile atmosphere of Moscow during the Ukraine crisis, the voices of restraint are fewer, and the consensus even among intelligent and educated citizens – encouraged by state-controlled media – appears to be that Russia is under siege and potentially subject to attack at any time. In particular, NATO's belated steps to enhance its capacity to defend the Baltic States and Poland are presented as an overtly hostile move, which heightens the perception of imminent threat (RT 2014). Stephen Cimbala adds an essential perspective according to which 'Russian military planners might reasonably assume that the initial period of war can be one of great danger. What seems politically absurd in a day and age of U.S.-Russian "reset" and post-post-Cold War Europe is not necessarily impossible from the standpoint of Russian military planners and analysts. Russian and Soviet historical experience so dictates' (Cimbala 2013).

The dissonance between public and private threat assessments may in part arise from a limited range of inputs into analyses of the range of threats that Russia faces. In the early stages of reform, Serdyukov and Makarov were criticised for embarking upon major change without having first put in place the academic or theoretical basis for managing this change or defining the desired end state – a significant departure from previous Soviet and Russian practice (McDermott et al. 2012). Informed Russian commentators note the relative dearth of military science, in the Russian sense of academic study of military affairs, resulting from a generation of underfunding in the 1990s and early 2000s, and the consequent deficiency in independent checks and balances on either military or political assessments of security challenges. This view is echoed by pessimistically inclined observers such as veteran commentator Pavel Felgenhauer:

> Serdyukov's military reform has been radical, but it lacked a clear strategic objective or a defined doctrine. The United States and NATO continued to be the presumed main enemy; and the Defence Ministry made massive investments into new strategic nuclear weapons and air defences. At the same time, attempts to meet all other possible threats resulted in thinly spreading out limited resources. Major military reform decisions have never been openly discussed in parliament or in the expert community.
> (Felgenhauer 2012)

This effect extended to a lack of consideration for a changing international political landscape, and to Russia's place in it. While partly justified by the very long perspective required for military planning, the apparent threat assessments remained unaffected even during temporary improved relations with the USA and a reduction in tensions in the South Caucasus following the armed conflict in Georgia in 2008. As put by Arbatov and Dvorkin (2013: 16), 'Russian military policy has to a large extent existed in a way independently of the state's international direction [...] These contradictions [...] suggest insufficient control by the political leadership over the military in developing the military doctrine as an important part of defence policy'. In effect, the new Russian military was taking shape while the threats it was intended to counter were in fact still being defined (Sokolov 2012).

Nuclear symbolism

At the beginning of the 1990s, Russia moved almost overnight from a comfortable position of strong conventional deterrence through the massive superiority of troop numbers of the Soviet Army, to a reliance on nuclear missiles as effectively the only deterrent, at strategic or other levels, that was available to the newly emergent Russian Federation. According to President Putin, speaking in 2006, the entire Russian Army had to be stripped of its combat-capable units and personnel in order to mount the limited campaign in Chechnya at the end of 1994. Throughout the following decade, Russian defence budgets continued a relative decline, with funding priority going to the nuclear forces. While perceived as of limited relevance by the USA and its allies, none of which intended to attack Russia, to the Russian leadership these nuclear forces constituted the last-ditch guarantee of Russian sovereignty and protection of its fundamental interests.

In the first decade after the end of the Soviet Union, the old quip comparing the country with 'Upper Volta with nuclear weapons' resurfaced regularly among Russia-watchers.[2] If nuclear weapons were all that stood between Russia and Third World status, the implications of taking the weapons away were clear enough. Regardless that Russia today is a very different country from the 1990s, the pre-eminent status of nuclear weapons in the national psyche remains the same. A temporary reduction in conventional military capability during the fundamental reorganisation of the forces during 2008–11 only reinforced the particular role that offensive nuclear weapons play in the Russian defence calculus, as not only the absolute guarantee of sovereignty, but also a symbol of great power status. According to Vladimir Putin (2012a), 'we will not under any circumstances turn our back on the potential for strategic deterrence, and we will reinforce it. It was precisely this which allowed us to maintain state sovereignty during the most difficult period of the 1990s'. Former US diplomat Wayne Merry explains this further:

> If all nuclear weapons were by magic to disappear from the earth over-night, American security would be enhanced due to our dominance in non-nuclear military technologies and forces; by contrast, Russia would face a fundamental crisis of national identity [...] Thus, American talk of global nuclear zero is viewed in Moscow as inspired by the goal of U.S. non-nuclear hegemony, rather than to free the world from nuclear fear.
> (Merry 2013)

The entry into force of the New START treaty in February 2011 saw the beginning of intensive Russian activity aimed at developing and introducing new strategic weapons systems, including at least three new intercontinental ballistic missile (ICBM) programmes. Tellingly, several of these are being conducted in conditions of secrecy, running counter to the common Russian habit of loudly proclaiming new advances in weapons technology (Schneider 2012). In addition, non-strategic nuclear weapons (NSNW) remain in the Russian inventory in large numbers and intended for use in a wide range of scenarios, including for de-escalation. Lying outside the bounds of New START, NSNW are, according to two Western analysts, 'prized and important assets to Moscow, and they have become even more prized and important assets as Russia's conventional military has become weaker. They are seen more and more as the fallback option if Russia one day faces some sort of defeat in a conventional conflict' (Renz and Thornton 2012: 45). 'The result is that when a threat escalates from armed conflict to local war, we will have to go over to the use of nuclear weapons', agrees one leading Russian analyst (Sivkov, in Lannon 2011).

Finally, a key consideration accentuating Russian reliance on nuclear weapons to a much greater extent than other major powers is the China factor. A sharp rise in Chinese strategic nuclear capabilities is expected over the next few decades, introducing both new submarines, heavy ICBMs with multiple independently targetable re-entry vehicles (MIRVs), and a strategic aviation capability to add an aerial arm of the nuclear triad. In Russia's view, the lack of any current obligation for China to disclose the size of its rapidly growing nuclear arsenal and capabilities leads to uncertainty and thereby 'a very dangerous situation' (Anonymous 2013). This underpins the Russian reluctance to engage in further arms-reduction talks bilaterally with the USA without expanding the negotiations to a multilateral basis – in other words, including China.

Russian defence spending

Also in contrast to the USA and most European militaries, which are seeing consistent reductions in their budgets, funding for the military in Russia is continuing its trend of rapid increase. After consistent impressive budget increases for the previous six years, the major arms purchasing programme announced in 2011 and scheduled to run to 2020 attracted excited headlines and broke all records for the proposed level of spending (Frolov 2011).

Yet, despite the experience of unrestrained arms spending contributing to the economic collapse of the Soviet Union, the spending plans have been pushed through regardless of Russia's capacity to afford them. The over-ambitious nature of the procurement plans was noted immediately on their announcement (Barabanov 2013). Both the capabilities of the defence industry (Pallin 2012) and the funding allocated were questioned (Arbatov 2013).

However, a denial of reality long coloured the debate over funding for procurement (Pukhov 2012), even well after former Minister of Finance Aleksey Kudrin was induced to resign after pointing out that the plans were unaffordable (*The Moscow Times* 2011). On his pre-election tours in early 2012, Vladimir Putin would observe that after the current spending plans 'there is no more money' – but not that there was not enough even to cover those plans (Latukhina 2012). Later, in June 2012, Putin re-emphasised that defence orders must be filled as agreed by manufacturers and no further funds would be forthcoming: 'There won't be other money, greater than the amount allocated to 2020. I've already talked about this 100 times. At one recent conference, proposals were again heard to increase it. We would be happy to increase it, perhaps, but there's no money!' (Putin 2012b).

Even before the impact of economic sanctions and the fall in the price of oil in 2014, adjustment of growth forecasts for the Russian economy had led to recognition that state spending must be reduced. During 2013 the Ministry of Finance (MoF) put forward a number of proposals for both reducing and rebalancing overall budget expenditure. At the same time, according to the MoF's *Basic Guidelines of Budgetary Policy Through 2016*, national defence was the only article of budget expenditure that would increase, not decrease, as a percentage of gross domestic product (GDP) during this period (Sergeyev 2013). Proposals for spending reductions consistently put forward by the MoF do not affect defence expenditure in the long term. Despite adjustments to the funding schedule of the State Armaments Programme (*Gosudarstvennaya programma vooruzheniya*, GPV), the overall procurement plans to 2020 remain unchanged. One MoF report identified potential savings of almost R1.2 trillion of the R19 trillion total GPV budget, through such means as deferrals and cancelling unnecessary credit agreements, and elimination of duplication in Ministry of Defence functions, but there was no indication that the report's recommendations had found a receptive audience in the Ministry of Defence (Samofalova 2013).

In particular, MoF proposals in 2013 to cut 5 per cent from the state budget gained widespread attention (*Interfax*, 5 September 2013), but in late September that year, Deputy Defence Minister Yuriy Borisov denied speculation that this reduction in overall government spending would affect military spending (*Interfax*, 26 September 2013). As clearly stated by Vladimir Putin, 'of course the overall extent of the State Armaments Program and the overall amount of those funds we envisaged for this must remain unchanged' (Centre for Analysis of World Arms Trade 2013). Furthermore, Deputy Chairman of the Military-Industrial Commission Oleg Bochkarev confirmed at the same time that budget adjustments would not affect overall defence spending plans, and noted a planned increase in the state defence order of 25–30 per cent annually in 2013–15 (*Interfax*, 20 September 2013). Although discussion between the MoF and defence agencies led to the rescheduling of some items of expenditure within the GPV, in large part these resulted not from a funding squeeze, but from recognition that some areas of the defence industry were simply not ready to spend the money.

Some savings have been found through not issuing a proportion of planned subsidised credits to industry (Tovkaylo 2013), but the large-scale state-guaranteed credits on offer to defence industry enterprises are both a means of supplementing the defence budget and an indication that budget constraints are relatively soft for leading defence contractors. Large credits with interest covered by the federal budget will add to domestic debt; in addition, they are unsecured, exposing the state budget to additional risk. Finally, they constitute both recognition that the original funding ambition for GPV-2020 was unrealisable, and a means to avoid dealing with the issue. Thus, again in striking contrast to other nations, increases in defence spending in order to enable transformation in the strictly Russian sense are being forced through regardless of whether or not the country can afford them. This trend has continued through the 2014 collapse in the rouble exchange rate and in Russia's earning power from energy sales. While other areas of government spending contract rapidly, President Putin has repeatedly voiced his commitment to maintaining defence spending regardless (Reuters 2015).

Real threats

If any potential major adversary is mentioned in public Russian discourse, it is almost inevitably one in the West. As always, the potential for a military threat from China is the exceptional case which, if discussed at all, is approached in exceedingly delicate terms, to the extent that China is conspicuous by its absence in Russia's National Security Strategy and Military Doctrine (Giles 2010). There is a mood of cautious optimism in assessments of relations with China (Kashin 2013), including the view that conflicts with countries that are not part of the Western bloc, including China, are 'very unlikely to materialise because there are very few areas where Russian interests are at odds with the interests of these countries' (Pukhov 2013a). Furthermore,

> China, aware of its growing competition with the United States, including in the military-political sphere, is doing its utmost not to threaten Russia. True, there exists the problem of China's gaining too much strength, which in a situation where there is no energetic policy for development of the Trans-Baikal region may result in 'Finlandization' of Russia, so to speak. But this risk is not a military one.
>
> (Karaganov 2012)

Nevertheless, the extremely long planning horizon required for military development means that despite current good relations, some preparations for military activity in the Russian Far East can be detected. Under the current procurement programme, each year an increasing proportion of new conventional weapons is directed to the Far East, with the Western Military District not receiving the most modern arms. At the same time, it is recognised that the concentration of population and infrastructure along the southern fringe of the Russian Far East makes it close to indefensible – especially since almost all major transport links in the region at some point pass within artillery range of the Chinese border. This situation and the limited options available to Russia to defend this territory, contribute to the strong relative weight accorded to the role of tactical nuclear weapons as a deterrent in Russian military thinking.

Meanwhile, a range of authoritative commentators in Russia and abroad agree that – Ukraine aside – the most immediate military threat facing Russia is an entirely different one, from an entirely different direction: central Russia's southern periphery (Arbatov and Dvorkin 2013: 5). The entirely predictable deterioration in security in Central Asia following the US and International Security Assistance Force (ISAF) drawdown in Afghanistan in 2014 causes genuine alarm among Russian military officers, and was a primary topic of discussion with NATO's Deputy Supreme Allied Commander Europe (DSACEUR) General Richard Shirreff in Moscow in late October 2013. Instability in the Middle East provides a further regional threat. The suggestion by Arbatov and Dvorkin (2013: 29) that 'in the near and medium term, destabilisation of South and Central Asia, the Near and Middle East, the South and North Caucasus are the greatest real military threat to Russia', is repeatedly echoed in private statements and briefings by Russian servicemen.

To Euro-Atlantic eyes the Middle East can appear tolerably remote from Russia, but this is to ignore Moscow's perception that the approaches to Russia's borders extend to a very considerable depth. According to James Sherr, the Russian state has historically 'maintained a set of security "needs" out of kilter and scale with those of most European powers', leading to the need to address these needs by 'creating client states and widening defence perimeters' (Sherr 2013). In Russian perceptions, the Middle East is 'right next door' (*sovsem ryadom*), and there are not only complex political networks between the Middle East and former Soviet states like Azerbaijan, but also major influences from Muslim ideology and political processes in the North Caucasus.

These wide perimeters of security consciousness mean that the consequences of military action in Syria or Iran are seen as a direct security problem for Russia. This is a factor not only in the intensive efforts that Russia devoted to preventing US-led military intervention in the Syrian civil war during 2013, but also to the ambivalent Russian attitude to operations against Islamic State (IS) in Syria and Iraq in the following year.

Concerns like these are reinforced by the Russian perception of lack of forethought by the USA and its allies when seeking regime change. The private internal debate over precisely why Russia needs a military is likely to have been influenced in later stages by the 'mild panic' experienced by the Russian leadership when observing the fate of Muammar Gaddafi (Segodnya 2012) – a reaction that lends colour to the Russian perception of a Western-backed *coup d'état* in Ukraine in 2014. The longer-term consequences of the Arab Spring are also of deep concern. These consequences, including arms proliferation, uncontrolled migration and socio-economic instability leading to increased attraction of radical Islam, are seen by Russian military thinkers as a danger not only to Russia, but to Europe as a whole: indeed, the likelihood of organised *jihadist* incursions from Afghan territory post-2014 is seen as a precursor for 'when the Islamists gain enough strength to mount a crusade against Europe' (Suvorov 2013).

In particular, the next destination of *jihadist* fighters from Syria is a serious preoccupation. As described by influential and well-informed defence commentator Ruslan Pukhov (2013b), 'the gold of the mediaeval Arab despots can in the blink of an eye redirect hordes of dehumanised fanatics from Syria to the steppes of Stavropol and Kazakhstan'. Stripped of the emotive language, a similar assessment is informing Russian military, as opposed to political, threat assessments. Stephen Cimbala, along with many Russian commentators, argues that it is this that should be the guiding influence for Russian defence planning:

> Russia is threatened neither primarily nor immediately by NATO. Instead, the threat of regional or smaller wars on Russia's periphery or terrorism and insurgent wars within Russia and other post-Soviet states must now take pride of place in General Staff and Ministry of Defence contingency planning. Preparedness for these contingencies of limited and local wars, regular and irregular, will require a smaller, more professional and more mobile military than post-Soviet Russia has fielded hitherto.
>
> (Cimbala 2013)

Yet preparations for lower-intensity conflicts involving the ground troops at present remain Russia's lowest funding priority. According to Lieutenant-General Andrey Tretyak,

> the significance of ground forces is diminishing in modern war. The VDV [Airborne Assault Forces] are not called rapid reaction forces, but fill that role, so the VDV still have priority [for funding] over ground forces. What money the ground forces get goes to their funding priority, the Spetsnaz. So motor-rifle divisions are right at the back of the queue.
>
> (Tretyak 2012)

It is this tiering of priorities for funding, equipment and training which leads to the disparity in appearance and professionalism between the Russian servicemen actually involved in Crimea and Ukraine, primarily from the Special Forces, and their line unit colleagues in the main force units behind the Russian border. In 2011, British academic and former soldier Rod Thornton had predicted that Russian foreign policy ambitions would 'inevitably result in occasional Russian military interventions abroad', and the implement of choice for this would be the VDV – still the most professional force available to Russia, he noted, and able to move with little visible preparation (Thornton 2011: 28). The seizure of Crimea proved him entirely correct.

The issue of force projection is another area where Russian aspirations differ from transformation as it is understood elsewhere. A capacity for expeditionary warfare is not a Russian aim. As explained in 2012 by the Swedish Defence Research Agency, FOI,

Up to 2020, the primary area of operations for the Army will probably remain Russia and its immediate surroundings. The Army's capability for operations outside Russia's territory is not necessarily dependent on the exact number of brigades and their location in each military district, but rather on whether they can, if required, be moved relatively quickly (within weeks or months).

(Pallin 2012: 124)

Indeed, a programme of major exercises and 'snap inspections' that continued through 2013 built up Russia's experience of deploying large numbers of troops briskly, and the results were visible in the rapid concentration of forces on the Ukrainian border in 2014. Strategic mobility from across Russia was executed on an impressive scale, using both rail and air movement, and troop movements overall demonstrated impressive agility and speed, to match the speed of decision making displayed in Crimea.

The fact that speed of movement is best achieved by different means in different parts of Russia was a key consideration in proposed plans to introduce 'light, medium and heavy' brigades in Russia's ground forces, with procurement of wheeled armour (Nikolskiy 2012), intended to provide for more agile, wheeled 'light' units more suitable for intervention in Russia's Western neighbours with a well-developed road network (Rikken 2013). An old adage runs that the Russian military only intervenes in places it can drive to. Further comments by Andrey Tretyak support this notion and the FOI assessment: in his words, there are no Russian plans for operations outside Russia except as part of an alliance, for example the Collective Security Treaty Organisation (CSTO), or through bilateral agreements, for example with Armenia or Belarus. Therefore there are no plans, 'not even the consideration of the possibility', of a military intervention in countries with no direct border with Russia. Naturally enough, to countries like Ukraine and the Baltic States which do have a border with Russia, this is small comfort.

Human capital

Difficulties in funding ambitious procurement plans, exacerbated by emphasis on expensive strategic deterrence weapons systems, are not the only obstacle to realising the desired new shape of the Russian military. Many of Russia's remaining problems in implementing its transformation aims are to do not with money or equipment, but with people. As noted by Arbatov and Dvorkin (2013: 45), 'the traditional Russian and Soviet approach has always been, from the times of the regular army and the wars of Peter the Great, down to the Second Chechen Campaign in 1999–2000, that servicemen are the Army and the Navy's cheapest consumable'.

Now, under fundamentally new circumstances where demographic change means that servicemen are at a premium, and furthermore they each require greater investment in order to be trained in operating ever more sophisticated equipment, this approach needs fundamental revision. However, difficulties in implementing plans for professional non-commissioned officers (NCOs), and for managing manpower overall, show that progress is slow.

The hangover from the long period of stagnation in military spending and development has continuing direct effects on personnel in individual arms of service. One indicative symptom is the Air Force continuing to suffer from a failure to retain junior officers, despite huge increases in salaries, due to flying hours only being allocated to senior officers – a problem that was supposed to have been rectified at the early stages of increased funding and fuel provision for the Air Force as part of the general increase in military spending resulting from Russia's increased oil revenues after 2005 (Mikhaylov 2012). The fact that fundamental issues such as this have not been resolved by the simple provision of money is indicative of the extent to which Russia's military was degraded during the years of relative neglect prior to 2005.

Furthermore, the change in the length of conscription in 2008 from two years to one not only doubles the number of conscripts required to maintain force numbers, but also works against the stated aim of more advanced training for operating more sophisticated weapons systems (Arbatov 2013). At the same time, conscripts are faced with an accelerated training pro-gramme, the nature of which depends on the time of year they are called up. Stephen Cimbala notes:

> Many of the 'permanent readiness' brigades would be undermanned and not capable of combat deployment with their full complement of per-sonnel. Further, most of the troops are conscripts serving one year terms and called up twice each year: at any given time, half of them have been in uniform less than six months and lack adequate training for battle.
>
> (Cimbala 2013)

FOI agrees:

> Although the Armed Forces often send new recruits on exercises and even commit them to combat operations, shorter training time means that both individual soldiers, and consequently their units, have a reduced capability.
>
> (Pallin 2012: 104)

There are clearly limitations on what 12-month conscripts, with their limited time in training, are capable of by comparison with volunteer, 'contract' servi-cemen who sign up for longer terms. This is tacitly recognised in decisions like the 31st Detached Guards Air Assault Brigade being assigned an additional 'peacekeeping' function 'because it is [the unit] with the highest proportion of contract manning' (Natsionalnaya oborona n.d.). Similarly, the Special Forces units deployed to Crimea in early 2014 left their recently conscripted personnel behind – because they were considered insufficiently trained to take part in such a complex operation (Howard and Pukhov 2014).

Meanwhile, the ground forces retain a higher proportion of conscript manpower, while contract servicemen are more prominent in permanent readiness units and posts involving more challenging tasks, as for instance in the Navy, VKO or VDV, but the range of posts for which a 12-month conscript can usefully be trained continues to narrow. On occasion, this gives rise to alarm over personnel performance in Russia's intensifying series of major exercises, as the proportion of servicemen with very little experience rises (n.a. 2011; Kravchuk 2011). Once again, the outcome of Russia's current plans is that the ground forces receive the lowest priority.

The target remains for a total of 425,000 contract servicemen in the Russian armed forces by 2017 (from a claimed 241,400 in 2013) (Ministry of Defence 2013). It appears that as with previous failed programmes to recruit contractors, at present Russian leaders would prefer to maintain the fiction that this is achievable, rather than adjust the target or institute major change in order to reach it. As is the case in all discussion of Russian military manpower, misleading information that understates the challenge is the norm, as with, for example, Chief of General Staff Valeriy Gerasimov stating in June 2013 that the target would be met by recruiting 60,000 contractors annually – without mentioning that many more than this figure would have to be recruited to allow for those leaving the service after their contract term expired (Safronov 2013).

A range of stopgap measures has been put in place to keep the junior command structure functioning while these targets remain unmet. In May 2012, it was announced that over 10,000 posts that had been downgraded to be filled by NCOs (still, at present, often one-year conscripts) would revert to requiring commissioned officers (*Agentstvo voyennykh novostey*, 23 May 2012; *Rossiyskaya Gazeta*, 29 May 2012). This followed sustained reporting of units being unable to carry out their functions since the NCOs or conscripts tasked with carrying out duties previously assigned to officers simply did not have the training or experience to do so, with examples including an anti-air missile unit deciding on its own initiative to re-hire dismissed officers after exercises proved conscripts were incapable of commanding Buk systems (*Krasnaya Zvezda*, 2 April 2012). This is a significant point when considering culpability for the Malaysia Airlines flight MH17 crash in July 2014, as it indicates that the perpetrators would have had to be highly trained system operators and therefore were most likely to be regular Russian troops. With the aim to recruit contractors, as with the related move to 'professional' NCOs, the Russian military's ambitions have run ahead of what is possible without detailed long-term planning and a corresponding fundamental cultural shift in the understanding of what precisely volunteer servicemen are and how they should be recruited and retained.

Despite these challenges, however, the trend is clear towards an overall improvement in the conditions endured by Russian servicemen. The well-equipped and highly professional troops seen in Crimea may not have been typical, but there have been improvements in status and personal equipment throughout the forces. Progress in the remainder of the army towards recognisably modern equipment is slow but definite. Meanwhile, morale and attitudes throughout the Russian armed forces had been transformed even before the prestige boost that came with success in Crimea. Huge increases in pay and allowances since 2005 (including tripling overnight) have combined with a recovery in social standing to leave Russian soldiers unrecognisably better off than a decade ago. As well as being better paid and enjoying a higher status, servicemen also appear to have recovered a sense of purpose. The striking increase in salaries has been earned through a much-increased workload. In the words of one Russian general, 'now we have something to get on with' (Giles 2014).

Conclusion and outlook

The seizure of Crimea established beyond doubt that Russia has a very different force available from the one that went into action in Georgia in 2008, and one which is more effective, flexible, adaptable and scalable for achieving Russia's foreign policy aims (Labarre 2012). The depth and scale of change that the Russian military has undergone in the last seven years is impossible to overstate, and few of the certainties that underpinned analysis of Russian military capability in the last decade still hold good. The fact that Russian servicemen throughout the military, and not just in the elite units seen in the Crimea, now resemble those of a modern military instead of their previous plainly post-Soviet appearance is also symbolic of much deeper transformation, and of readiness to change further. As noted by FOI, 'although Russia will probably not be able to reach all of the ambitious goals of its reform programme for the Armed Forces, there is little doubt that its overall military capability will have increased by 2020' (Pallin 2012: 21).

The primary aim of this increased capability is to close the gap with other major powers, in order both to reduce the perceived vulnerability to a devastating first strike, but also to return to a situation where the Russian military can no longer be disregarded as a deterrent factor and a tool of influence – not only in strictly military terms, but also in foreign policy more broadly. This is sometimes expressed in very simplistic terms by senior Russian military officers: the Soviet Union was respected because it possessed a 4.5 million-strong army, and a military that needs to be taken into serious consideration will once again ensure Russia's voice is heard and heeded internationally.

In particular, one eventual goal is to provide a deterrent to US actions, in order that the USA is not the only state with unlimited freedom of movement globally, including in Russia's self-designated 'sphere of privileged interest'. This is a long-term aspiration: a closed conference in London in December 2013 heard a reference by a senior Russian diplomat to a previous phase of Russian long-term military preparations while not capable of campaigning against the prime enemy, following the Treaty of Tilsit in 1807 and leading up to confrontation with Napoleon in 1812 (Lieven 2010). In the present day, the timescales for military reorganisation and preparation are even longer, but at the time of writing we are already close to the 2020 strategic horizon set by Russia's National Security Strategy and Military Doctrine – and the related deadline for the transformation aim and desired end-state of having usable armed forces for twenty-first-century conflict as viewed by Russia.

In addition, for Russia, a strong military is an essential attribute of a great power, whether needed for actual security challenges or not (Arbatov and Dvorkin 2013). In the words of Sergey Karaganov (2012), 'it looks like the military build-up is expected to compensate for the relative weakness in other respects – economic, technological, ideological and psychological'. Thus, the Russian military build-up can be expected to continue regardless of the state of relations with partners and competitors, and in particular while relations with the USA and NATO run through their familiar predictable cycles of thaw and freeze (Giles 2011).

The text of Russia's latest Military Doctrine, approved on 26 December 2014, shows that in declaratory policy at least, Russia's threat perception has not substantially changed (Office of the President of the Russian Federation 2014). Russia might feel after NATO's 2014 Wales Summit that its pre-conceived notions of NATO as a threat might be a little more realistic and not simply hypothetical, but in the Doctrine NATO remains just a 'military risk' as opposed to a threat. The difference in Russian doctrinal lexicon is significant, and the distinction makes an important political statement, with NATO and its members the intended audience.

The results of the Georgian war in 2008 validated military force as a foreign policy tool for Russia, appearing as it did to bring long-term strategic gains for short-term and limited economic and reputational pain. At the time of writing, economic upsets are disrupting the application of this calculus to operations in Ukraine, but they have done little to challenge the euphoria resultant from the successful seizure of Crimea – and the impression that bold military strokes, if designed not to trouble NATO members with consideration of an Article 5 response, are unlikely to meet with significant resistance or challenge. Russia's neighbours should therefore be prepared for more military interventions as the parts of the armed forces that are considered ready and fit for use expand (Giles and Rogovoy n.d., forthcoming).

Notes

1 For an exploration of how apparently common security terminology in fact masks significant differences in interpretation, see Andrew Monaghan, 'The Indivisibility of Security: Russia and Euro-Atlantic Security', NATO Defense College, January 2010, www.ndc.nato.int/research/series.php?icode=2.
2 The comment is widely, but not exclusively, attributed to German Chancellor Helmut Schmidt in the late 1980s.

Bibliography

Anonymous (2013, 16 December) Seminar on 'Russia's Strategic Overhaul', Chatham House, London.

Arbatov, A. (2013, 15 April) 'Real and Imaginary Threats: Military Power in World Politics in the 21st Century', Russia in Global Affairs. http://eng.globalaffairs.ru/number/Real-and-Imaginary-Threats-15925 (accessed 8 January 2015).

Arbatov, A. and Dvorkin, V. (2013) *Voyennaya reforma Rossii: sostoyaniye i perspektivy* (Russia's Military Reform: Status and Prospects), Moscow: Moscow Carnegie Centre.

Barabanov, M. (2013, 8 January) 'Kriticheskii vzgliad na GPV-2020' (A critical look at the State Arms Programme-2020), *Voenno-promyshlennyi kur'er – Military-industrial courier*, no. 1.

Borisov, Y. (2013, 29 June) *Deputy Defence Minister*, interviewed on *Ekho Moskvy radio*.

CCTV.com (2013, 21 June) 'Putin: Russia Not to Reduce Nuclear Forces'. http://english.cntv.cn/program/newsupdate/20130621/102936.shtml (accessed 8 January 2015).

Centre for Analysis of World Arms Trade (2013) *Partial Postponement of GPV-2020 Expenditures to a Later Time is Possible Under State Budget Optimization*. http://www.armstrade.org (accessed 8 January 2015).

Chatham House (2015, 6 February) *Ukraine Test Bed for Russia's New Army*. http://www.chathamhouse.org/expert/comment/16856 (accessed 17 February 2015).

Chekinov, S. (2012, 27 November) *Speech at a Briefing at NATO Defence College*.

Cimbala, S.J. (2013) 'Russian Threat Perceptions and Security Policies: Soviet Shadows and Contemporary Challenges', *The Journal of Power Institutions in Post-Soviet Societies*, No. 14/15. http://pipss.revues.org/4000 (accessed 8 January 2015).

Cohen, A. and Hamilton, R. (2011) *The Russian Military and the Georgia War: Lessons and Implications*, Carlisle, PA: US Army War College Strategic Studies Institute.

Felgenhauer, P. (2012, 28 June) 'The Failure of Military Reform in Russia', *Eurasia Daily Monitor*, Vol. 9, No. 123. http://www.jamestown.org/single/?tx_ttnews%5Btt_news%5D=39554&no_cache=1#.VRKTovmsXTo (accessed 8 January 2015).

Finch, R.C. (n.d.) *Why the Russian Military Failed in Chechnya*, Fort Leavenworth, KS: Foreign Military Studies Office. http://fmso.leavenworth.army.mil/documents/yrusfail/yrusfail.htm (accessed 8 January 2015).

Frolov, A. (2011) *Russian Military Spending in 2011–2020*, Moscow Defence Brief, No. 1.

Frolov, A. and Barabanov, M. (2012) *Russian Military Reform from Administrative Reorganization to Structural Reform*, Centre for Analysis of Strategies and Technologies (CAST), Presentation at US National Defence University, 26 April.

Gareyev, M. (2013, 23 January) 'Na poroge epokhi potryaseniy: dlya obespecheniya bezopasnosti trebuyetsya obyektivnaya otsenka ugroz' (On the threshold of an epoch of upheaval: in order to provide security, an objective assessment of the threats is required), *Voyenno-promyshlennyy kurer*, Vol. 3, No. 471.

Giles, K. (2006) *Russian Regional Commands*, Conflict Studies Research Centre. http://www.academia.edu/929854/Russian_regional_commands (accessed 8 January 2015).

Giles, K. (2007) *Military Service in Russia – No New Model Army*, Conflict Studies Research Centre. http://www.academia.edu/929855/Military_Service_in_Russia_-_No_New_Model_Army (accessed 8 January 2014).

Giles, K. (2010) *The Military Doctrine of the Russian Federation 2010*, Rome: NATO Defence College.

Giles, K. (2011) *The State of the NATO-Russia Reset*, Conflict Studies Research Centre.

Giles, K. (2014) *Interview with Russian General (Anonymous)*, Skype, August.

Giles, K. (n.d., forthcoming) *European Missile Defense and Russia*, US Army War College Strategic Studies Institute.

Giles, K. and Rogovoy, A. (n.d., forthcoming) *A Russian View on Land Power*, US Army War College.

Grau, L. (ed.) (1996) *The Bear Went Over The Mountain: Soviet Combat Tactics in Afghanistan*, Washington: National Defence University Press.

Howard, C. and Pukhov, R. (eds) (2014) *Brothers Armed: Military Aspects of the Crisis in Ukraine*, Eastview Press.

Karaganov, S. (2012, 26 October) 'Security Strategy: Why Arms?' *Russia in Global Affairs*. http://eng.globalaffairs.ru/pubcol/Security-Strategy-Why-Arms-15716 (accessed 8 January 2015).

Kashin, V. (2013, 15 April) 'The Sum Total of All Fears. The Chinese Threat Factor in Russian Politics', *Russia in Global Affairs*, http://eng.globalaffairs.ru/number/The-Sum-Total-of-All-Fears-15935 (accessed 8 January 2015).

Kravchuk, I. (2011, 20 September) 'Takogo pozora VMF RF eshche ne znal. Poka-zushnyye ucheniya na Kamchatke' (The Russian Navy has Never Seen Such an Embarrassment. Show Exercise in Kamchatka), *Gaidpark*, http://gidepark.ru/user/2976644430/article/424394.

Labarre, F. (2012) 'Defence Innovation and Russian Foreign Policy', in Black, J.L., *Russia after 2012*, London: Routledge.

Lannon, G. (2011) 'Russia's New Look Army Reforms and Russian Foreign Policy', *The Journal of Slavic Military Studies*, Vol. 24, No. 1, pp. 26–54.

LarouchePAC (2013, 21 June) *Putin: Be Aware of Plans for First Strike Capability.* http://archive.larouchepac.com/node/27054 (accessed 8 January 2015).

Latukhina, K. (2012, 21 February) 'Lomat' stereotypy', *Rossiyskaya Gazeta*.

Lavrov, A. (2010) 'Nachalo reformy Vozdushno-desantnykh voysk', in Barabanov, M. (ed.) *Novaya armiya Rossii*, Moscow: CAST.

Lieven, D. (2010) *Russia against Napoleon: The True Story of the Campaigns of War and Peace*, New York: Viking.

McDermott, R.N., Nygren, B. and Pallin, C.V. (eds) (2012) *The Russian Armed Forces in Transition*, London: Routledge.

Merry, E.W. (2013) 'Ballistic Missile Defense Through Russian Eyes', *Defense Dossier*, American Foreign Policy Council.

Mikhaylov, A. (2012, 6 August), 'Molodyye letchiki begut iz VVS', *Izvestiya*. http://izvestia.ru/news/531968 (accessed 8 January 2015).

Ministry of Defence (2003) *Urgent Tasks of the Development of the Russian Federation Armed Forces.* http://red-stars.org/doctrine.pdf (accessed 8 January 2015).

Ministry of Defence (2013) *Activity Plan for the Ministry of Defence 2013–2020.* http://mil.ru/mod_activity_plan/doc.htm (accessed 8 January 2015).

The Moscow Times (2011, 10 October) 'Kudrin Stands Firm on Defense Spending During "Timeout"'.

n.a. (2011, 22 September) 'Ucheniya na Kamchatke: rakety s kreysera "Varyag" ne doletali do tseli, boyevaya tekhnika zastrevala v peske' (Exercise in Kamchatka: Missiles from the Cruiser *Varyag* Don't Reach their Target, Military Equipment Stuck in the Sand), *Novyy region*, http://nr2.ru/society/349713.html.

Natsionalnayaoborona (n.d.) *V VDV poyavyatsya mirotvorcheskiye batalyony* (Peacekeeping Battalions Will Make their Appearance in The Airborne Assault

Forces). http://www.oborona.ru/pages/mainpage/news/index.shtml (accessed 8 January 2015).

Nikolskiy, A. (2012, 12 May) 'Rossiya ispytyvayet italyanskiye kolesnyye tanki' (Russia testing Italian wheeled tanks), *Vedomosti.ru*. http://www.vedomosti.ru/poli tics/news/1732497/rossiya_ispytyvaet_italyanskie_tanki (accessed 8 January 2015).

Office of the President of the Russian Federation (2014) *Military Doctrine of the Russian Federation*. http://news.kremlin.ru/media/events/files/41d527556bec8deb3530.pdf (accessed 8 January 2015).

Orlenko, L. (2013, 20 May) 'Twice as Much Money Is Needed: Twenty Trillion Released for Rearming the Army and Navy Clearly is Not Enough', *Voyenno-promyshlennyy kuryer.*

Pallin, C.V. (ed.) (2012) *Russian Military Capability in a Ten-Year Perspective – 2011*, FOI.

Pukhov, R. (2012, 16 March) 'Natsionalnaya oborona: vozmozhna ekonomiya', *Nezavisimoye voyennoye obozreniye*. http://nvo.ng.ru/forces/2012-03-16/11_economy.html (accessed 8 January 2015).

Pukhov, R. (2013a, 13 August) 'The World vs Russia', *Force*, August. http://www.cast.ru/eng/?id=508 (accessed 8 January 2015).

Pukhov, R. (2013b, 11 December) *Kak nam obustroit voyennyy byudzhet, Vedomosti*. http://www.vedomosti.ru/opinion/news/19976231/kak-nam-obus troit-voyennyj-byudzhet (accessed 8 January 2015).

Putin, V. (2006, 6 May) *Poslaniye Federalnomu Sobraniyu Rossiyskoy Federatsii* (Address to the Federal Assembly of the Russian Federation). http://archive.krem lin.ru/text/appears/2006/05/105546.shtml (accessed 8 January 2015).

Putin, V. (2012a, 20 February) 'Byt silnymi: garantiya natsionalnoy bezopasnosti dlya Rossii' (Being strong is a guarantee of national security for Russia), *Rossiyskaya gazeta.*

Putin, V. (2012b, 14 June) 'Soveshchaniya po vypolneniyu gosudarstvennoy programmy v oblasti aviatsionnoy tekhniki', http://kremlin.ru/transcripts/15646 (accessed 8 January 2015).

Putin, V. (2013, 19 June) *Meeting on Implementing the 2011–2020 State Arms Procurement Programme.* http://eng.kremlin.ru/news/5615 (accessed 8 January 2015).

Renz, B. (2014) 'Russian Military Capabilities after 20 Years of Reform', *Survival: Global Politics and Strategy*, Vol. 56, pp. 61–84.

Renz, B. and Thornton, R. (2012) 'Russian Military Modernization: Cause, Course and Consequences', *Problems of Post-Communism*, Vol. 59, No. 1, pp. 44–54.

Reuters (2015, 16 January) 'Putin's Defense Fixation Deepens Russian Budget Problems'. http://uk.reuters.com/article/2015/01/16/russia-crisis-budget-idUSL6N0UU4 NG20150116 (accessed 17 February 2015).

Rikken, K. (2013, 13 February) 'Meanwhile, Over at the Massive Russian Military Buildup …', *ERR News*. http://news.err.ee/v/features/582a4ad5-d634-40b4-b3c7-b2f26 e6071a3 (accessed 8 January 2015).

RossiyskayaGazeta (2013, 3 July) 'Five War Scenarios: Dmitriy Rogozin: Russia Must Be Independent and Strong, or It Will Not Exist at All'.

RT (2014, 1 December) 'NATO Destabilizing Baltic by Stationing Nuke-capable Aircraft – Moscow'. http://rt.com/news/210383-nato-baltic-troops-russia/ (accessed 8 January 2015).

Safronov, I. (2013, 28 June) 'Planned Readiness Declared in Defence Ministry: The Military Told About its Work for the Next Seven Years', *Kommersant*.

Samofalova, O. (2013, 6 September) 'A Farewell to Arms. State Armaments Program May Fall Victim to Budget Spending Cuts', *Vzglyad*, 6 September.

Schneider, M.B. (2012) 'Russian Nuclear Modernization', Presentation at National Institute for Public Policy, 20 June.

Segodnya, L. (2012, 8 March) 'Zapreshchennoye nastupleniye: Intervyu prezidenta Akademii geopoliticheskikh problem general-polkovnika Leonida Ivashova', *Segodnya*. http://www.segodnia.ru/content/106674 (accessed 8 January 2015).

Sergeyev, M. (2013, 12 September) 'Defense Industry Fails to Keep Pace with Government's Plans', *Nezavisimaya gazeta*.

Sherr, J. (2013) *Russia and the Rest of Us: The Dynamics of Discontent*. http://www.sta tecraft.org.uk/research/russia-and-rest-us-dynamics-discontent (accessed 8 January 2015).

Slipchenko, V. and Gareyev, M. (2005) *Budushchaya voyna* (Future War), Moscow: Polit.ru.

Sokolov, B. (2012, 8 August) 'Orientirovat Vooruzhennye Sily nado na otrazheniye realnykh, a ne fantasticheskikh ugroz', *Voyenno-promyshlennyy kuryer*, http://vp k-news.ru/articles/9127 (accessed 8 January 2015).

Suvorov, V., Maj.-Gen. (2013, 27 November) *Briefing for Russian General Staff Academy visit to NATO Defense College*, Rome.

TASS (2015, 1 July) 'Russia Could Not Let NATO Troops Enter Sevastopol – Putin'. http://itar-tass.com/en/russia/738508 (accessed 8 January 2015).

Thomas, L.T. (2011) *Recasting the Red Star*, Fort Leavenworth, KS: Foreign Military Studies Office.

Thornton, R. (2011) *Organizational Change in the Russian Airborne Forces: The Lessons of the Georgian Conflict*, USAWC Strategic Studies Institute.

Tovkaylo, M. (2013, 10 July) 'The Military Beat Back the Budget', *Vedomosti*.

Tretyak, A. (2012, 27 November) *Speech at a briefing at NATO Defence College*.

PART III
Asia

7 Great power identity, security imaginary and military transformation in China

Rex Li

Over the past two decades, China has made a sustained effort to modernise its armed forces. While most defence analysts agree that China's military power is still behind that of the USA, Chinese military capabilities have increased substantially. This is supported by a consistently rising defence budget. There is no shortage of general and specialised studies of China's military modernisation and defence capabilities (Wortzel 2013; Cole 2010; Hallion et al. 2012; Shambaugh 2002; Blasko 2012). However, little attention has been paid to the analysis of how changes in Chinese military doctrine and force development have been influenced by US military transformation within the context of China's great power aspirations and its expanding global interests and activities (Lai 2012).

This chapter seeks to analyse Chinese defence modernisation as a response to US military transformation. It argues that the US Revolution in Military Affairs (RMA) has played an instrumental role in shaping the nature and direction of China's military transformation. However, US influence on Chinese military developments must be examined in relation to Chinese leaders' threat perceptions and attempts to construct a great power identity for their country. Thus, the chapter argues further that the most important driver of China's military transformation is its great power ambition, which is embedded in Chinese 'security imaginary'. It is this longstanding aspiration that has motivated Chinese leaders and defence planners to follow, analyse and learn from the military transformation and war-fighting experience of the USA, the sole superpower in the post-Cold War world. Nevertheless, the scope and dynamics of the transformation of the People's Liberation Army (PLA) are shaped by a variety of domestic and external factors.

The chapter begins with an analysis of the main drivers for China's military transformation from the theoretical perspectives of neo-realism and constructivism. The second section examines the nature and dynamics of the transformation, focusing on the changes in the PLA's military doctrines and the key aspects of China's defence modernisation in relation to its threat perceptions and strategic goals. This will be followed by a discussion of Chinese military developments within the framework of the US transformation agenda. It concludes by considering whether America's RMA has fundamentally changed the strategic thinking behind Beijing's military reforms.

Why transformation? Threat perceptions, security imaginary and great power identity

There is no doubt that the Chinese military has been going through a process of significant transformation in the past 20 years. The key question is what has made Chinese leaders decide to launch a major overhaul of their armed forces? To be sure, defence modernisation has long been a main component of the 'Four Modernisations' programme advocated by Deng Xiaoping in the 1970s, which includes the modernisation of agriculture, industry, science and technology, and defence, but Deng's priority was to build 'a good economic foundation' without which, he believed, China would not be able to build up its military capabilities. His advice was, therefore, to 'wait patiently' until China quadrupled its gross national product. He was certain that this goal could be achieved by the end of the twentieth century (Deng 1985). Why is it that the Chinese leaders felt the urgency of pushing for military transformation ahead of the schedule recommended by Deng? More importantly, why have Chinese leaders and defence planners been emulating America's RMA assiduously since the early 1990s?

The diffusion of new military technology and ideas is not a new phenomenon in international relations (Goldman and Eliason 2003). As Emily Goldman argues, 'diffusion can restructure power relations as states leverage new capabilities to increase their military power and enhance their international influence' (Goldman 2006: 91). From a neo-realist perspective, the international system is characterised by relentless competition for power and influence among states, especially the great powers. In such an anarchic system, it is not surprising that Chinese leaders seek to 'imitate the military innovations contrived by the country of greatest capability and ingenuity' (Waltz 1979: 127). However, to understand why Chinese leaders have decided to accelerate the pace of China's defence modernisation, one needs to look at its threat perceptions. After all, military responses are seen by many political leaders as the most effective means of dealing with external threats to their country's security, as the Realists would argue (Morgenthau 1978).

China's security environment has improved enormously since the end of the Cold War. The People's Republic of China (PRC) no longer faces any immediate external threat to its national security and survival. In the view of the Chinese, there is no possibility of a global war, nor is there any prospect of a foreign invasion of China. This is acknowledged in China's 2006 defence White Paper: 'China's overall security environment remains sound. China [...] enjoys steady economic growth, political stability, ethnic harmony and social progress. Its overall national strength has considerably increased, as has its international standing and influence' (Ministry of National Defence 2007). So what are Chinese leaders' primary security concerns?

Their anxieties began in 1990–91 when the United States demonstrated its extraordinary military power in the Gulf War. In common with other states examined in this collection, such as Russia and India, Chinese military analysts were truly shocked by America's advanced military technology and its effective application in fighting the war (Zhang et al. 1992). Their concern with US military superiority was exacerbated following the US-led air campaign in Kosovo in 1999, the military operations in Afghanistan in 2001, and the US invasion of Iraq in 2003. The possession of strong military capabilities alone does not necessarily constitute a threat, however. Beijing's concerns about US power are best explicated by Stephen Walt's (1987) theory of balance of threat. China is worried about America's military superiority precisely because it is perceived as a potential threat to Chinese security interests.

Of the greatest concern to Chinese leaders is the possibility for Taiwan to gain *de jure* independence, particularly during the Lee Teng-hui and Chen Shui-bian eras. The Clinton Administration's decision to send two aircraft carriers to the areas near Taiwan during the 1995–96 Taiwan Strait crisis was seen as a clear signal of American support for Taipei (Ross 2000). Soon after he came to office, President George W. Bush approved the sale of a massive arms package to Taipei. The April 2002 package included four Kidd-class destroyers, eight diesel-electric patrol submarines, 12 P-3 Orion maritime patrol aircraft, submarine- and surface-launched torpedoes and other naval systems. Together, they enhanced Taiwan's capability to break potential Chinese blockades. Indeed, President Bush made it clear in public that the USA would do 'whatever it took to help Taiwan' defend itself (Sanger 2001). Similarly, the Obama Administration approved an arms sales package to Taipei worth US \$6.4 billion in January 2010. The package encompassed 114 Patriot missiles, 60 Black Hawk helicopters, communications equipment for Taiwan's F-16 fleet, Harpoon missiles and mine-hunting ships (Branigan and Harris 2010). In September 2011, the Obama Administration approved another arms sales package to Taiwan worth \$5.8 billion which attracted strong reactions from China. The arms package included upgrades to Taiwan's F-16 fighter fleet, an extension of F-16 pilot training in the USA for five years, and spare parts for the maintenance of three other types of plane (CNN 2011; Jacobs 2011). Taiwan is treated by the Chinese government as an integral part of China, therefore the issue of Taiwanese independence becomes a matter of national unity and territorial integrity. To PRC leaders, there is a pressing need to develop China's military capabilities to thwart Taiwan's efforts to seek independence and deter American intervention in the event of a cross-strait military conflict.

Taiwan is not the only area where China has security concerns. While China has settled most of its border disputes in recent years, it still has unresolved territorial disputes with Brunei, Malaysia, the Philippines, Taiwan and Vietnam in the South China Sea. Their competing claims over the Spratly and Paracel islands are a major source of conflict in the region. The United States is not a claimant to any part of the South China Sea but it has vital interests in maintaining freedom of navigation. Washington is concerned about the destabilising effects of a potential conflict among the claimants. Indeed, tensions between China and US allies such as the Philippines have escalated in the past few years, as China becomes more assertive in pressing for its claims (Landingin and Hille 2011; Thayer 2012). While America's position on the disputes is neutral, Washington has made it clear that it has treaty obligations to support its allies in the region. This policy is known as the Obama Administration's 'pivot' or 'rebalance' to Asia (Clinton 2011; Clinton 2014: 45–46). The US-Japan and US-Philippines relationships are examined by Hughes and Eadie, respectively, in this volume.

Indeed, the United States signed a new military pact with the Philippines in April 2014. The ten-year military agreement, in the words of President Obama, indicates that American 'commitment to the defence of the Philippines is iron-clad', and that 'the United States will keep that commitment because allies never stand alone' (Felsenthal and Spetalnick 2014). He reiterated his point in November 2014: 'any effective security order for Asia must be based – not on spheres of influence, or coercion or intimidation where big nations bully the small – but on alliances for mutual security, international law and norms that are upheld, and the peaceful resolution of disputes' (Lee and Taylor 2014). To Chinese leaders, any US involvement in the South China Sea disputes, direct or indirect, is an attempt to dominate Asia-Pacific security and constrain China in particular. They suspect that America would deploy its formidable naval forces to prevent China from asserting its claims by force over the disputed waters in the South China Sea. The development of China's maritime capabilities is seen by Chinese military planners as a crucial step in safeguarding what they consider to be their national sovereignty and territorial integrity.

Another security issue that has caused grave concern to Chinese leaders is the territorial dispute between China and Japan over the sovereignty of the Diaoyu/Senkaku islands in the East China Sea. For many years, the two East Asian powers were able to contain the dispute so that it would not seriously damage their political and economic relations. However, their contesting claims have intensified in the past few years, which have led to significant diplomatic strains between them. Indeed, tensions in the East China Sea have escalated since September 2012, when the Japanese government announced its decision to nationalise the disputed islands (Ryall 2012). With seemingly widespread domestic support, the Chinese and Japanese governments are unwilling to compromise on their territorial claims, and they accuse each other of ignoring historical facts and defying international law. Both the Chinese maritime surveillance ships and Japanese coast guard vessels have been deployed in the contested area to demonstrate their resolve to defend what they regard as their territorial waters. In January 2014 a Chinese frigate allegedly locked its radar on a Japanese destroyer in the East China Sea.

What worries Chinese leaders most is the US-Japan security alliance, which has been strengthened substantially since the end of the Cold War. They are deeply concerned about the extension of the scope of US-Japanese security cooperation to include 'the situation in Japan's surrounding areas' (Xiao

1998: 8). During his recent visit to Japan, President Obama stated that the US-Japan security treaty 'covers all territories under Japan's administration including [the] Senkaku islands' (BBC 2014). Not surprisingly, the Chinese government responded by saying that the security alliance is 'a bilateral arrangement' that is used to 'damage China's sovereignty and legitimate interest' (Ng 2014). Indeed, China has long been suspicious of Japan's strategic intentions despite a high degree of economic interaction between the two countries. Chinese leaders and elites are convinced that Japan is collaborating with the USA in impeding China from rising as a great power (Li 1999; Li 2010).

In Beijing's view, the USA is the biggest military power in the world that is capable of challenging China's security interests. It has a strategic interest and strong military presence in the Asia-Pacific. It also has many close friends and allies in the region, including Japan, Taiwan, South Korea, Australia and various South-East Asian countries. Washington is believed to have both the intention and military capability to frustrate China's attempts to assert its territorial claims and to intervene in a regional conflict (Qi 2013). President Obama's policy of rebalance to the Asia-Pacific is seen by the Chinese as a clear indication of America's support for its Asian allies that have unresolved maritime disputes with China (He 2014; Wu 2012).

This assessment is consistent with the Chinese discourse of the United States as a threatening 'other' (Li, R. 2009: chs 2 and 3). A Realist response to the perceived challenge would be 'internal balancing' (Mearsheimer 2001: 157), in the sense that Beijing would strengthen its military capabilities to deter US intervention. Neo-realists would argue that a menacing security environment could encourage a threatened state 'to adopt new military methods, frequently by emulating the most successful states in the system' (Goldman 2006: 69). From this perspective, it makes sense for China to observe and follow the US RMA. In fact, 'the threatening development', argues Theo Farrell, 'may itself be military innovation by an opponent (a new weapon or way of war) that demands an innovative response' (Farrell 2008: 780; see also Evangelista 1988). America's impressive performance in Operation Desert Storm in 1991 certainly forced Chinese leaders and military planners to respond to the high-tech challenge in war-fighting and to undertake its own 'transformation in military affairs' (军事变革) (You 2004; Newmyer 2010). This fits in with the argument that the intervention of civilian policymakers is significant in driving military innovation (Posen 1984: 224–26; Zisk 1993: 178–79; Grissom 2006: 908–910).

In 1993 Jiang Zemin, the then Chinese president, issued a new set of military strategic guidelines (Finkelstein 2006) for the PLA to develop its capability to fight and win 'local wars under high-tech conditions' (高技术条件下的局部战争) (Jiang, Z. 1997).

Chinese leaders were acutely aware that they had to transform their armed forces while continuing to develop the Chinese economy (Sun 2003). They also recognised that their military was still going through the process of mechanisation. However, they could not afford to wait until this process was completed to start the development of the capabilities of what they call 'informationised warfare'. Therefore, they had to pursue the path of 'leapfrog development' (跨越式发展) – that is, developing mechanisation and informationisation simultaneously. According to this strategy, the modernisation of China's armed forces would undergo three stages starting with the first step of building a solid foundation by 2010, which would be followed by the completion of mechanisation with major progress in informationisation by 2020. The ultimate goal of defence modernisation and military transformation should be reached by the mid-twenty-first century. China's plan is summed up clearly in the following statement:

> Persisting in taking mechanization as the foundation and informationization as focus, China is stepping up the composite development of mechanization and informationization. Persisting in strengthening the military by means of science and technology, China is working to develop new and high-tech weaponry and equipment, carry out the strategic project of training talented people, conduct military training in conditions of informationization, and build a modern logistics system in an all-round way, so as to change the mode of formation of war-fighting capabilities. Persisting in laying stress on priorities, China distinguishes between the primary and the secondary, and refrains from doing certain things, striving to achieve leapfrog development in key areas.
>
> (Ministry of National Defence n.d.)

To be sure, neo-Realism has offered some convincing explanations for PRC leaders' decision to modernise their armed forces and initiate a Chinese version of RMA. However, to understand fully the drivers for China's military transformation, one needs to go beyond the rationalist approach to include an analysis of the relevant cultural factors. Culture can be defined as 'the context within which people make sense of the world around them and which is indeed the source of their impetus to act in a certain way and not another' (Pretorius 2008: 100). Realists tend to perceive a 'threat' to state security as something that exists objectively. What they fail to consider is the cultural context within which the threat is constructed 'through the fixing of meanings to things'. This kind of 'security imaginary', as Joelien Pretorius argues, has 'a powerful presence in political and social life that amply evidences and reproduces itself' (Pretorius 2008: 100). The conception of security imaginary derives from the studies on social imaginaries that focus on how people imagine their social environment, which forms the basis for a shared understanding and legitimacy of certain common practices in society (Taylor 2004).

Essentially, a security imaginary is underpinned by a particular social and political discourse that serves to constitute and legitimise specific interpretations of a security situation and responses to any perceived threat arising from it (Pretorius 2008). This concept challenges the positivist presumption that security decisions are based on an 'objective' assessment of the external security environment. It argues that security discourse and practice are rooted in the history and culture of a country, which has a strong element of subjectivity. Security imaginaries, like 'national interests', are arguably a product of social construction (Weldes 1996). This constructivist perspective is especially pertinent to our analysis of the forces driving China's defence modernisation and its decisions to emulate the US model of military transformation in particular. The adoption of and adaptation to America's RMA in China are intimately linked to the security imaginary embedded in Chinese society.

As discussed earlier, Chinese leaders feel that they are facing a range of external security threats. From a neo-Realist standpoint, it seems sensible for China to adapt the model of its military development to the country with 'greatest capability and ingenuity' (Waltz 1979: 127) – that is, the United States. However, the PRC's external threats may not exist as an objective reality as the positivists would argue. Rather, they can be seen as the product of subjective interpretations of China's security environment in the context of its historical memory and future aspirations. Much of China's external security concern is related to its historical legacy, such as various territorial disputes with neighbouring countries. Many Chinese leaders are deeply scarred by the 'century of national humiliation' (百年国耻), when China was defeated by the superior military might of Western powers and Japan in the nineteenth century (Wang 2012). With the demise of the Sino-centric order in Asia, China lost not only the control of its territories but its dominant position in the region.

For decades, the shame and humiliation associated with external invasion and domination of China became a significant part of Chinese security discourse. The decline of China's pre-eminence in Asia and its conquest by Japan and European colonial powers are often explicated by its inadequate defence capabilities. Chinese elites and citizens are constantly reminded that 'past experience, if not forgotten, is a guide to the future' (前事不忘, 后事之师). From a psycho-political perspective, perceptions of history are a major dimension of national self-imagery and they 'generate powerful needs to avoid past experiences which are felt as humiliating, dangerous, or deadly'. To Chinese intellectuals and policy elites, there is a psychological need to 'restore honour, dignity, and strength to the nation' and to 'demand and gain respect from the rest of the world' (Kaplowitz 1990: 51–52).

Both Deng Xiaoping and Jiang Zemin placed a strong emphasis on the development of China's military capabilities as a major part of its modernisation agenda. As the Chinese economy expanded in the 2000s, Hu Jintao called for the building of a 'prosperous country with powerful armed forces' (富国强军) at the 17th National Congress of the Chinese Communist Party (CCP) (Hu 2007). This provided clear strategic guidance for both the CCP and the PLA in China's modernisation drive (Zhang 2012). Indeed, the 'dream of a powerful military' (强军梦) is presented as a vital and inseparable part of the 'dream of a powerful nation' (强国梦) or the 'China dream' (中国梦) under the current leadership of Xi Jinping (Li 2013; Sui 2013; Huang 2014).

Alexander Wendt (1999: 263) argues that 'collective self-esteem' is often considered by political elites as a national interest. Since the end of the Cold War, Chinese elites have been engaged assiduously in the construction of a great power identity for China (Li, R. 2009: ch. 6). In social identity theory this is known as a socio-cognitive process of 'self-enhancement' in that 'people have a basic need to see themselves in a positive light in relation to relevant others' (Hogg et al. 1995). Thus, it can be argued that the most important driver of Chinese military transformation is the PRC leaders' aspiration to achieve the 'rejuvenation of the Chinese nation' (中华民族复兴) (Xi 2013). Through intensive education and socialisation, this aspiration is ingrained in China's security imaginary which, in turn, provides a powerful impetus for an RMA with Chinese characteristics.

To Chinese leaders, there is an inextricable link between 'internal instability and external invasion' (内忧外患). The severe domestic weaknesses of the Qing dynasty are thought to have contributed significantly to China's inability to defend itself from external attacks. This explains why maintaining internal stability is viewed by Chinese leaders as indispensable to the protection of China's national sovereignty and territorial integrity. In particular, they are profoundly suspicious of alleged Western/US attempts to undermine the PRC's legitimacy and regime security through regular criticisms of its political ideology and encouragement of separatist activities in Tibet and Xinjiang. More recently, America has been accused of actively supporting the 'Occupy Central' movement in Hong Kong, with the aim of undermining China's domestic stability and political system (Bradsher 2014; Hua 2014). Meanwhile, there is a widespread supposition in Chinese elite and popular discourse that Washington is seeking to encircle China strategically by fortifying security ties with its allies in the Asia-Pacific and abetting the countries that have unsettled territorial disputes with the PRC. Consequently, it is considered essential for Chinese leaders to have an accurate assessment of America's military strength, particularly its defence transformation. The domestic/external linkage in Chinese perceptions is thus central to the construction of China's security imaginary. The PLA is expected to play a critical role in preserving China's internal security as well as defending its external borders.

With the emergence of China as a key economic player in the world, the conception of its security interests has been broadened considerably. Between 1993 and 2013 the annual gross domestic product (GDP) growth rate in the PRC averaged 10 per cent (see Figure 7.1). In 2011, China surpassed Japan as the world's second largest economy (Moore 2011). Indeed, China's economic and trade relations with most countries have expanded enormously in the past few decades. It is now a major trading nation with imported and exported goods valued at $4.16 trillion in 2013. By January 2014 China overtook the United States as the world's biggest goods trading nation, although America remained the largest overall trading nation in the world (Rushton 2014). This 'shift in the trading pecking order' according to *The Guardian*, 'reflected China's rising global dominance' (Monaghan 2014). As China's economy is growing rapidly and its consumption of oil and other commodities increases, Chinese

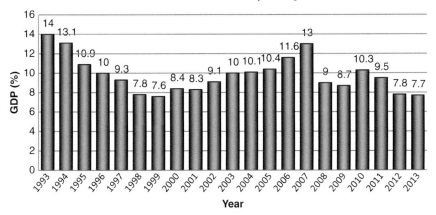

Figure 7.1 China's GDP growth rate, 1993–2013
Source: World Bank, various years; Xinhua, 20 January 2014.

energy companies have been buying foreign energy assets in many countries, including Angola, Iran, Kazakhstan, Nigeria, Sudan and Venezuela. State-owned companies have reportedly received low-interest loans and direct capital injections from the government to fund takeovers or mergers with resource firms abroad (Spencer 2009; Klare 2010). China was estimated to have spent $35 billion on joint ventures and outright purchases in 2012 alone. Since 2009 Chinese companies have spent $100 billion on oil and gas assets in Africa, the Middle East and other countries, including the United States (United Press International 2013). Given the global reach of Chinese trade and investment, China's conception of security interests has been expanded to encompass economic and energy security.

Clearly, China's economic growth relies significantly on the exports of its products as well as imports of raw materials and other goods. The security of sea lines of communication (SLOC) in East Asia is therefore extremely important to Chinese shipping. In addition, its trade and economic activities depend heavily on external resources. However, over 30 per cent of the PRC's oil supply is imported from Central Asia. This explains why Beijing has been pursuing cooperation on the construction of oil pipelines and oil exploration with various countries in the region. Similarly, 90 per cent of China's imported oil passes through the Strait of Malacca. If this strategic sea lane were to be obstructed, China's economic development would be seriously jeopardised. Thus, China needs to build up its naval capabilities in order to protect its energy security in the Malacca Strait. China's security concerns are summarised in the 2012 defence White Paper as follows:

> Security issues are increasingly prominent, involving overseas energy and resources, strategic sea lines of communication (SLOCs), and Chinese nationals and legal persons overseas.

> (Ministry of National Defence 2007)

In the meantime, Chinese leaders are increasingly aware of the implications of non-traditional security issues. The 'new' security challenge is summed up succinctly in China's 2004 defence White Paper:

> Non-traditional security threats present greater danger [...] Security issues related to energy, resources, finance, information and international shipping routes are mounting. International terrorist forces remain active, shocking terrorist acts keep occurring. Natural disasters, serious communicable diseases, environmental degradation, international crime and other transnational problems are becoming more damaging in nature.
>
> (Ministry of National Defence 2005)

Since the mid-2000s, Beijing has become much more proactive in dealing with different types of non-conventional security threats and willing to cooperate with other countries in tackling the problems. This is partly because these security issues affect China and partly because it hopes to use the opportunity to project China as a peaceful and responsible rising power.

On 24 December 2004, the CCP leader and Chinese President Hu Jintao presented a new set of strategic guidelines at the Central Military Commission. According to the guidelines, the PLA would be expected to fulfil its 'new historical missions' (新的历史使命) in the new century: first, to provide an important guarantee of strength for consolidating the CCP's ruling position; second, to provide a strong security guarantee for safeguarding the important period of strategic opportunity for national development; third, to provide powerful strategic support for safeguarding national interests; and fourth, to play an important role in safeguarding world peace and promoting common development. This is known as 'three provides and one role' (三个提供, 一个发挥) (Zhang and Yang 2008; Zheng and Liu 2005; Zhou 2008). These guidelines reveal Chinese leaders' strategic priorities. The most important mission of the PLA is to maintain domestic and regime security, which is linked to various external security concerns as discussed earlier. Moreover, the Chinese military is tasked to defend China's economic development and expanding national interests both within and beyond its territorial boundary, including the maritime environment, outer space and the electromagnetic spectrum. Last but not least is the PLA's role in safeguarding world peace in that it is required to deal with a range of traditional and non-traditional security issues and conduct 'military operations other than war' (MOOTW) (非战争军事行动).

Since 2008 the PLA has participated in a variety of MOOTW, which are regarded as an important part of what the Chinese leaders call 'diversified military tasks' (多样化军事任务). Under the direction of the Central Military Commission, a MOOTW Capacity-Building Plan has been issued with the establishment of 'leading groups' in the PLA's four general departments and seven military regions to handle emergencies. In addition, a mapping, meteorology and communication system is being constructed to support MOOTW. The Emergency Office of the PLA General Staff Headquarters is coordinating with more than 20 government departments, including those of public security, civil affairs, water conservancy, forestry, earthquake, oceans and weather, to enable information sharing at the headquarters level. The PLA has also built professional state-level emergency response teams of 50,000 people in eight categories, as well as provincial emergency response teams of 45,000 people in nine categories in all the military area commands (Wu et al. 2011). More significantly, the PLA has constructed five specialised forces for carrying out MOOTW, including a flood and disaster relief force, a post-earthquake emergent rescue force, an emergent rescue force for nuclear, chemical and biological disasters, an emergent relief force for transportation facilities, and an international peacekeeping force (Kamphausen 2013).

The development that has attracted much attention is China's involvement in international peacekeeping. China has deployed over 21,000 troops to peacekeeping operations (PKOs) in total (Ministry of National Defence 2013). As of 30 November 2014, it had contributed 1,975 troops, 32 military experts and 174 police to nine United Nations (UN) PKOs (United Nations 2014). UN Secretary-General Ban Ki-moon has acknowledged that China provides more peacekeepers to the UN than all of the other four permanent Security Council members combined. Some 14 Chinese have lost their lives during peacekeeping activities (Ban 2013). Another prominent contribution by China to UN peacekeeping is the establishment of two peacekeeping training centres in Langfang (Hebei) and Huairou (Beijing).

There is no doubt that China's peacekeeping role has expanded considerably in the past decade (Gill and Huang 2009; Hirono and Lanteigne 2011). Hitherto, the types of capabilities the PLA deployed focused primarily on engineering, transportation, logistics and military medical assistance. In December 2013 China sent a 395-strong peacekeeping force including security forces to Mali to protect the peacekeeping mission's headquarters and its surrounding areas. From December 2014 China will send 700 combat troops to South Sudan, including 121 officers and 579 soldiers (Smith 2013). This is the first time the PLA will dispatch an infantry battalion to participate in a UN peacekeeping mission. Mindful of Western apprehensions of China's growing activities in Africa, the Chinese media state that the operation should be seen as a demonstration of China's international responsibilities rather than building an overseas Chinese military base (Li 2014).

Another area of MOOTW in which the PLA has been enthusiastically involved is anti-piracy. China has participated in numerous anti-piracy escort missions in the Gulf of Aden since 2008. These operations have provided the PLA Navy (PLAN) with an opportunity to gain experience in operating in the sea far beyond Chinese borders: 13 task forces have been deployed, involving 10,000 personnel on 37 warships with 28 helicopters. These naval escort task forces have protected more than 5,000 Chinese and foreign commercial vessels. Four ships loaded with World Food Programme cargo have been saved from pirates by the PLAN (Erickson and Strange 2013). These anti-piracy deployments have enabled the Chinese Navy to work closely with foreign militaries, thus learning lessons in 'far seas' operations (Kamphausen 2013: 4). While the PLAN's current out-of-area capabilities may be limited, the experience from its anti-piracy missions will certainly contribute to the future development of Chinese maritime capability.

Moreover, the PLA has been involved in numerous disaster relief operations both at home and abroad. High-profile PLA domestic relief operations include the Wenchuan earthquake (2008), the Zhouqu landslide (2010), Yushu county earthquake (2010), the Lushan earthquake (2013), the Ludian earthquake (2014), and the Xinjiang earthquake (2014). While a well-integrated and streamlined response mechanism is in place for disaster relief operations, there are some capability gaps in implementing relief operations. For example, inadequate pilot training and ageing and limited aircraft are believed to have undermined effective air relief efforts. Insufficient heavy construction and earth-moving equipment and assault and transport helicopters for moving troops are also a noticeable deficiency in ground-based relief efforts (Patel 2009). The PLA seems to be aware of these problems and is seeking to deal with the challenges relating to MOOTW equipment (Kamphausen 2013: 6–7).

Meanwhile, the PLA has been active in joining international disaster relief missions, contributing to a range of relief efforts from South-East Asia to Africa, such as the Haiti earthquake (2010), Typhoon Haiyan in the Philippines (2013), the Ebola outbreak in West Africa (2014), and the search for the missing Malaysian Airline flight MH370 and the Air Asia flight QZ8501 (2014). The contribution of the PLA Air Force (PLAAF) and the PLAN is particularly conspicuous in overseas disaster relief operations. The Chinese hospital ship 'Peace Ark', which provides free medical goods and services, has visited various parts of the world including Asia, the South Pacific, the Middle East and Africa. This clearly plays a key role in achieving China's maritime diplomacy in the twenty-first century (Le Mière 2014).

The PLA's active involvement in MOOTW may be seen as China's responses to the broad range of security threats it is facing, but these operations offered the PLA opportunities to gain some valuable operational experience. They are also useful for China to project a positive image to the international community that it is making an important contribution to maintaining global peace and stability. Despite their political and military values, PRC leaders have made it clear that the primary role of the Chinese armed forces is still war-fighting. In this sense, Hu Jintao's new historical missions are of huge significance in laying the strategic foundation for China to develop a 'prosperous country with powerful armed forces' (富国强军).

What transformation? China's doctrinal changes and force modernisation

Any analysis of China's military transformation must begin by examining its changing strategic doctrine in recent years. While there is no one single document that provides an overarching strategic and operational guidance for the PLA, Chinese strategic doctrine can be identified from the military strategic guidelines and other important documents issued by PRC leaders. From the mid-1930s to the late 1970s, the concept of 'people's war' (人民战争) created by Mao Zedong was adopted as the Chinese military doctrine, which was based on the idea that foreign invading forces could be lured into the strategic depth of China and then overwhelmed by its military forces with the support of the civilian population. After the Sino–Vietnamese border war in 1979, the people's war doctrine was modified to become the doctrine of 'people's war under modern conditions' (现代条件下的人民战争) to reflect a re-assessment of the nature of modern warfare and China's changing strategic environment (Joffe 1987: 559–60). In the mid-1980s, Deng Xiaoping reached the conclusion that China no longer faced the prospects of a total war and that future conflicts would likely be small wars along China's periphery. Thus, China's military doctrine was changed to 'local war under modern conditions' (现代条件下的局步战争). As discussed earlier, the doctrine was further changed to 'local war under high-tech conditions' (高技术条件下的局部战争) by Jiang Zemin in 1993, following close observations of the 1990–91 Gulf War. This signified China's recognition of the centrality of high technology to fighting a modern war and its implications for the modernisation of the PLA. The 2003 Iraq War convinced the Chinese leaders that effective utilisation of information technology in war-fighting is the key to success. America's network-centric warfare highlighted the need for China to learn from US military transformation in modernising its armed forces (see Chapter 4 in this volume). Thus, a new doctrine of 'local war under modern informationised conditions' (现代信息化条件下的局部战争) was introduced in 2004 (Information Office of the State Council of the People's Republic of China 2004).

Basically, what this military doctrine indicates is that China's future wars are likely to be short in duration, limited in geographical scope, and specific in political/military objectives. Chinese military leaders understand that the success of this type of warfare would depend on the PLA's ability to exploit IT to integrate computer, communication and command systems. According to General Xiong Guangkai, former PLA deputy chief of staff, there are five main features in America's military transformation (军事变革) that would offer useful lessons for China. These include artificial intelligence for weapon systems, streamlining the organisation of the armed forces, computerisation of command and control, multi-dimensional battlespace encompassing land, sea, air, outer space and magnetic space, and integration of combat systems (Xiong 2003a, 2003b). Of particular interest to Chinese defence analysts is the integrated nature of US military operations, which is seen as the key feature of informationised warfare. They have been keen to follow the US model of 'joint integrated operations' (联合作战).

With the promulgation of the 'Principles of Joint Campaigns of the Chinese People's Liberation Army' (中国人民解放军联合战役纲要) in January 1999, Chinese leaders clearly endorsed the significance of jointness in China's military operations (*Liberation Army Daily* 1999: 1). To achieve joint integrated operations in China, they have called for the strengthening of 'eight integrations' (八个一体化), including integrated thinking among officers, integrated services and combat power, integrated command systems, integrated information systems, integrated weapon systems, integrated logistics systems, integrated quality for military personnel, and integrated education and training (Shang 2008). Indeed, the building of joint operation systems has been highlighted in China's defence White Papers since 2008. Special attention has been paid to the research into the doctrines relating to joint operations, the building of 'a system of streamlined, joint, multi-functional and efficient system of combat forces', improving operational command systems to ensure 'lean, agile and efficient operational capability', and enhancing integrated support capabilities 'linking strategic, operational and tactical levels' (Ministry of National Defence 2012).

China's military transformation has been funded by a generous defence budget for over two decades (see Figure 7.2). It is also supported by an expanding and increasingly innovative defence industry (Cheung 2011). Undoubtedly, China has introduced a wide-ranging programme to reform its armed forces and improve their capabilities with the aim of fighting and winning 'local war under modern informationised conditions'. The modernisation of the PLA Army, Navy and Air Force has been driven substantially by the consideration of conducting network-centric warfare, effect-based operations, and expeditionary warfare. All these are the key components of America's transformation agenda (US Department of Defense 2003).

If one looks at the structure of the PLA ground force, there has been a substantial reduction in its manpower in the past three decades, with 1.25 million personnel today. The rationale behind this reduction is to create a smaller, more mobile and agile force capable of responding to contingencies along China's periphery (Blasko 2012). Meanwhile, the obsolescent equipment designed primarily to fight 'people's war' has gradually been upgraded or replaced by modern weapons systems with third-generational capabilities, including main

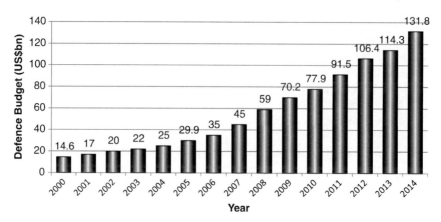

Figure 7.2 China's official defence budget, 2000–14
Source: IISS, *The Military Balance*, various years; Xinhua, 5 March 2013, 5 March 2014.

battle tanks (MBTs), armoured infantry fighting vehicles (AIFVs), armoured personnel carriers (APCs) and self-propelled artillery. A major focus of the reform is to improve the ground force's armoured, air defence, aviation, ground-air coordination, and electronic warfare capabilities. According to the 2013 Pentagon report on China's military developments, the PLA ground force has acquired new air defence equipment such as its first medium-range surface-to-air missile (SAM), the CSA-16, in addition to the indigenous CSA-15s and a new advanced self-propelled air defence artillery system, the PGZ-07 (US Department of Defense 2013: 9). In addition, considerable efforts have been made in providing training for mobilising forces rapidly and efficiently across long distances involving several military regions. Finally, the ground force is keen to conduct joint operations training with other military services in order to increase its power projection capability to deal with regional contingencies like a Taiwan Strait crisis.

While China has the largest army in the world, it is the modernisation of its naval forces that has attracted most attention. This is because the PRC's unresolved territorial disputes are primarily maritime disputes covering a wide range of areas in the South China Sea and East China Sea. It is also due to the more assertive stance taken by Beijing on these disputes in the past few years. Importantly, Presidents Hu Jintao and Xi Jinping have advocated the building of China as a maritime power in the twenty-first century (Xinhua 2012, 2013).

The PLAN has made tremendous progress in its modernisation efforts, and is at the forefront of safeguarding China's increasingly expansive security interests (Saunders et al. 2012). China's naval modernisation is also consistent with its changing naval strategy in the last three decades (Li, N. 2009; Office of Naval Intelligence 2009). With the diminishing Soviet threat in the mid-1980s, the doctrine of 'near-coast defence' (近岸防御) was gradually replaced by one of 'offshore defence' (近海防御) or 'near-seas active defence' (近海积极防御). The main mission for the PLAN was no longer the provision of naval assistance for land-based defence through counter-amphibious landing and other operations that would help defend China's coastal military assets and bases. Instead, the PLAN's 'near-seas' defence activities would cover a much broader area, including the first island chain, the Yellow Sea, East China Sea and South China Sea. This clearly went beyond the 200 nautical miles (nm) from China's coastal baseline, its exclusive economic zone as defined by the 1982 UN Convention on the Law of the Sea (UNCLOS). Undoubtedly, this strategy was formulated to develop Chinese naval capabilities for preventing Taiwan from seeking *de jure* independence, gaining control over the territorial waters and islands in the disputed areas, ensuring the security of SLOC to protect China's trade activities and energy supply, defending the country against any foreign attacks from the sea, and providing effective nuclear deterrence.

Since mid-2000, the concept of 'far-seas defence' (远海防卫) has been advocated by PRC military analysts with official endorsement. This concept extends the PLAN's operational reach to the second island chain covering the

Kurile Islands through Japan, the Bonin Islands, the Mariana Islands, the Caroline Islands, and Indonesia. The rationale behind 'far-seas defence' is to enhance China's naval capabilities to meet existing and potential challenges, reflecting China's growing economic power and expanding global interests. It would allow the PLAN to conduct long-range surface and submarine patrols, defend Chinese interests in distant waters, and undertake military operations other than war such as counter-piracy, humanitarian missions and PKOs.

To achieve its strategic goals, the PLAN has introduced an extensive modernisation programme encompassing a wide range of platforms and weapon acquisition programmes. They include programmes for anti-ship ballistic missiles (ASBMs), anti-ship cruise missiles (ASCMs), land-attack cruise missiles (LACMs), SAMs, mines, manned aircraft, unmanned aircraft, submarines, aircraft carriers, destroyers, frigates, corvettes, patrol craft, amphibious ships, mine counter-measures (MCM) ships, underway replenishment ships, hospital ships, and supporting C4ISR systems (O'Rourke 2014: 2–3). The emphasis of China's naval modernisation is on qualitative improvement of its platforms. With the removal of many obsolete platforms, the PLAN now possesses a variety of up-to-date and proficient platforms.

The PLAN currently has approximately 77 principal surface combatants, over 60 submarines, 55 medium and large amphibious ships, and about 85 missile-equipped small combatants (US Department of Defense 2014: 7–9; Karotkin 2014). The traditional single-mission ships have gradually been replaced by larger, multi-mission ships, equipped with advanced anti-ship, anti-air and anti-submarine weapons and sensors. One recent report has indicated that over 50 naval ships were laid down, launched or commissioned in 2013 alone (Karotkin 2014).

A main focus of China's naval modernisation is its submarine force. Three JIN-class nuclear-powered ballistic missile submarines (SSBNs) (Type 094) are operational and China is planning to field five more before developing the next-generation SSBN (Type 096) in the coming decade. The JIN-class SSBN and the JL-2 submarine-launched ballistic missile it carries can reach a range of over 4,000 nm, which would provide China with its first credible sea-based nuclear deterrent (US Department of Defense 2014: 7–9). There has also been an expansion in China's nuclear-powered attack submarines (SSN). Two SHANG-class SSNs (Type 093) are currently in service and China has been building four improved variants of its SHANG-class SSN since 2012 to replace the antiquated HAN-class SSNs (Type 091). In addition, China is developing two new classes of nuclear submarine: the Type 095 guided-missile attack submarine (SSGN) and the Type 096 SSBN. The growth and improvement of China's nuclear and conventional submarines are expected to increase the PLAN's capabilities in engaging opposing surface ships throughout the Western Pacific and to defend future nuclear deterrent patrols and aircraft carrier task groups.

Another main area of expansion in China's submarine force is related to its modern diesel-powered attack submarines (SS). Over the past two decades China has acquired 12 KILO-class submarines from Russia, eight of which are equipped with the SS-N-27 anti-ship cruise missiles. Other diesel-powered attack submarines in the PLAN's inventory include 13 SONG-class SS (Type 039) and 12 YUAN-class SSP (Type 039A). The production of 20 more YUAN-class SSPs is anticipated to be in the pipeline (US Department of Defense 2013: 7; US Department of Defense 2014: 8).

The construction of various classes of Chinese surface combatant in the past six years has attracted considerable attention, which includes both guided missile destroyers (DDGs) and guided missile frigates (FFGs). Apart from continuing to produce the LUYANG II-class DDG (Type 052C), China launched the LUYANG III-class DDG (Type 052D) which will likely enter service this year. The LUYANG III incorporates the PLAN's first multipurpose vertical-launch system, which is believed to be capable of launching ASCMs, LACMs, SAMs and anti-submarine rockets. China is expected to build over a dozen LUYANG III-class DDGs to replace the ageing LUDA-class destroyers (DD). Moreover, China has continued serial production of the JIANGKAI II-class FFG (Type 054A), most of which will likely be operational by 2015 (US Department of Defense 2013: 7; US Department of Defense 2014: 8). In addition, the PLAN has acquired four Sovremenny-class (Type 956E and Type 956EM) DDGs from Russia. These acquisitions, combined with systematic upgrades of China's destroyers and frigates, have no doubt enhanced its capabilities to project power in the Taiwan Strait, the South China Sea, the East China Sea and the Western Pacific. This would also enable the PLAN to perform various non-traditional security missions well beyond China's near coast.

In 2012 the PLAN launched the JIANGDAO-class corvettes (FFL) (Type 056) with the intention of producing 20 to 30 more of this new class of small combatants (US Department of Defense 2013: 7; US Department of Defense 2014: 8), which are particularly useful for supporting China's 'near-seas defence' strategy. In the same year, the PLAN commissioned two new YUZHAO amphibious transport docks (LPD), bringing its total number of LPDs to three. It is intending to introduce a new landing helicopter assault ship, called the Type 081, by 2018. The YUZHAO LPD is capable of carrying a mix of air-cushion landing craft, amphibious armoured vehicles, helicopters and marines. This would help improve the PLAN's capabilities to take military action against Taiwan as well as fulfilling such non-traditional missions as humanitarian assistance and counter-piracy (O'Rourke 2014).

For Chinese civilian and military leaders, there has long been a desire to build aircraft carriers, which are considered a symbol of great power status. In 1998 China purchased an ex-Soviet aircraft carrier, *Varyag*, from Ukraine. After approximately six years of renovation work and one year of sea trials, China commissioned its first aircraft carrier, the *Liaoning* (辽宁舰) in September 2012 (Global Military n.d.). The main value of this refurbished vessel is to build the PLAN's proficiency in aircraft carrier operations until it develops a carrier aviation capability later. China is seeking to pursue an indigenous aircraft carrier programme, which is indicative of its blue water ambition. The plan is to build at least three more aircraft carriers in the coming years, the first of which is being built in Dalian and will likely be completed by 2018 (Wan 2014). China's aircraft carrier capability will certainly enhance its capability to project air power in the Asia-Pacific and to undertake a range of other missions, including airborne early warning, anti-submarine warfare, helicopter support to ground forces, humanitarian assistance, search and rescue, and other naval operations (US Department of Defense 2013: 7; US Department of Defense 2014: 8).

Given China's concern about potential American military intervention in a Taiwan Strait crisis and territorial disputes in the South and East China Seas, a main goal of its naval modernisation efforts is to acquire anti-access/area-denial (A2/AD) capability (Mahnken 2011). The deployment of DF-21D ASBMs in 2010, combined with China's long-range ASCMs, would strengthen Chinese capabilities to intimidate US aircraft carriers in the Western Pacific region. China is believed to be fielding additional DF-21D missiles and developing a longer-range variant (Erickson 2013). All this is clearly aimed at deterring US intervention or undermining its effectiveness in the event of a conflict between China and its neighbouring countries. Indeed, C4ISR systems, ASBMs, ASCMs, LACMs, attack submarines, among others, are seen as significant elements of China's maritime A2/AD force. Chinese defence planners are, as Geoffrey Till argues, 'developing the capabilities they feel they need in order to turn their A2/AD thinking into reality' (Till 2012: 87).

Apart from the Chinese Navy, there has been considerable progress in the modernisation of the Air Force. The PLAAF is seeking to improve its capability to conduct a range of offensive and defensive operations, such as strike, air and missile defence, power projection, and early warning and reconnaissance. In order to increase its strike capabilities, the PLAAF has been developing fourth-generation multi-role aircraft, a new H-6K bomber, and fifth-generation fighters. However, most Chinese aircraft still belong to second- and third-generation or upgraded variants. Following the first flight of the J-20 stealth fighter in January 2011, China tested a second next-generation fighter prototype J-31 and conducted its first flight in October 2012. The J-31 is similar in size to a US F-35 fighter. Meanwhile, China continues to upgrade its H-6 bomber fleet with a new variant that possesses greater range and is armed with a long-range cruise missile. Finally, China has been developing a wide range of unmanned aerial vehicles (UAVs), including long-range and low-observable systems that are capable of conducting reconnaissance and strike missions (US Department of Defense 2014: 9–10).

China's military transformation: emulating the US model?

The success or failure of China's military transformation should not be measured purely by the extent to which it is able to match US capabilities (Mulvenon et al. 2006). Despite making substantial advances in its modernisation drive, the military capabilities of the PRC still lag behind those of America and there are many weaknesses in its defence capabilities. However, the progress of the PLA's transformation is best measured by its ability to appreciate and adapt to the changing technological environment within which modern warfare is conducted. Apart from upgrading its military hardware, the PLA has focused heavily on the application of IT to the development of weapons systems and military training. Indeed, the power of the Chinese military is not based on its capability to confront the most advanced military forces. Rather, it lies in China's ability to conduct asymmetric operations, which are designed to deter and defeat a much more powerful adversary.

Back in 1999, Thomas Mahnken already predicted that 'potential adversaries […] may […] develop ways to deny the United States and its allies the ability to project power into their spheres of influence' (Mahnken 1999: 26). China certainly considers the Asia-Pacific as its sphere of influence and much of current Chinese defence planning is associated with the development of asymmetric strategies to tackle 'counter-intervention' in this region. China's A2/AD capabilities are developed precisely for the purpose of thwarting US military intervention in a conflict in the South and East China Seas. The expansion and improvement of China's submarine force, the acquisition and upgrading of its destroyers and frigates, and the development of its cruise missile and ballistic missile force are all parts of an extensive programme to fortify Chinese asymmetric warfare capabilities. The DF-21A, for example, is a formidable anti-ship ballistic missile that could be used to deter US aircraft carrier battle groups from intervening in a regional conflict involving China. As such, the PLA's transformation 'is war driven, catering for particular external security threats, specific adversaries and anticipated combat modes' (You 2014).

In recent years, China has also been paying particular attention to the role of space and satellite communications in fighting 'local war under modern informationised conditions'. The PLA has made some headway in developing its anti-satellite (ASAT) weapons. In January 2007 China fired its first ASAT missile, destroying an ageing Chinese weather satellite in outer space. There has been considerable progress in China's space programme, with an increasing number of satellite launches. In 2012 alone, China conducted 18 space launches. In May 2013 China allegedly tested a new ASAT missile, the Dong Ning-2, which is a ground-based, high Earth-orbit attack missile (Keck 2014). In July 2014 a US State Department official said that the Chinese government had conducted another ASAT test (Gruss 2014a, 2014b), although China claimed that the test was on its land-based anti-missile interception system (Zhao 2014b). There is evidence of an expansion in China's space-based intelligence, surveillance, reconnaissance, navigation, meteorological and communications satellite constellations (US Department of Defense 2013: 9). All this is believed to be aiming at the USA, which relies heavily on space and satellite communications for military operations. Thus, the use of ASAT weapons falls within the remit of China's asymmetric capabilities. Similarly, cyber warfare features prominently in China's defence calculation, as the ability to gain control over information in military campaigns is crucial to the success of modern warfare. The PLA is actively building its capabilities for information advantage through advanced electronic warfare systems, counter-space weapons and computer network operations (US Department of Defense 2014: 32). These developments will definitely strengthen China's A2/AD capabilities. Indeed, military information operations are central to network-centric warfare, which is a major component of America's military transformation.

Chinese leaders and strategic planners are fascinated by US network-centric warfare and its application to various military operations. This is why they have paid particular attention to integrated joint operations accentuating the importance of running coordinated and simultaneous military operations that employ real-time integration of C4ISR to conduct effective precision strikes against adversaries. There is a strong emphasis on joint operations in a realistic and 'complex electromagnetic environment' in PLA training and military exercises. Under the 2008 Outline of Military Training and Evaluation, the focus of Chinese military training is on system-of-systems operations, which would link up various forces and capabilities from different geographical areas into an integrated system. It has recently been reported that China is planning to establish a joint operational command system 'in due course' with the intention of building more coordinated and combat-capable forces to respond to a crisis efficiently. According to this proposal, Chinese military regions would be reorganised and reduced from seven to five. Each new military region would create a joint operations command having the responsibility to control its army, navy and air force and a strategic missile unit (Zhao 2014a). However, it is not clear when and how the proposal will be implemented (Zhang 2014). Despite some progress in promoting coordinated joint operations, China's joint capabilities remain rather limited, lacking the close service integration and command and coordination flexibility that exist in Western militaries (McCauley 2014).

Another key aspect of US military transformation, an effects-based approach to military operation, has had a considerable influence on China's defence modernisation. As mentioned earlier, the PLA has been closely observing how the United States has used its air power to achieve specific strategic effects since the early 1990s. The North Atlantic Treaty Organization's (NATO) air campaign in Kosovo further convinced Chinese military leaders of the importance of effect-oriented use of precision force. An effects-based approach is particularly attractive to China in dealing with a Taiwan contingency, where civilian casualties should be minimised in any military engagement. From Beijing's point of view, the main purpose of such operations is not to destroy the island but to achieve the 'reunification' of the PRC and Taiwan. Thus, the use of missile strikes and artillery-delivered high-precision munitions, such as short-range ballistic missiles and the PHL-03 300 mm multiple-rocket launcher, is seen by China as a much more effective means of attaining its political objective. This kind of non-contact warfare would allow Chinese leaders to employ precision-strike forces for different scenarios in the South China Sea. China's medium-range ballistic missiles could be used to carry out precision strikes against land targets and warships around the first island chain. Meanwhile, China is developing conventional intermediate-range ballistic missiles to increase its capability for near-precision strike against targets as far as the second island chain. Other Chinese precision-guided munitions that have been developed for effects-based operations include air- and ground-launched LACMs, air-launched cruise missiles, ASCMs, tactical air-to-surface missiles, satellite-guided bombs, anti-radiation missiles and laser-guided bombs (US Department of Defense 2013: 42).

Finally, China has been developing its capabilities for expeditionary warfare, which is a prominent component of US military transformation. Like America and other Western countries, China has to face a variety of 'new' security challenges ranging from global terrorism to piracy at sea. The PLA is increasingly called upon to undertake missions far beyond Chinese borders, particularly UN peacekeeping, anti-piracy operations and disaster relief operations. This would require expeditionary capabilities such as maritime power projection capability. It also fits in with the PRC's global aspirations and broadening security agenda. In recent years, China has been accelerating its naval modernisation with the aim of achieving maritime power status. As China's global activities expand, Chinese leaders feel that they need to have the maritime capabilities to defend Chinese interests. At the same time, the ability to conduct expeditionary operations is consistent with China's 'far-seas' defence doctrine in the sense that its armed forces are expected to go as far as necessary to defend Chinese national interests. Thus, building aircraft carriers capability will aid the PLA in carrying out expeditionary missions, whether in areas close to China or far from it.

Conclusion: military transformation with Chinese characteristics?

The military transformation in China over the past two decades is truly astonishing. The transformation agenda has undeniably had an enormous impact on Chinese military developments. The question is whether and to what extent America's RMA has changed Chinese strategic thinking fundamentally. The available evidence suggests that China's emulation of US transformation is selective due to various cultural, political and practical factors. Despite an appreciation of the technological significance of the US military model, Chinese leaders have not abandoned their traditional military doctrine and strategic thought.

To start with, Chinese perspectives on asymmetric warfare are closely linked to Mao's philosophical thinking in that one does not need to be as strong as one's opponents to win a war (Jiang, L. 1997; Wang 2004). Although the 'people's war' doctrine has been modified substantially due to China's changing strategic environment, there is still considerable emphasis on the importance of involving the 'people' in military planning and war preparation. The ideas of utilising non-military means to defeat enemies and the manipulation of intelligence and deception can be traced to Sun Zi's *Art of War* (孙子兵法) (Fairbank 1974; Scobell 2005; Lai 2012: 118–22). Moreover,

China has always been apprehensive of the limits of learning from other countries due to its sense of cultural superiority and traumatic experience in the nineteenth century. This is derived from the traditional thinking of 'Chinese learning for the essence, Western learning for practical use' (中学为体, 西学为用). Indeed, China has made several unsuccessful attempts at modernising its military since the Qing dynasty. It is not a new idea for Chinese leaders to acquire the skills and knowledge from the West in the hope that they could be used to defeat Western adversaries.

Another constraint on Chinese learning of US military transformation is related to political considerations. For example, a true emulation of the American model of joint integrated operations would inevitably involve a shake-up of the existing military structures, which could have far-reaching political implications. More significantly, catching up with US military capabilities is a costly business that China cannot afford. From Beijing's perspective, economic development is still its priority. Military transformation and regime security can only be sustained by continued economic growth. This is why Chinese leaders do not wish to follow the Soviet path of military development, which eventually led to the demise of the Soviet Union. Finally, China has found it difficult to get access to some advanced Western military technology because of Western suspicions of its future strategic intentions.

For all these reasons, China's military transformation is bound to be different from the transformation in the USA and other Western nations. In recent years, the Chinese armed forces have been called upon to perform a whole range of MOOTW. By involvement in these activities, the Chinese military is engaging in the process of social learning in military transformation. While these diversified military operations have put additional pressure on the Chinese armed forces, they should be seen as a contribution to the PRC's defence modernisation efforts rather than a diversion from them. To be sure, the PLA is still essentially a platform-centric force, despite making significant progress in its modernisation. It will be some time before China's military is completely transformed and capable of conducting effective network-centric operations. Nevertheless, China seems determined to transform the PLA into a modern force capable of fighting 'local wars under modern informationised conditions'. Chinese leaders regard a strong and modernised military as a guarantee for the national security and territorial integrity of their country. More important, a powerful military force is viewed as a key element in the formation of China's great power identity. While it is difficult to predict exactly how the PLA will develop, one can expect to see a much more advanced and formidable Chinese military in the coming decades.

Bibliography

Ban, K.-M. (2013, 19 June) *Remarks at the China Peacekeeping Military Training Centre*, Beijing. http://www.un.org/apps/news/infocus/sgspeeches/statments_full.asp?statID=1900#.VKLlrdV1A (accessed 8 January 2015).

BBC (2014, 24 April) 'Obama Asia Tour: US-Japan Treaty "Covers Disputed Islands"'. http://www.bbc.co.uk/news/world-asia-27137272 (accessed 8 January 2015).

Blasko, D.J. (2012) *The Chinese Army Today: Tradition and Transformation for the 21st Century*, New York: Routledge.

Bradsher, K. (2014, 10 October) 'Some Chinese Leaders Claim U.S. and Britain are behind Hong Kong Protests', *The New York Times*. http://www.nytimes.com/2014/10/11/world/asia/some-chinese-leaders-claim-us-and-britain-are-behind-hong-kong-protests-.html (accessed 8 January 2015).

Branigan, T. and Harris, P. (2010, 30 January) 'China Fumes at US Arms Sale to Taiwan', *The Guardian*. http://www.guardian.co.uk/world/2010/jan/30/china-reaction-us-arms-sale-taiwan (accessed 8 January 2015).

Cheung, T.M. (2011) 'The Chinese Defence Economy's Long March from Imitation to Innovation', *The Journal of Strategic Studies*, Vol. 34, No. 3, pp. 325–354.

Clinton, H. (2011, 11 October) 'America's Pacific Century', *Foreign Policy*. http://foreignpolicy.com/2011/10/11/americas-pacific-century/ (accessed 8 January 2015).

Clinton, H. (2014) *Hard Choice*, London: Simon & Schuster.

CNN (2011, 22 September) 'China Warns U.S. Against Arms Sales to Taiwan'. http://articles.cnn.com/2011-09-22/asia/world_asia_china-us-taiwan-arms-sale_1_taiwan-relations-act-taiwan-strait-renegade-province?_s=PM:ASIA (accessed 8 January 2015).

Cole, B.D. (2010) *The Great Wall at Sea: China's Navy in the Twenty-First Century*, Maryland: Naval Institute Press.

Deng, X.P. (邓小平) (1985, 4 June) 'Speech at an Enlarged Meeting of the Military Commission of the Central Committee of the Communist Party of China'. http://english.peopledaily.com.cn/dengxp/vol3/text/c1410.html (accessed 8 January 2015).

Erickson, A. (2013) 'How China Got There First: Beijing's Unique Path to ASBM Development and Deployment', *China Brief*, Vol. 13, No. 12.

Erickson, A.S. and Strange, A.M. (2013) *No Substitute for Experience: Chinese Antipiracy Operations in the Gulf of Aden*, Newport: US Naval War College.

Evangelista, M.A. (1988) *Innovation and the Arms Race: How the United States and the Soviet Union Develop New Military Technologies*, Ithaca, NY: Cornell University Press.

Fairbank, J.K. (1974) *Chinese Ways in Warfare*, Harvard: Harvard University Press.

Farrell, T. (2008) 'The Dynamics of British Military Transformation', *International Affairs*, Vol. 84, No. 4, pp. 777–807.

Felsenthal, M. and Spetalnick, M. (2014, 29 April) 'Obama Says U.S. Commitment to Defend Philippines "Ironclad"', Reuters. http://www.reuters.com/article/2014/04/29/us-philippines-usa-obama-idUSBREA3S02T20140429 (accessed 8 January 2015).

Finkelstein, D. (2006) 'China's National Military Strategy: An Overview of the "Military Strategic Guidelines"', in Kamphausen, R. and Scobell, A. (eds) *Right-Sizing the People's Liberation Army: Exploring the Contours of China's Military*, Carlisle: Strategic Studies Institute, pp. 92–102.

Gill, B. and Huang, C.H. (2009) 'China's Expanding Peacekeeping Role: Its Significance and the Policy Implications', SIPRI Policy Brief.

Global Military (环球军事) (n.d.) '辽宁舰' (*Liaoning* Aircraft Carrier). http://weapon.huanqiu.com/liaoningaircraftcarrier.

Goldman, E.O. (2006) 'Cultural Foundations of Military Diffusion', *Review of International Studies*, Vol. 32, No. 1, pp. 69–91.

Goldman, E.O. and Eliason, L.C. (eds) (2003) *The Diffusion of Military Technology and Ideas*, Stanford, CA: Stanford University Press.

Grissom, A. (2006) 'The Future of Military Innovation Studies', *The Journal of Strategic Studies*, Vol. 29, No. 5, pp. 905–934.

Gruss, M. (2014a, 18 July) 'U.S. State Department: China Tested Anti-satellite Weapon', *SpaceNews*. http://spacenews.com/41413us-state-department-china-tested-anti-satellite-weapon/ (accessed 8 January 2015).

Gruss, M. (2014b, 25 August) 'Senior U.S. Official Insists China Tested ASAT Weapon', *SpaceNews*. http://spacenews.com/41676senior-us-official-insists-china-tested-asat-weapon/.

Hallion, R.P., Cliff, R. and Saunders, P.C. (eds) (2012) *The Chinese Air Force: Evolving Concepts, Roles, and Capabilities*, Washington, DC: National Defence University Press.

He, Y.F. (何亚非) (2014, 16 September) '美国的亚太版"离岸平衡"战略' (The Asian Version of America's 'Offshore Balance' Strategy), 中国新闻周刊 (*China Newsweek*), No. 674.

Hirono, M. and Lanteigne, M. (2011) 'Introduction: China and UN Peacekeeping', *International Peacekeeping*, Vol. 18, No. 3, pp. 243–256.

Hogg, M.A., Terry, D.J. and White, K.M. (1995) 'A Tale of Two Theories: A Critical Comparison of Identity Theory with Social Identity Theory', *Social Psychology Quarterly*, Vol. 58, No. 4 (December), pp. 255–269.

Hu, J.T. (胡锦涛) (2007, 15 October) *Report to the 17th National Congress of the Communist Party of China*. http://www.china.org.cn/english/congress/229611.htm (accessed 8 January 2015).

Hua, Y.W. (华益文) (2014, 10 October) '美国对"颜色革命"为何乐此不疲?' (Why is America so Enthusiastic about the 'Colour Revolutions'?), 人民日报 [海外版] (*People's Daily* – Overseas Edition), p. 1.

Huang, Y.X. (黄迎旭) (2014, 27 January) '中国梦视阈里的强军梦' (The Dream of a Powerful Military from the Perspective of the China Dream), 学习时报 (*Study Times*).

Information Office of the State Council of the People's Republic of China (2004) *China's National Defence in 2004*. http://www.china.org.cn/e-white/20041227/III.htm#3 (accessed 8 January 2015).

Jacobs, A. (2011, 22 September) 'Arms Sale Draws Angry, but Familiar, Reaction' *The New York Times*. http://www.nytimes.com/2011/09/23/world/asia/china-expresses-anger-over-latest-us-arms-sales-to-taiwan.html?_r=1 (accessed 8 January 2015).

Jiang, L. (蒋磊) (1997) 现代以劣胜优战略 (*Modern Strategy for Using the Inferior to Defeat the Superior*), 北京: 国防大学出版社.

Jiang, Z.M. (江泽民) (1997, 12 September) 'Hold High the Great Banner of Deng Xiaoping Theory for an All-round Advancement of the Cause of Building Socialism with Chinese Characteristics into the 21st Century', Report delivered at the 15th National Congress of the Communist Party of China, *Beijing Review*. http://www.bjreview.com.cn/document/txt/2011-03/25/content_363499.htm (accessed 8 January 2015).

Joffe, E. (1987) 'People's War under Modern Conditions: A Doctrine for Modern War', *The China Quarterly*, No. 112, pp. 555–571.

Kai, C. (2012, 14 November) 'China Voice: Building China into Maritime Power Essential for Future Development'. http://news.xinhuanet.com/english/special/18cpcnc/2012-11/14/c_131973164.htm (accessed 8 January 2015).

Kai, C. (2013, 31 July) 'Xi Advocates Efforts to Boost China's Maritime Power'. http://news.xinhuanet.com/english/china/2013-07/31/c_132591246.htm (accessed 8 January 2015).

Kamphausen, R.D. (2013) 'China's Military Operations Other than War: The Military Legacy of Hu Jintao', Paper presented at the SIPRI conference, Stockholm, 18–19 April.

Kaplowitz, N. (1990) 'National Self-images, Perception of Enemies, and Conflict Strategies: Psychopolitical Dimensions of International Relations', *Political Psychology*, Vol. 11, No. 1 (March), pp. 39–82.

Karotkin, J.L. (2014) 'Trends in China's Naval Modernization: US-China Economic and Security Review Commission Testimony'. http://www.uscc.gov/sites/default/files/Karotkin_Testimony1.30.14.pdf.

Keck, Z. (2014, 19 March) 'China Secretly Tested an Anti-Satellite Missile', *The Diplomat*. http://thediplomat.com/2014/03/china-secretly-tested-an-anti-satellite-missile/ (accessed 8 January 2015).

Klare, M.T. (2010, 7 April) 'China Tilts Resource Balance', *Asia Times*. http://www.atimes.com/atimes/Global_Economy/LD07Dj06.html.

Lai, D. (2012) 'The Agony of Learning: The PLA's Transformation in Military Affairs', in Kamphausen, R., Lai, D. and Tanner, T. (eds) *Learning by Doing: The PLA Trains at Home and Abroad*, Carlisle: Strategic Studies Institute, pp. 337–380.

Landingin, R. and Hille, K. (2011, 1 June) 'China and Philippines Tensions Mount', *Financial Times*. http://www.ft.com/cms/s/0/ba85f500-8c47-11e0-b1c8-00144feab49a.html#axzz30J0tuJj2 (accessed 8 January 2015).

Lee, C.E. and Taylor, R. (2014, 15 November) 'Obama Seeks to Reassure Asia Allies on Pivot', *The Wall Street Journal*. http://www.wsj.com/articles/u-s-president-seeks-to-reassure-asia-allies-on-asia-pivot-1416021193 (accessed 8 January 2015).

Le Mière, C. (2014) *Maritime Diplomacy in the 21st Century: Drivers and Challenges*, London: Routledge.

Li, N. (2009) 'The Evolution of China's Naval Strategy and Capabilities: From "Near Coast" and "Near Seas" to "Far Seas"', *Asian Security*, Vol. 5, No. 2, pp. 144–169.

Li, R. (1999) 'Partners or Rivals? Chinese Perceptions of Japan's Security Strategy in the Asia-Pacific Region', *The Journal of Strategic Studies*, Vol. 22, No. 4, pp. 1–25.

Li, R. (2009) *A Rising China and Security in East Asia: Identity Construction and Security Discourse*, London: Routledge.

Li, R. (2010) 'A Regional Partner or a Threatening Other? Chinese Discourse of Japan's Changing Security Role in East Asia', in Dent, C.M. (ed.) *China, Japan and Regional Leadership in East Asia*, Cheltenham: Edward Elgar, pp. 101–128.

Li, Y. (2014, 26 September) 'Peace-keeping Mission in South Sudan is China's Duty', *China Daily*. http://www.chinadaily.com.cn/opinion/2014-09/26/content_18669133.htm (accessed 8 January 2015).

Li, Y.M. (李玉梅) (2013, 18 November) '深入学习贯彻强军目标重大战略思想确保召之即来来之能战战之必胜' (Study Thoroughly and Implement the Major Strategic Thinking on the Aim of Strengthening the Armed Forces to Ensure Military Victory in the Future), 学习时报 (*Study Times*).

Liberation Army Daily (解放军报) (1999, 8 January) '江主席签署中国人民解放军联合战役纲要' (Chairman Jiang Signed the Principles of Joint Campaigns of the Chinese People's Liberation Army).

Mahnken, T.G. (1999) 'Uncovering Foreign Military Innovation', *The Journal of Strategic Studies*, Vol. 22, No. 4, pp. 26–54.

Mahnken, T.G. (2011) 'China's Anti-Access Strategy in Historical and Theoretical Perspective', *The Journal of Strategic Studies*, Vol. 34, No. 3, pp. 299–323.

McCauley, K. (2014) 'PLA Joint Operations Developments and Military Reform', *China Brief*, Vol. 14, No. 7.

Mearsheimer, J.J. (2001) *The Tragedy of Great Power Politics*, New York: W.W. Norton.

Ministry of National Defence (2005) *China's National Defense in 2004*. http://eng.mod.gov.cn/Database/WhitePapers/2007-01/15/content_4004365.htm (accessed 8 January 2015).

Ministry of National Defence (2007) *China's National Defense in 2006*. http://eng.mod.gov.cn/Database/WhitePapers/2007-01/15/content_4004365.htm (accessed 15 January 2007).

Ministry of National Defence (2012, 2 April) *China's National Defense in 2010*. http://eng.mod.gov.cn/Database/WhitePapers/2011-04/02/content_4442745_5.htm (accessed 8 January 2015).

Ministry of National Defence (2013) *China's National Defense in 2012*. http://eng.mod.gov.cn/Database/WhitePapers/2013-04/16/content_4442755.htm (accessed 8 January 2015).

Ministry of National Defence (n.d.) *Defence Policy*. http://eng.mod.gov.cn/Database/DefensePolicy/index.htm (accessed 8 January 2015).

Monaghan, A. (2014, 10 January) 'China Surpasses US as World's Largest Trading Nation', *The Guardian*. http://www.theguardian.com/business/2014/jan/10/china-surpasses-us-world-largest-trading-nation (accessed 8 January 2015).

Moore, M. (2011, 14 February) 'China is the World's Second Largest Economy', *The Telegraph*. http://www.telegraph.co.uk/finance/economics/8322550/China-is-the-worlds-second-largest-economy.html (accessed 8 January 2015).

Morgenthau, H.J. (1978) *Politics among Nations: The Struggle for Power and Peace*, New York: Alfred A. Knopf.

Mulvenon, J.C. et al. (2006) *Chinese Responses to U.S. Military Transformation and Implications for the Department of Defense*, Santa Monica: RAND.

Newmyer, J. (2010) 'The Revolution in Military Affairs with Chinese Characteristics', *The Journal of Strategic Studies*, Vol. 33, No. 4, pp. 483–504.

Ng, T. (2014, 12 April) 'Beijing Angered by Obama's Stance on Disputed Diaoyu Islands', *South China Morning Post*. http://www.scmp.com/news/asia/article/1494942/obama-says-disputed-islands-within-scope-us-japan-security-treaty (accessed 8 January 2015).

Office of Naval Intelligence (2009) *The People's Liberation Army Navy: A Modern Navy with Chinese Characteristics*.

O'Rourke, R. (2014, 10 April) *China Naval Modernization: Implications for U.S. Navy Capabilities – Background and Issues for Congress*.

Patel, N. (2009) 'Chinese Disaster Relief Operations: Identifying Critical Capability Gaps', *Joint Force Quarterly*, Vol. 52, No. 1, pp. 111–117.

Posen, B.P. (1984) *The Sources of Military Doctrine: France, Britain, and Germany Between the World Wars*, Ithaca, NY: Cornell University Press.

Pretorius, J. (2008) 'The Security Imaginary: Explaining Military Isomorphism', *Security Dialogue*, Vol. 39, No. 1, pp. 99–120.

Qi, J.G., Lt-Gen. (戚建国) (2013, 21 January) '前所未有的大变局: 对世界战略形势和我国家安全环境的认识与思考' (Unprecedented Great Changing Situation: Understanding and Thoughts on the Global Strategic Situations and Our Country's National Security Environment), 学习时报 (*Study Times*).

Ross, R.S. (2000) 'The 1995–1996 Taiwan Strait Confrontation: Coercion, Credibility, and the Use of Force', *International Security*, Vol. 25, No. 2, pp 87–123.

Rushton, K. (2014, 10 January) 'China Overtakes US to Become World's Biggest Goods Trading Nation', *The Telegraph*. http://www.telegraph.co.uk/finance/economics/10565166/China-overtakes-US-to-become-worlds-biggest-goods-trading-nation.html (accessed 8 January 2015).

Ryall, J. (2012, 5 September) 'Japan Agrees to Buy Disputed Senkaku Islands', *The Telegraph*. http://www.telegraph.co.uk/news/worldnews/asia/japan/9521793/Japan-agrees-to-buy-disputed-Senkaku-islands.html (accessed 8 January 2015).

Sanger, D.E. (2001, 26 April) 'U.S. Would Defend Taiwan, Bush Says', *The New York Times*. http://www.nytimes.com/2001/04/26/world/us-would-defend-taiwan-bush-says.html (accessed 8 January 2015).

Saunders, P.C., Yung, C.D., Swaine, M. and Yang, A.N.D. (eds) (2012) *The Chinese Navy: Expanding Capabilities, Evolving Roles*, Washington, DC: National University Press.

Scobell, A. (2005) 'Is there a Chinese Way of War', *Parameters*, Vol. 35, No. 1, pp. 118–122.

Shambaugh, D. (2002) *Modernizing China's Military: Progress, Problems and Prospects*, Berkeley: University of California Press.

Shang, C.M. (商春明) (2008, 2 September) '联合作战应强化"八个一体化"' (The Strengthening of 'Eight Integrations' in Joint Integrated Operations), 解放军报 (*Liberation Army Daily*). http://www.chinamil.com.cn/site1/xwpdxw/2008-09/02/content_1456744.htm (accessed 8 January 2015).

Smith, D. (2013, 23 December) 'China to Send 700 Combat Troops to South Sudan', *The Guardian*. http://www.theguardian.com/world/2014/dec/23/china-700- combat-troops-south-sudan-africa-battalion-un-peacekeeping (accessed 8 January 2015).

Spencer, R. (2009, 22 February) 'China Prepares to Buy up Foreign Oil Companies', *The Telegraph*. http://www.telegraph.co.uk/finance/newsbysector/energy/4781037/China-prepares-to-buy-up-foreign-oil-companies.html (accessed 8 January 2015).

Sui, X.F. (隋笑飞) (2013, 31 July) '强军梦为实现中国梦提供坚强力量保证' (The Dream of a Powerful Military Provides a Strong Guarantee for the Realisation of the China Dream), 解放军报 (*Liberation Army Daily*).

Sun, K.J. (孙科佳) (2003) '试论中国特色军事变革' (On Military Transformation with Chinese Characteristics), 中国军事科学 (*China Military Science*), Vol. 16, No. 1.

Taylor, C. (2004) *Modern Social Imaginaries*, London: Duke University Press.

Thayer, C.A. (2012, 12 June) 'Standoff in the South China Sea', *YaleGlobal*. http://yaleglobal.yale.edu/content/standoff-south-china-sea (accessed 8 January 2015).

Till, G. (2012) *Asia's Naval Expansion: An Arms Race in the Making?* London: Routledge/IISS.

United Nations (2014) *Contributors to United Nations Peacekeeping Operations, Monthly Summary of Contributions*. http://www.un.org/en/peacekeeping/contributors/2014/nov14_1.pdf. (accessed 8 January 2015).

United Press International (2013, 26 June) 'Chinese Secure Foreign Oil in $100B Buying Spree'. http://www.upi.com/Business_News/Energy-Resources/2013/06/26/Chinese-secure-foreign-oil-in-100B-buying-spree/UPI-41271372279165/.

US Department of Defense (2003) *Military Transformation: A Strategic Approach*.

US Department of Defense (2013) *Annual Report to Congress on China's Military Power, Military and Security Developments Involving the People's Republic of China 2013*, Washington, DC.

US Department of Defense (2014) *Annual Report to Congress on China's Military Power, Military and Security Developments Involving the People's Republic of China 2014*, Washington, DC.

Walt, S.M. (1987) *The Origins of Alliances*, Ithaca, NY: Cornell University Press.

Waltz, K.N. (1979) *Theory of International Politics*, Reading, MA: Addison-Wesley.

Wan, J. (万钧) (2014, 24 January) '中国首艘国产航母有望2018年竣工' (The Building of China's First Indigenous Aircraft Carrier is Likely to be Completed in 2018), 中国网 (China.com). http://military.china.com/important/11132797/20140124/18313188.html (accessed 8 January 2015).

Wang, S.M. (王硕民) (2004) '论毛泽东以劣胜优战略思维及其现实意义' (On Mao Zedong's Strategic Thinking on Using the Inferior to Defeat the Superior and its Practical Significance), 毛泽东思想研究 (*Mao Zedong Thought Study*), Vol. 21, No. 2 (March), pp. 77–80.

Wang, Z. (2012) *Never Forget National Humiliation: Historical Memory in Chinese Politics and Foreign Relations*, Columbia: Columbia University Press.

Weldes, J. (1996) 'Constructing National Interests', *European Journal of International Relations*, Vol. 2, No. 3, pp. 275–318.

Wendt, A. (1999) *Social Theory of International Politics*, Cambridge: Cambridge University Press.

Wortzel, L. (2013) *The Dragon Extends Its Reach: Chinese Military Power Goes Global*, Washington, DC: Potomac Books.

Wu, T.M., Han, G.X. and Li, Y. (2011, 5 September) 'Chinese Military Operations Other than War Since 2008', *PLA Daily*. http://eng.mod.gov.cn/DefenseNews/2011-09/05/content_4295580_2.htm (accessed 8 January 2015).

Wu, X.B. (2012) 'Not Backing Down: China Responds to the US Rebalance to Asia', *Global Asia*, Vol. 7, No. 4, pp. 18–21

Xi, J.P. (习近平) (2013, 17 March) '习近平在十二届全国人大一次会议闭幕会上发表重要讲话' (Xi Jinping Delivered an Important Speech at the Closing Meeting of the First Session of the 12th National People's Congress), 中国中央电视台 (CCTV). http://news.cntv.cn/special/xijinpingjianghua/.

Xiao, F. (晓风) (1998) '后冷战时期冷战思维的产物 – 日美新防卫合作指针评析' (The Product of the Cold War Mentality in the Post-Cold War Era – Comments on the New Guidelines for US-Japan Defence Co-operation), 东北亚论坛 (*Northeast Asia Forum*), No. 1, pp. 8–12.

Xiong, G.K. (熊光楷) (2003a, 4 August) '熊光楷谈世界新军事变革的现状与未来趋势' (Xiong Guangkai on the Current Situation and Future Trends in the World's New Transformation in Military Affairs), 半月谈 (*Bi-monthly Discussions*). http://news.xinhuanet.com/mil/2003-08/04/content_1009538.htm (accessed 8 January 2015).

Xiong, G.K. (熊光楷) (2003b) 国际战略与新军事变革 (*International Strategy and New Transformation in Military Affairs*), 北京: 清华大学出版社.

You, J. (2004) 'Learning and Catching up: China's RMA Initiative', in Goldman, E. and Mahnken, T. (eds) *Information Revolution in Military Affairs in Asia*, New York: Palgrave Macmillan, pp. 97–124.

You, J. (2014, 19 March) 'PLA Transformation and Australia-Chinese Military Relations', Australian Centre on China in the World, 2013. http://www.thechinastory.org/agenda2013/pla-transformation-and-australia-chinese-military-relations/ (accessed 8 January 2014).

Zhang, D. and Liu, M.F. (郑卫平, 刘明福) (eds) (2005) 军队新的历史使命论 (*On the New Historical Missions of the Armed Forces*), 北京: 人民武警出版社.

Zhang, D.H. and Yang, C.Z. (张东辉, 杨春长) (eds) (2008) 新世纪新阶段军队历史使命研究 (*Study on the Historical Missions of the Armed Forces at a New Stage in the New Century*), 北京: 军事科学出版社.

Zhang, T. (2014, 6 January) 'MND Clarifies Rumors about "Joint Operational Command"', *China Military Online*. http://eng.chinamil.com.cn/news-channels/china-military-news/2014-01/06/content_5722583.htm.

Zhang, X.T. (张晓彤) (2012, 16 September) '中国特色军事变革: 强军在四大历史使命下推进' (Military Transformation with Chinese Characteristics: Advancing Military Power under the Four Historical Missions), 瞭望 (*Outlook*).

Zhang, X.Y., Wang, Y. and Hu, D.H. (张相元, 王勇, 胡东华) (eds) (1992) 海湾战争纵缆 (*A Comprehensive Survey of the Gulf War*), 北京: 海军海潮出版社.

Zhao, S.N. (2014a, 3 January) 'New Joint Command System "On Way"', *China Daily*. http://usa.chinadaily.com.cn/china/2014-01/03/content_17212780.htm (accessed 8 January 2015).

Zhao, S.N. (2014b, 25 July) 'Latest Round of Anti-missile Tests Hits "Preset Goal"', *China Daily*. http://www.chinadaily.com.cn/china/2014-07/25/content_17920445.htm (accessed 8 January 2015).

Zhou, B. (周奔) (2008, 8 October) '胡主席提出新世纪新阶段我军历史使命' (Chairman Hu has Put forward the Historical Missions of our Armed Forces at a New Stage in the New Century), 解放军报 (*Liberation Army Daily*).

Zisk, K.M. (1993) *Engaging the Enemy: Organization Theory and Soviet Military Innovation 1955–1991*, Princeton University Press.

8 Japan's military transformation

Catching up on 'traditional' security agendas via 'non-traditional' justifications?

Christopher W. Hughes

Introduction: Japan's fundamental military transformation

Japan's security planners and wider society have been contemplating the regional and global challenges of military transformation for much of the post-Cold War period, with moves accelerating especially over the last decade for concomitant revisions of national defence policies, doctrines and capabilities. Indeed, Japan's engagement with and response to trends in military transformation might be argued as the most fraught and potentially radical amongst the advanced industrial democracies, given the pronounced disparities between its defence posture and that of other states for most of the post-war period. The strictures of the post-war security environment – characterised internationally by total defeat, initial demilitarisation, alienation from East Asia and incorporation into the protection of US hegemony and bilateral alliance systems, and domestically by the 'peace' constitution and deep-rooted anti-militaristic sentiment amongst its citizenry – have ensured that Japan's security and defence policy often developed at a pace and in directions strongly deviating from that of other so-called 'normal' military powers. Japan was known in particular for preferring a broader 'comprehensive' approach to security, generally espousing diplomatic and economic responses and eschewing military force as only a last resort (Chapman et al. 1982).

Japan's famously highly constrained post-war military stance, however, has found it harder to endure in the post-Cold War period. A range of re-emergent or newly emergent international security challenges, and most particularly North Korea's nuclearisation and the rise of China militarily, and an accompanying revived domestic debate on security, have obliged Japan to reappraise fundamentally its national security situation. Japan has thus begun to consider shifting away from its previously sheltered Cold War security stance and onto a new trajectory more in perceived accord with regional and global military developments. Japanese policymakers now debate the necessity of catching up with other 'normal' powers through their own programme of military transformation, involving the dismantlement of constraints on the state's exercise of military force for national interests and the upgrading of the Japan Self-Defence Forces (JSDF).

Japan, therefore, in engaging with issues of military transformation, is not simply making adjustments to its defence policy but instead contemplating questions of the need to fundamentally revise and overturn its entire post-war security stance, and to reassert for the first time in the post-war period the identity of a major military international actor. In this sense, Japan's response to issues of military transformation may be marked by greater relative change than Germany, the state that often functions as a key comparator due to its shared status as a defeated and constrained military power in the post-war period (Berger 1988). Japan's facing of a greater magnitude of 'frontline' security challenges in East Asia, its lack of embedding in the reassurances of multilateral frameworks such as the North Atlantic Treaty Organization (NATO), and thus the need to seek security through the major enhancement of alliance ties with the USA and the potential rapid build-up of its own national capabilities, all ensure it must travel further in military transformation agendas.

The objective of this paper, given the very significant questions posed by issues of military transformation, is to examine just exactly how fundamentally transformative these agendas have proven for Japan in recent years and are likely to prove in the future. The paper seeks to investigate the ways in which Japan has started to reshape its approach to security policy and military capabilities in order to respond to a range of non-traditional and traditional security challenges. In turn, it considers the impact of Japan's search for a more 'normal' and militarised security role in regional and global security. The paper argues that Japan's response to military transformation carries deep implications in helping to consolidate long-term trends for its re-emergence as a more assertive player in international security. Japan is set to become a more engaged and reliable alliance partner for the USA regionally and globally, as well as to enhance its own potential for more autonomous military action internationally.

However, at the same time that the chapter acknowledges Japanese intent to 'catch up' with military transformation trends and to respond to both traditional and non-traditional security concerns, it will also argue that Japan's security focus still remains in certain ways adrift from these trends. In part, this is due to the continuing domestic and international constraints that mean Japan will continue to lag behind its US ally and other 'normal' powers in the exercise of military power. Just as importantly, though, Japan, despite maintaining a genuine interest in responding to non-traditional security issues globally and regionally, is likely to lag behind by now placing its principal emphasis on traditional security issues limited to its own East Asia region. Japan's own military transformation will probably take most radical effect across a narrower range of traditional military contingency roles, rather than adopting the more diversified stance of other advanced industrial powers' militaries (Midford 2011: 186–191). Moreover, the chapter will argue that Japan is in many cases utilising the discourse of non-traditional security to legitimise or obfuscate the dismantling of the constraints on the state's use of military force and to effect the traditional security agenda. In this way, Japan's military transformation may contain something of an irony in that whilst it may enable catch-up with other states through acquiring a more militarised international security role, it will also achieve this by diverging from many of its own traditions of comprehensive security and the more recent stances of other states that emphasise the importance of non-traditional issues in global security. In this way, Japan is likely to function less as a power seeking to tackle the types of new challenges with which the militaries of many other advanced states are currently preoccupied, and develop more into a power seeking to deal with older-style state-to-state major conflicts. Japan may then emerge as a more capable military power, but one at times less able to work with those very states with which it is seeking to catch up, and less oriented to deal with a wider range of extant and pressing security issues beyond East Asia.

This chapter proceeds in three sections to make these arguments. The first section provides key background information on the past conceptions and traditions of Japan's security policy in the Cold War and early post-Cold War periods. This section outlines Japan's status as something of an 'outlier' in military developments and its development of 'comprehensive' notions of security to respond to both traditional and non-traditional agendas, and thus provides the context and baselines by which to assess the significance of subsequent developments and divergences from Japan's past military trajectory.

The second section then examines Japan's evolving perceptions of regional and global security challenges in the post-Cold War period, as well as interlinked domestic debates on security, and the specific ways this has begun to feed into Japanese military transformation and degrees of convergence with trends in other advanced industrial states and military power. The section examines plans for the revision of JSDF doctrines and capabilities and Japan's record of responding to a variety of traditional and non-traditional security issues.

The third section and conclusion then provide an overall assessment of the trajectory of Japan's military transformation, examining the tactics employed by the Japanese state to legitimise JSDF transformation and the ways in which this reveals the changing degree of relative emphasis ascribed to responding to a range of traditional and non-traditional security issues. Questions are raised around the implications for Japan's military transformation trajectory for convergence or divergence in cooperating with other states in international security.

Japan's post-war military trajectory: the 'Yoshida Doctrine' and comprehensive security

Although it is important to be wary of attributing the label of unique to Japan's security situation in the post-war period, there can be no doubt that its military posture was subject to particularly intense pressures that made for it to diverge markedly from international trends for most of the Cold War. Japan's experience of the atomic bombings, total defeat and economic devastation at the end of the Pacific War, and then the process of initial demilitarisation and the US-led Occupation from 1945 to 1952, eliminated at a stroke its previous role as a great military power in East Asia. Japan was rendered as lacking sovereign state autonomy and essentially defenceless in an increasingly hostile region due to the legacy of colonial history and the onset of Cold War confrontation (Hook et al. 2012: 28–31).

In addition, Japan's catastrophic defeat and the introduction of the 1947 Constitution and famed Article 9 'peace clause' reinforced domestically a deep sense of anti-militarism. Japanese anti-militarism, rather than manifested in pacifism *per se*, was more accurately characterised by a general suspicion of the utility of military power and resistance to the elevation of the status of the military in society. In turn, Japan's anti-militarism was reflected in divides amongst political elites about the future course of post-war security. Conservative right-wing politicians, later to form the Liberal Democratic Party (LDP) in 1955 which was to govern for nearly the entire post-war period, debated the need to revise the constraints of Article 9 and to restore national autonomy through large-scale rearmament and the renewal of multiple alliance partnerships. On the left of the political spectrum, the main opposition Japan Socialist Party (JSP) – later renamed the Social Democratic Party of Japan (SDPJ) – argued that Japan should maintain a position of unarmed neutrality (Hook 1996: 26–41).

Japan was eventually able to thread its way between these conflicting positions by settling for Prime Minister Yoshida Shigeru's formulation of a new 'grand strategy' for post-war national security. In order to restore national sovereignty and guarantee its future security, Yoshida committed Japan to signing simultaneously the 1951 San Francisco Peace Treaty and USA-Japan Security Treaty. Japan forged a strategic bargain for the continued provision of bases to the US military on its territory for Cold War power projection in East Asia in return for implicit US security guarantees, including the extended nuclear deterrent, and the ending of the Occupation. Japan consented to minimal rearmament to assist in its own security, with the eventual formation of the JSDF in 1954, but was essentially freed from the costs of large-scale military build-up and could focus instead on its own economic reconstruction. Japan's policymakers, and most especially Yoshida himself, recognised that the choice of alignment in the Cold War with its former US adversary was not entirely cost free. Japan risked becoming embroiled in US military strategy as a target for the USSR or even being persuaded by the USA to despatch the JSDF in support of the US military in East Asian conflicts (Hughes and Fukushima 2004: 55–86). Conversely, Japanese policymakers were cognisant that the USA as a superpower maintained global security interests that might supersede those relating to Japan, and thus that there was always a risk, however remote given the importance of Japan to the US strategic presence in the region, that the USA might not fulfil its security guarantees. Japanese policymakers were thus always careful to hedge their military commitments to the USA, resisting the build-up of JSDF capabilities that might be used to support US-led expeditionary warfare.

Notwithstanding Japanese policymakers' – and indeed much of the wider citizenry's – concerns about alignment with the USA, the 'Yoshida Doctrine' of dependence on the USA militarily, light rearmament and concentration on economic reconstruction proved a highly resilient formula for post-war security. The Yoshida Doctrine failed to satisfy either the conservative LDP 'Revisionists' who agitated for a more assertive military stance, or the left-wing 'Pacifists' who viewed the JSDF and USA-Japan security treaty as a transgression of Article 9 (Samuels 2007: 29–37), but the dominant main-stream of policymakers in the LDP and central bureaucracy, and wider societal opinion, acquiesced and then grew more supportive of the strategy as it removed the highly contentious issue of security from the centre of political debate and paid strong dividends with Japan's rapid economic growth from the late 1950s onwards.

Japan's Yoshida Doctrine did undergo a number of adjustments in the latter stages of the Cold War. The revised 'mutual' 1960 security treaty made more explicit US obligations to defend Japan under Article 5, as well as indicating in Article 6 the importance of the treaty for the wider peace and security of the East Asia region. Moreover, throughout the 1980s the JSDF undertook a major quantitative and qualitative expansion of capabilities in response to the build-up of Soviet forces and threat of invasion, and also began to explore for the first time bilateral military coordination with the USA under Article 6 of the security treaty to contribute to its own and wider regional security through the formulation of the USA-Japan Defence Guidelines in 1978. Japan's leaders also began for the first time in 1981, 30 years after the signing of the treaty, to refer to the USA-Japan security arrangements as an 'alliance' (Tanaka 1997: 265–304).

Japanese policymakers, nevertheless, continued to hedge military commitments throughout this period to avoid alliance dilemmas of 'abandonment' and most especially 'entrapment'. The JSDF concentrated on developing capabilities that were designed solely for the defence of national land and sea space, including large numbers of Maritime Self-Defence Force (MSDF) advanced destroyers, Air Self-Defence Force (ASDF) interceptors and Ground Self-Defence Force (GSDF) main battle tanks, and which could thereby help to act as a defensive shield for US forces projecting power from bases in Japan, but which were not integrated tactically or in command and control with the US military, and which were highly limited in their own power projection so as to avoid involvement in US expeditionary warfare.

Japan's hedging through complementary but essentially separate forces with those of the USA, was reinforced by a range of constitutional prohibitions and anti-militaristic principles derived from Article 9 of the Constitution. Japan promotes an 'exclusively defence-oriented defence policy', and since 1954 has held to the interpretation that whilst Japan possesses as a sovereign nation under the United Nations (UN) Charter the right of collective self-defence, its exercise of this right is prohibited by Article 9 of the Constitution. Japan was thus barred from using armed force to assist its US ally or other states outside its own territory. Similarly, Japan has expounded the Three Non-Nuclear Principles since 1967 (not to produce, possess or introduce nuclear weapons); a complete ban on the export of military technology since 1976 (with the exception of a limited number of technological projects with the USA); the 'peaceful' use of outer space since 1969; and the 1 per cent of gross national product (GNP) limit on defence expenditure since 1976. Individually and combined, these principles made for a highly restrained military stance during the Cold War period, although none of them – despite originating from the spirit of the Constitution – were legally binding on the Japanese state (Hughes 2004a: 31–35).

In turn, Japan's 'culture of antimilitarism' gave rise to particularistic perspectives on security overall. Japan in the 1980s began to develop a concept of 'comprehensive national security' that acknowledged in the depths of the Cold War the need for a robust military posture, but also stressed that notions of security had to expand to a range of other threats to the lives of the citizenry, including resources and food supplies. Japan's policymakers posited that there was need for diplomacy and economic cooperation to address the underlying causes of military conflict. One result of the Comprehensive Security concept was that Japan was to acquire a new strategic logic for the expansion in quantity and global geographical scope of its official development assistance (ODA) (Hughes 2004b: 150). Japanese reticence to accept the utility of military force for achieving security ends was also reflected in societal attitudes towards the JSDF. For most of its post-war existence the JSDF's primary role in opinion polls has been regarded as not for national military defence, but overwhelmingly instead for national disaster relief from earthquakes and typhoons (Hughes 2009: 100). In this sense, Japan can be seen to have long had – and perhaps far in advance of other developed states which have recently discovered this agenda – a highly embedded attachment to 'non-traditional' security concerns in its national security posture.

Japan's post-war security transformation

Japan's distinctive defence posture and reticence over the use of military force, and consequent predilection to focus on non-traditional security concerns, thus made for something of an outlier position during the Cold War in terms of its functioning as an ally for the USA and more generally in terms of aligning with military trends amongst other developed industrial powers. However, in the wake of the end of the Cold War globally and its winding down in East Asia, and along with the emergence of other international security challenges, Japan's maintenance of its past security stance has come under severe stress. This has triggered for Japan a process of seeking military transformation and greater convergence with the security agendas of the USA and other states.

Japan was forced for the first time after the Cold War to confront new global security issues that it had largely been shielded from previously by the USA. The Gulf War of 1990–91 proved a major security shock for Japan, as for the first time it perceived a demand from the USA and the international community to provide a 'human contribution' to the war effort in the form of the overseas despatch of the JSDF, but in the end was only able to provide a financial contribution of US$13 billion to support the coalition forces. The Gulf War reopened the domestic fissures in the debate over national security with the SDPJ working to block LDP plans for the dispatch to the Gulf of the JSDF on non-combat logistical support missions. Japan after the cessation was able to despatch MSDF minesweepers to the Gulf in 1991, but there still ensued a full-scale domestic debate on Japan's future international security role. Japan thus eventually settled on the passing of a new International Peace Cooperation Law (IPCL) in June 1992 to allow JSDF despatch on non-combat UN peacekeeping operations (PKOs) for the first time.

Japan's awareness of the need to respond to new global security challenges was further sparked in the aftermath of the events of 11 September 2001 and the onset of the 'war on terror'. Japanese policymakers once again argued for the perceived need to demonstrate solidarity with the USA and international community to expunge the threats of terrorism and weapons of mass destruction, and to do so through the despatch of the JSDF. Moreover, policymakers feared that if Japan did not show a sufficient response, then even though there were risks of entrapment in US-led expeditionary coalitions in the Indian Ocean and Gulf regions, there was an even higher risk of abandonment by the USA as an unreliable ally.

For Japanese policymakers, potential abandonment by the USA in the post-Cold War period has been a central concern because of the greater national security challenges posed by the East Asian region. Japan's most prominent security concern has been North Korea's gradual acquisition since the mid-1990s of nuclear weapons and its related development and proliferation of ballistic missile technology. The North Korean nuclear crisis of 1993–94 proved particularly problematic for Japan, not only because it highlighted for the first time the North's nuclear ambitions, but also because it exposed the USA-Japan alliance's inability to respond to regional contingencies. Japan's concentration on Article 5 rather than Article 6 bilateral cooperation under the USA-Japan Defence Guidelines meant that it was unprepared to respond to US requests for military logistical support in the event of a conflict on the Korean Peninsula, and the spectre of abandonment as an unreliable ally was thus raised again (Smith 1999: 69–93). Japanese concerns about North Korea have only grown since the mid-1990s as it has conducted nuclear tests in 2006, 2009 and 2013, and ballistic missile tests around and over Japanese airspace in 1998, 2006, 2009 and 2012. These concerns have been compounded by continuing fears of US abandonment, with the principal anxiety being that the USA might not fulfil its security guarantees to Japan in the event that North Korea acquires a nuclear blackmail capability against US forces in the Asia-Pacific or the US homeland.

Looming behind North Korea, however, China's rise and its military modernisation have posed for Japan far greater regional security concerns. Japanese policymakers since the Taiwan Strait crisis of 1995–96 have become increasingly aware of China's willingness and capabilities to project military forces in the pursuit of its national interests beyond its immediate territory. From the Japanese perspective, China since the mid-1990s has demonstrated a new willingness not just to use military force to enforce its will on Taiwan to prevent moves towards independence, but now also to challenge the wider military and territorial *status quo* in the Asia-Pacific. China's rapid expansion of defence budgets and military modernisation is seen to lack transparency, and the Japanese suspicion is that China's design is to utilise its growing asymmetric anti-access, area denial (A2/AD) capabilities, and newly increasingly symmetric capabilities, progressively to undermine US military hegemony and intervention in the region. Japan's particular national security concerns vis-à-vis China revolve around the latter's territorial claims to the Senkaku/Diaoyu islets in the East China Sea under the administrative control of Japan, as well as to other disputed resource-rich sea spaces further to the north in the East China Sea – the Japanese anxiety being that China's expanded naval activities in and around these areas will impede the sea lines of communication (SLOC) or even presage China attempting to acquire these territories by force.

Japanese fears over China's potentially aggressive intentions have been fed by the People's Liberation Army's (PLA) acquisition of key power projection capabilities. The ASDF senses that the airpower balance is now tipping against Japan, with the PLA Air Force's (PLAAF) procurement of fourth-generation fighters. The PLA's ballistic missile capabilities pose a growing and direct threat to JSDF and US military bases in Japan. MSDF concerns focus on the PLA Navy's (PLAN) introduction of more advanced submarines which complicate its traditional defensive role of keeping the sea space around Japan clear for the US Seventh Fleet's projection of offensive power. The PLAN's development of new classes of destroyers and anti-ship ballistic missiles capable of attacking the USA's aircraft carriers is seen to complicate greatly the past naval dominance of the US Navy and MSDF in the region, and China's initiation of its own aircraft carrier programme is perceived as a major threat to the SLOC and US control of the 'global commons'. Finally, China's increasing emphasis on cyber warfare – manifested in repeated attacks on Japan's foreign and defence ministry infrastructure and arms producers – has become a key concern for military transformation (Hughes 2012b: 199–205; Yahuda 2013: 115–124).

All this is not to say that Japan has lost sight entirely of its traditions of comprehensive security. Indeed, Japanese policymakers have sought in various ways to mainstream comprehensive security more effectively through supporting the promotion of the concept of 'human security' since the late 1990s. The Japanese articulation of human security, emphasising in the main 'freedom from want' and the linkages between economic development and the alleviation of the sources of conflict, clearly fits well Japan's past emphasis on ODA and non-military approaches to security. Japan thus established the Trust Fund for Human Security at the UN in 1998, providing over $340 million in funding since, and then took a prominent role in the UN's Commission on Human Security in 2003. Japan has further developed since the late 1990s a new role equating to humanitarian assistance and disaster relief (HADR). In response to the Asian tsunami in 2004–05, the JSDF despatched around 1,500 personnel, supported by GSDF helicopters and an MSDF amphibious ship, to help in the disaster relief effort in Thailand and Indonesia. The Haiyan cyclone disaster in the Philippines in 2013 led to the despatch of over 1,000 JSDF personnel for relief operations around the Leyte Gulf. The importance of humanitarian relief has only been brought all that much closer to home for Japan's policy-makers by the triple disasters of the great east Japan earthquake, tsunami and Fukushima nuclear plant failure in March 2011, all of which required the mobilisation of 100,000 JSDF personnel (Samuels 2013: 80–109).

In addition to HADR-type missions, the JSDF has taken on a role in anti-piracy mission in recent years, with the despatch of MSDF destroyers and P3-C patrol aircraft to the Gulf of Aden since 2009 to support international efforts in this region, and the JSDF constructing its first post-war overseas base for these operations, in Djibouti in 2011. The JSDF has further maintained its role in UN PKOs, conducting non-combat logistical support and reconstruction missions in Cambodia (1992–93), Mozambique (1993–95), Golan Heights (1996–2013), East Timor (2002), Nepal (2007), Sudan (2008–09), Haiti (2010), Timor (2010–12), and South Sudan (2011–present). Japan has adhered rigidly to this limited range of UN PKO missions, despite discussion over lifting the restrictions on JSDF activities to take on more core peacekeeping activities including the possibility of a combat role, and has been even firmer in steering away from the consideration of undertaking humanitarian intervention or responsibility to protect (R2P)-type responsibilities.

Japan's pursuit of military transformation

Japan's encounter of a range of new international security challenges has been accompanied by, or in fact has been an important trigger for, shifts in the domestic policymaking environment which have opened the way for military transformation. The cessation of the relative stability of the Cold War and the series of ensuing global and regional security crises from the 1990s onwards helped generate a process of domestic regime change. The former ideological and security divides between the LDP on the right and SDPJ on the left of the political spectrum became less relevant domestically with the collapse of Soviet communism, whilst at the same time the SDPJ's anti-militaristic stance resonated less with the electorate in the face of readily extant regional and global security crises. The bursting of the Japanese 'bubble economy' in the early 1990s similarly engineered a slow-burn economic crisis, only staved off through government pump priming for close to two decades, but which eventually undermined the legitimacy of the LDP mainstream to govern effectively. The result of these domestic and international ructions was for the SDPJ to be displaced by the rise of the more centrist Democratic Party of

Japan (DPJ) and for it eventually to remove the LDP from power for a brief spell between 2009 and 2012. In the meantime, the revisionist and more neo-liberal economics-oriented wing of the party has increasingly moved to capture the leadership of the LDP. The two most prominent of these Revisionist LDP prime ministers have been Koizumi Junichirō (2001–06) and Abe Shinzō (2006–07) and (2012–present), espousing a stronger nationalist agenda and a more dynamic security policy.

The return of the LDP Revisionists, but also the rise and fall of the DPJ, itself converging on a position of arguing for a more assertive security policy, has strongly tested the former consensus around the Yoshida Doctrine focused on the pursuit of a low defence profile, largely passive exploitation of the shield of US hegemony, and mercantilist economic growth (Hughes 2012a). Instead, the new security discourse in Japan debates the need for a more 'normal' security role, both for defence of the national homeland and for undertaking a range of 'international peace cooperation activities', encompassing more active support regionally and globally for the USA as an ally and engagement in UN and other international security operations.

The declining status of the Yoshida Doctrine as grand strategy has initiated a range of fundamental revisions in Japan's defence principles, operational doctrines and JSDF capabilities. At the highest level of national strategic culture, Japan's policymakers have started to investigate the dismantling of Article 9 of the Constitution as setting the overall constraints on the exercise of military force for security ends in the post-war period, and have already made significant inroads into the related sets of anti-militaristic principles (Hughes 2013). LDP Revisionists have long sought to revise the Constitution, which is seen as foreign-imposed, rendering Japan as lacking the capacity for its own defence, and in turn depriving the country of national identity and international presence. The DPJ and other political parties, with the exception of the SDPJ, have also increasingly accepted the need for some form of revision to make the Constitution more congruent with the realities of Japan's growing security role. The LDP under Koizumi and Abe has brought forward drafts for revision since the mid-2000s. The most recent and radical version in 2012 includes not only the explicit recognition for the first time of the existence and then renaming of the JSDF as a 'national defence military' but also lays down the duty of the state to defend all national territory and resources, the expecta- tion that citizens should cooperate with the state for national defence, and strengthened emergency powers for the prime minister in the event of a military attack – all very much the antithesis of the strict anti-militaristic spirit of the existing Constitution (Minshutō 2012).

Abe's government, despite avowed plans to ease the pathway towards general constitutional revision by removing the current clause requiring the need for a two-thirds majority in both houses of the National Diet to enact amendments, to require instead a straight majority, is still likely to find formal revision a difficult struggle. The LDP, following election victories in 2012 and 2013, controls both houses with a straight majority, but just lacks a two-thirds majority in its own right in the Lower House and requires the support of the New Kōmeitō coalition partner to achieve that majority. Similarly, the LDP-New Kōmeitō in the Upper House is just shy of a two-thirds majority. The New Kōmeitō is known for its dovish stance on defence issues and is thus opposed to radical constitutional revision. The LDP would thus need to reach out to the opposition parties for support on revision, so creating relatively high domestic political costs. The LDP is likely instead to concentrate more immediately on the possibilities of informal revision through a process of government reinterpretation, especially in the lifting of the ban on the exercise of collective self-defence.

Abe during his first period of office instituted a Council on the Recon-struction for the Legal Basis of Security which reported in 2008 and argued that in a set of key contingency scenarios – including responding to attacks on US warships engaged in joint exercises with the MSDF, and a ballistic missile launch targeted at the USA – Japan should have no choice but to change its constitutional interpretations and to breach the ban on the exercise of collective self-defence. The Council's recommendations were not implemented because of Abe's fall from power in 2007, but on returning to office Abe reconvened the Council in 2013. The Council reported in May 2014, arguing this time round not only for the implementation of its original recommendations but now to expand the exercise of collective security to include the USA and its regional allies and partners, such as Australia, the Philippines and India, in situations that also threaten Japan's security (*The Japan Times*, 2013). Abe's government then moved in July 2014 to produce a Cabinet Decision which effectively breached previous constitutional interpretations and enabled Japan to exercise a 'limited' form of collective self-defence in situations that posed a threat to national existence and there is no other means to counter that threat, for the support of states in a close relationship with Japan, and restricting the use of force to the minimum possible.

Japan's move to exercise collective self-defence, even hedged round with conditions for precipitating military action, marks the essential discarding of much of its post-war hedging and emergence as a 'normal' military power in the sense of now agreeing to fight alongside its US ally rather than just provide logistical support.

Japan's policymakers have further gradually chipped away at the range of anti-militaristic principles derived from the spirit, if not the letter, of Article 9. The 1 per cent GNP limit on defence expenditure has remained broadly in place as a military constraint, although it was overtly breached in the mid-1980s with the JSDF's build-up, and depending on how the defence budget is calculated has been consistently breached by small margins since then. Japan in effect overturned its principle on the peaceful use of space by shifting to one of 'defensive' use in the early 2000s in order to open the way for the increased use of military spy satellites. Japan has now moved to abandon the 1976 total ban on the export of military technology in order to help sustain its defence industrial base, which has been under pressure from constrained

JSDF budgets and the lack of economies of scale and access to export opportunities (Hughes 2011). Japan is thus reverting to a policy akin to the original 1967 ban, which permitted military exports on a licensed basis to states not involved in conflicts or communist in nature, and is already exploring exports of equipment to South-East Asia and India, or basic military technology exchange agreements with the United Kingdom and France. As for the Three Non-Nuclear Principles, these were consistently breached, even from their initial declaration, with the USA's transport from the 1960s onwards of nuclear weapons on its ships through Japanese ports. Japan has long maintained, in fact, that its acquisition of nuclear weapons is constitutional, if for defensive purposes, and its more hawkish policymakers in recent years, including Abe, have publicly toyed with the need to reconsider their non-nuclear stance in the face of North Korea's nuclearisation and China's growing conventional and nuclear modernisation (Hughes 2009: 102–112).

Japan's policymakers have further moved to develop institutional and legal infrastructures to facilitate a more proactive defence posture. The Prime Minister's Office has acquired an enhanced role in determining national security policy through internal reforms leading to the integration of different ministerial expertise under the direction of the prime minister and chief cabinet secretary. The establishment of Japan's first National Security Council (NSC) in December 2013, concentrating crisis management amongst the four key positions of the prime minister, chief cabinet secretary, and foreign and defence ministers, has further boosted the central coordinating role of the core executive. Prime Minister Abe was then able in December 2013 to instruct the drafting of the very first National Security Strategy to be overseen by the NSC (Chief Cabinet Secretary of Japan 2013). Japan crafted its first national emergency legislation in 2003 and 2004, enabling the more effective mobilisation of national and local government resources to respond to armed attacks on Japanese territory and to provide civilian facilities for US forces. In December 2013, Abe's administration passed a State Secrecy Law placing tighter controls on the handling of information, and so promoting closer intelligence sharing with the USA and other partners.

In turn, Japan's renewed seriousness of purpose in defence was demonstrated by the establishment in 2004 of the Ministry of Defence (MoD), replacing the former Japan Defence Agency (JDA) created in 1954. The JDA had been very much under the domination of the other ministries in the making of security policy, but its elevation to full ministerial status provided it with greater autonomy and a place alongside the Ministry of Foreign Affairs, and US Departments of State and Defense in managing the alliance in the bilateral Security Consultative Committee. Inside the MoD itself there has also been a gradual shift in civilian control mechanisms, with the uniformed officers of the JSDF approaching greater equality with the civilian bureaucrats in the devising of defence policy and operations (Hughes 2009: 53–66).

Japan's revision of its security policymaking structures has facilitated major changes in doctrines and capabilities. The National Defense Program Guidelines

(NDPG), the document that sets out doctrine and necessary capabilities, has been revised four times since its original inception in 1976, with the latest iteration in 2013. Although as with most developments in Japanese security policy, change has been incremental to obscure overall trajectories until finally revealed, the most recent versions of the NDPG have now moved essentially to overturn much of post-war doctrine. The 2010 NDPG abandoned the previous doctrine of the Basic Defence Force (BDF) and instituted a new Dynamic Defence Force (DDF) concept (Ministry of Defence Japan 2010). The BDF was first established during the Cold War and was designed to maintain the minimal force posture necessary to help repulse a Soviet land invasion. It therefore made for a JSDF force posture limited to the static defence of Japanese territory and the build-up of heavy ground forces. The new DDF, in contrast, and mindful of the North Korean and Chinese threats, stresses a more proactive JSDF posture in and around Japanese territory, with increasing deployments of forces southwards, and capable of power projection. The latest iteration of the NDPG, in 2013, looks set to refine this concept further to seek a 'Dynamic Joint Defence Force' which enables improved cooperation amongst the GSDF, ASDF and MSDF (*Asahi Shimbun* 2013). In turn, the accompanying Medium-term Defense Programs that lay out military procurement priorities have emphasised for the JSDF the characteristics of readiness, flexibility, sustainability, versatility and jointness, which in practice has meant the continuing build-down of GSDF numbers of main battle tanks and artillery, and a switch to investment in lighter, more mobile and technologically advanced forces capable of responding to regional contingencies.

Japan has largely sought to counter China's modernisation with a symmetrical build-up of JSDF assets. The ASDF has sought to slow any adverse movement in the balance of air defence power by investing in fifth-generation fighters to trump China's current fourth-generation inventory. Japan's decision in December 2011 to procure 42 F-35As with stealth capabilities indicates that it is interested not only in restoring its traditional air interceptor superiority but also now adding air defence penetration to strike against North Korean missile bases and even the Chinese mainland in a contingency. Japan's reaction to Chinese and North Korean missile forces has again been largely symmetrical in attempting to neutralise these capabilities through the deployment of ballistic missile defence (BMD). Japan now deploys after the USA the most sophisticated BMD capabilities in the Asia-Pacific, as well as contemplating deterrence by denial through the F-35A and the possible acquisition of cruise missile capability.

Matching Japan's recent primary concerns over China relating to maritime security, it is the MSDF that has embarked on the most significant build-up of capabilities, many of which are designed to negate both the PLAN's access-denial and blue water naval strategies. The MSDF under the 2010 NDPG increased the submarine fleet by more than one-third, from 15 to 22 boats. The destroyer force is maintained at 48, and Japan as part of this build-up continues to introduce destroyer-helicopter warships (DDH). The MSDF has taken delivery of two 7,000-ton Hyūga-class 16DDHs, with a regular complement of four helicopters but capable of carrying up to 11. It is then set to procure a further two 19,000-ton 22DDs, capable of carrying up to 14 helicopters, the first of the Izumo-class launched in August 2013. MSDF DDHs are the largest vessels built for the service in the post-war period and are in all but name light helicopter carriers. The prime function of these assets is to provide a very powerful anti-submarine warfare (ASW) capability, clearly aimed against China's access-denial strategy. However, Japan's venturing back into carrier technology is resonant of a possible Sino–Japanese carrier arms race, and the suspicion of analysts is that the MSDF might eventually attempt to operate fixed-wing aircraft from the DDH-22s, such as the maritime variant of the F-35. Japan's maritime air and ASW capability is to be further strengthened through the procurement of a replacement for its P-3Cs with the introduction of an indigenously developed P-1 patrol surveillance aircraft able to sweep over an 8,000-kilometre range and thus deep into the South China Sea.

The GSDF has not been left out of this drive to upgrade its capabilities, establishing in 2007 a Central Readiness Force comprising airborne and Special Forces for rapid despatch to contingencies, and it is now considering the formation for the first time of an amphibious unit, akin to a marine corps, for responding to incursions against Japan's outlying islands. In addition, Japan has strengthened its intelligence capabilities through an ambitious information-gathering satellite programme since the late 1990s, and formed an MoD Cyber Defence Unit in 2014.

Japan's transformation of its national defence doctrines and capabilities has been accompanied by significant shifts in its external military commitments. The exposure by the North Korean and Taiwan Strait crises of the mid-1990s of the lack of interoperability in the USA-Japan alliance to respond to regional contingences has led to attempts to consolidate bilateral military cooperation. Japan and the USA revised the Guidelines for Defence Cooperation from 1996 to 1997, thereby clarifying the extent of Japanese rear area logistical support for the USA in a regional contingency. Japan and the USA embarked on a further process of revision of the Guidelines for Defence Cooperation in February 2013, completed in April 2015, this time looking to step-up bilateral activities around Japan's vicinity, including enhanced BMD cooperation; maritime security; intelligence, surveillance and reconnaissance; and cyber defence (Ministry of Defence Japan 2015). For Japan the revision of the Defence Guidelines has been a key component to bolster the USA's 'rebalance' towards the Asia-Pacific and counter rising Chinese power, with the latest iteration now permitting Japan to promote 'seamless' cooperation with the USA both regionally and globally.

US-Japanese cooperation has been further promoted through responding not just to regional but also global security issues. Japan, in order to support the US-led international coalition in Afghanistan after 9/11, passed an Anti-Terrorism Special Measures Law, which enabled the despatch of the MSDF to conduct non-combat refuelling operations for coalition shipping in the Indian Ocean from 2002 to 2009. Furthermore, in response to expectations from the

USA for support from its allies in the intervention in Iraq, Japan passed an Iraqi Reconstruction Law which enabled the despatch of the JSDF on non-combat logistical and reconstruction missions in southern Iraq from 2004 to 2008.

In undertaking to expand the scope of US-Japanese security cooperation, Japan has been careful to maintain its hedging tactics where possible. In the case of regional contingencies, Japan has been anxious to ensure that the JSDF's role under the Defence Guidelines remains one of logistical support, and policy-makers have been careful not to specify the exact geographical extent of this support, preferring to stress a 'situational' definition of the scope of the USA-Japan security treaty so as to avoid designating particular contingencies such as the Taiwan Strait which might drag Japan into a conflict with China. Similarly, for global security cooperation, in the case of the Indian Ocean and Iraq despatch Japan was careful to ensure that the JSDF missions were non-combat, and time bound by different sets of legislation to delimit operations and avoid problems of entrapment (Hughes 2009: 126–136). Nevertheless, Japan's increasing moves towards bilateral cooperation and integration of missions with the USA, and its participation in US-led multinational coalitions, marks a major departure from its previous attempts to maintain a defence posture complementary to but separate from the USA for fear of entrapment. Moreover, Japanese moves towards the exercise of collective self-defence will only work for the increased integration of the JSDF into US regional and global military strategy, and thus further deviation from the Yoshida Doctrine, and shift instead towards the trajectory of becoming a 'normal' ally. Finally, Japan's experimentation with enhanced bilateral cooperation with the USA outside traditional geographical and functional parameters has opened the way for new external commitments with other US allies and partners. Japan has thus looked to forge closer cooperation with Australia through the announcement in 2007 of a Joint Security Declaration, and then concluded in 2010 a bilateral acquisition and cross-serving agreement to provide logistical support in peace-time operations. Japan has further sought to strengthen military ties with South Korea, India and the states of South-East Asia.

Japan's pursuit of 'old' security through 'new' agendas

Japan's military transformation has clearly been driven predominantly by the resurgence of 'traditional' threats of inter-state conflict, and the need to augment the Japanese state's constitutional and legal preparedness and the JSDF's capacity to engage in defensive warfare if necessary. At the same time, policymakers have ensured that Japan maintains a contribution to a security agenda often considered non-traditional in other states but in many ways more traditional for Japan because of the approximation with long-held notions of comprehensive security.

However, what is striking is that Japan's adherence to this comprehensive security agenda has arguably slipped in its overall set of security priorities, even though it has been increasingly utilised to legitimise the pursuit of new 'traditional' security concerns involving the potential use of force. It is clear that whilst Japan has now developed a considerable history of participation in UN PKOs, its overall devotion of policy energy and resources to this agenda has remained limited. The JSDF has taken part in many UN PKO missions with some major deployments, as in East Timor and Haiti, but in most cases the number of personnel deployed has been in single figures, which represents a very small proportion of a military establishment numbering close to 250,000 (Bōeishōhen 2013).

Moreover, the government has failed to lift restrictions on the range of JSDF UN PKO missions, again suggesting that it remains a marginal mission for Japan's military other than to provide legitimacy and experience for the JSDF in overseas despatch, and when compared to the energy poured into freeing up the restrictions on JSDF deployments in other contexts. Indeed, it is notable that the Japanese government has tended to find most energy for UN PKOs and establishing a military presence when these missions appear to further its core national interests, as with the despatch of the GSDF to South Sudan, a region perhaps not coincidentally perceived to be falling under growing Chinese influence and offering rich energy resources.

Instead, the Japanese government has focused on other types of mission under the broad heading of 'international peace cooperation activities'. Japan's despatch of the JSDF to the Indian Ocean and Iraq has been designated under this heading and derived legitimacy from the labels of 'international' and 'peace', as in a sense equating with UN missions. However, the reality is that these deployments, generally the largest and most extensive for the JSDF in terms of personnel despatched, and even if non-combat in nature and seemingly serving non-traditional security concerns, have been designed to support US-led coalitions and therefore to acquire for the JSDF knowledge of working in multinational settings: a knowledge particularly useful for enhancing inter-operability for the US-Japanese alliance and with other US allies and partners for potential war-fighting in the future (Hughes 2009: 82–84). The MSDF's despatch on anti-piracy missions has served a similar function of utilising a non-combat mission to expand and make nearly indefinite a Japanese naval presence in the Persian Gulf region, including an overseas base, in order to rehearse cooperation with the USA and other powers to guard SLOC, with a particular eye on China's expanding interests in this area.

Non-traditional security concerns have been employed to boost the legitimacy of military transformation in a range of other related ways. The 2010 NDPG introduced the idea that the JSDF now had a role in human security, even though this concept was largely unrelated to JSDF activities, and thus the concept was seemingly being stretched to add legitimacy to the overturning of past doctrines and moving to a harder-edged military stance (Ministry of Defence Japan 2010). Similarly, the JSDF has acquired a range of new capabilities such as the DDHs, helicopters and air transport aircraft on the basis that they can be used for humanitarian relief efforts. These capabilities have indeed been used for these missions, but the use of such justifications for procurement conveniently distracts from the fact that many of these capabilities are very new in Japan's military arsenal and their primary function is for military deterrence.

Conclusion: Japan's trajectory and significance for international security

Japan's military transformation in the post-Cold War period has been genuinely fundamental. Japan has moved from a status as one of the most highly constrained military powers anywhere on the globe in the post-war period, and seemingly immovable from that status, to one now moving along an accelerating trajectory of discarding many of these constraints. The result is that it is now emerging as an increasingly unfettered and highly capable military power in its own right and a more reliable US ally, even if domestic resistance to this trajectory has not been totally extinguished and policymakers continue to try to hedge against over-dependence on the USA for security. In moving on this trajectory, Japan has not abandoned its earlier conceptions of comprehensive security but nevertheless has shifted its prime focus to issues of inter-state war, and in certain cases used a concern with that older comprehensive security agenda to legitimate and camouflage the impulse towards a 'normal' security policy.

Hence, in this way, Japan's newly emergent security policy can be judged to be both in and out of synch with military transformation developments globally. Japan has embarked on a military transformation agenda similar to many other developed states of creating more technologically advanced forces capable of undertaking a broader range of roles to deal with diverse 'new' security challenges. However, above all for Japan, the prime aim of this transformation has been not to engage in these agendas but rather to address the older agenda of inter-state conflict. The outcome is that Japan is likely to remain oriented to confronting threats from China and North Korea, and to lock itself into supporting the US 'rebalance' in East Asia, all with attendant risks for destabilising security dilemmas in the region. The consequence of this is that Japan will remain divorced to a degree from wider international security efforts in other regions that involve peacekeeping, HADR and interventionism, and will prove a less forthcoming partner on these issues for other states despite its very military transformation and very considerable capabilities.

Bibliography

Asahi Shimbun (2013) '*Shūdan-teki Jieiken, Doko made Kōshi Yōnin, Hadome Shōten*', 18 September, p. 3.

Berger, T.U. (1988) *Cultures of Antimilitarism: National Security in Germany and Japan*, Baltimore, MA: Johns Hopkins University Press.

Bōeishōhen (2013) *Bōeishō Hakusho 2013*, Tokyo: Zaimushō Insatsukyoku.

Chapman, J.M.W., Drifte, R. and Gow, I.T.M. (1982) *Japan's Quest for Comprehensive Security: Defence, Diplomacy and Dependence*, New York: St Martin's Press.

Chief Cabinet Secretary of Japan (2013) *Kokka Anzen Hoshō ni Tsuite*, 17 December. http://www.kantei.go.jp/jp/kakugikettei/2013/__icsFiles/afieldfile/2013/12/17/20131217-1_1.pdf.

Hook, G.D. (1996) *Demilitarization and Remilitarization in Contemporary Japan*, London: Routledge.

Hook, G.D., Gilson, J., Hughes, C.W. and Dobson, H. (2012) *Japan's International Relations: Politics, Economics and Security*, London: Routledge.

Hughes, C.W. (2004a) *Japan's Re-emergence as a 'Normal' Military Power*, Oxford: Oxford University Press.

Hughes, C.W. (2004b) *Japan's Security Agenda: Military, Economic and Environmental Dimensions*, Boulder, CO: Lynne Rienner Publishers.

Hughes, C.W. (2009) *Japan's Remilitarisation*, London: Routledge.

Hughes, C.W. (2011) 'The Slow Death of Japanese Techno-Nationalism? Emerging Comparative Lessons for China's Defence Production', *The Journal of Strategic Studies*, Vol. 34, No. 3, pp. 451–479.

Hughes, C.W. (2012a) 'The Democratic Party of Japan's New (but Failing) Grand Strategy: From Reluctant Realism to Resentful Realism?' *Journal of Japanese Studies*, Vol. 38, No. 1, pp. 109–140.

Hughes, C.W. (2012b) 'China's Military Modernization: US Partners in Northeast Asia', in Tellis, A. and Tanner, T. (eds) *Strategic Asia 2012–13: China's Military Challenge*, Seattle, WA: National Bureau of Asian Research.

Hughes, C.W. (2013) 'Japan's Remilitarization and Constitutional Revision', in Stearns, P.N. (ed.) *Demilitarization in the Contemporary World*, Chicago, IL: University of Illinois Press.

Hughes, C.W. and Fukushima, A. (2004) 'Japan-US Security Relations: Toward "Bilateralism-plus"?' in Krauss, E.S. and Pempel, T.J. (eds) *Beyond Bilateralism: The US-Japan Relationship in the New Asia-Pacific*, Stanford, CA: Stanford University Press, pp. 55–86.

The Japan Times (2013) 'Panel to Propose Japan Help Defend All Allies, Not Just U.S.', 13 August. http://www.japantimes.co.jp/news/2013/08/13/national/panel-to-propose-japan-help-defend-all-allies-not-just-u-s/#.UpyqqxZChz8.

Midford, P. (2011) *Rethinking Japanese Public Opinion: From Pacifism to Realism?* Stanford, CA: Stanford University Press.

Ministry of Defence Japan (2010) *National Defense Program Guidelines for FY2011 and Beyond*, 17 December. http://www.tr.emb-japan.go.jp/T_06/files/National_Defense_Program_FY2011.pdf.

Ministry of Defence Japan (2015) *The Guidelines for Japan-US Defense Cooperation*, 27 April. http://www.mod.go.jp/e/d_act/anpo/pdf/shishin_20150427e.pdf.

Ministry of Foreign Affairs Japan (2009), *The Trust Fund for Human Security: For the 'Human Centred' 21st Century.* http://www.mofa.go.jp/policy/human_secu/t_fund21.pdf.

Ministry of Foreign Affairs Japan (2013) *Joint Statement of the Security Consultative Committee: Toward a More Robust Alliance and Greater Shared Responsibilities*, 3 October. http://www.mofa.go.jp/mofaj/files/000016028.pdf.

Minshutō, J. (2012) *Draft of Revised Constitution.* http://www.jimin.jp/policy/policy_topics/pdf/seisaku-109.pdf.

Oros, A.L. (2008) *Normalizing Japan: Politics, Identity and the Evolution of Security Practice*, Stanford, CA: Stanford University Press.

Pyle, K.B. (2007) *Japan Rising. The Resurgence of Japanese Power and Purpose*, New York: Public Affairs.

Samuels, R.J. (2007) *Securing Japan: Tokyo's Grand Strategy and the Future of East Asia*, Ithaca, NY: Cornell University Press.

Samuels, R.J. (2013) *3.11: Disaster and Change in Japan*, Ithaca, NY: Cornell University Press.

Smith, S.A. (1999) 'The Evolution of Military Cooperation in the US-Japan Alliance', in Green, M.J. and Cronin, P.M. (eds) *The US-Japan Alliance: Past, Present and Future*, New York: Council on Foreign Relations.

Soeya, Y., Tadakoro, M. and Welch, D.A. (eds) (2011) *Japan as a 'Normal Country': A Nation in Search of its Place in the World*, Toronto: University of Toronto Press.

Tanaka, A. (1997) *Anzen Hoshō*, Tokyo: Yomiuri Shimbunsha.

Yahuda, M. (2013) *Sino-Japanese Relations; Two Tigers Sharing a Mountain*, London: Routledge.

9 Indian military transformation in the twenty-first century

Rajat Ganguly

Introduction

In the new millennium, India's military has gradually transformed into a major force in the world. According to Global Firepower (2013), the Indian military today is the world's fourth largest after the US, Russian and Chinese militaries. The Indian Army (IA) is a 1 million plus volunteer force that is well trained, disciplined and equipped with modern armaments. The Indian Air Force (IAF) has acquired the capacity to project power within and beyond India's immediate neighbourhood and is capable of playing both offensive and defensive roles. The Indian Navy (IN) has been transformed into a blue water-capable navy with the acquisition and development of aircraft carriers, destroyers, submarines and various other naval assets; it is also constructing new and refurbishing existing bases. Since 1998, India has also officially become a nuclear weapons state with the ability to deliver nuclear warheads beyond its immediate region through land- and air-based delivery vehicles. It may very soon acquire the capacity to deliver nuclear weapons from the sea, thus completing its strategic triad.

To facilitate this transition, between 2001 and 2013 India's spending on defence increased by 64 per cent (SIPRI 2013). As expected, the lion's share of this defence spending has gone to the Army (approximately 49 per cent), followed by the Air Force (28 per cent), the Navy (18 per cent) and the Defence Research and Development Organization (DRDO) (5 per cent) (Behera 2013: 2). Approximately 40 per cent of the total defence expenditure was spent on capital outlays (consisting of expenditure on arms procurement, construction, infrastructure and other military equipment) across the three services (CSIS 2011). IHS Jane's Defence Budgets has projected that India's spending on defence is likely to increase from US$46 billion in 2013 to $65.4 billion in 2020, which would make India the fourth largest defence spender after the USA, China and Russia. Although as a percentage of gross domestic product (GDP) India's defence spending has remained steady at 2.5–3.0 per cent, with the Indian economy emerging as the fastest growing large economy in the world the Indian government should be able to sustain increased spending on defence in the 2015–20 period (Kumar 2014).

'Military transformation' means something more than simply a 'revolution in military affairs'. While the latter concept denotes the integration of advanced information technology with weapons systems in order to develop smart weapons, the former signals the fusion of high-technology weapons with new ways of thinking about threats and strategy. In India's case, both concepts are highly relevant. Threatening developments within India and the surrounding region, an uncertain and fluid global strategic environment, and growing unreliability of traditional defence suppliers in the post-Cold War era have influenced Indian political and military elites into new ways of thinking. At a broad level, there is consensus that India faces multiple threats – conventional, non-conventional, nuclear and cyber, to national security. These threats are posed by both state and non-state actors and by old as well as new enemies; these threats are unpredictable and dangerous. The Indian military must therefore change in order to better defend against these threats.

Over the past two decades, the Indian military has focused on procuring modern high-tech weapons for all three services. The main aim of these procurements has been to give the military not only a more robust defensive capability but also to enable the military to project offensive power in India's immediate region and beyond, to mobilise quickly and launch counter-insurgency and special operations, and to undertake humanitarian missions when required. The three services are also developing and revising their strategic doctrines to reflect better upon the key changes to India's immediate, regional and global strategic environments, their own rising prowess and the various tasks and challenges confronting the forces.

India's post-Cold War threat perceptions

When the Cold War ended and the Soviet Union disintegrated, India's national security was left in a very difficult and vulnerable place. The Soviet Union's disintegration robbed India of a loyal ally that had stood by the country during its times of crisis. Russia was engulfed in economic, financial and political turmoil and its forces had to be deployed to prevent disgruntled regions from seceding from the state. Russia was therefore in no position to offer India uninterrupted defence supplies on extremely favourable terms of trade, as the Soviet Union had done previously. Russia's emergence as an unreliable defence supplier adversely affected India's military whose weapons were predominantly Soviet-made. Indian leaders therefore understood the imperative for India to diversify its defence procurement and build and consolidate the country's strategic autonomy in the face of a deteriorating and uncertain international strategic and political milieu.

Since the disastrous 1962 Sino–Indian war (Kavic 1967; Maxwell 1970; Hoffmann 1990; Vertzberger 1984; Gupta 1971), India has viewed China as its foremost enemy. India shares with China a 4,000 km-long land border, parts of which are in dispute. The military threat from China across the disputed land border was magnified after the 1962 war with the modernisation of the People's Liberation Army (PLA), the establishment and consolidation of strategic ties between China and Pakistan, and the construction by the Chinese of an all-weather road linking Tibet with Xinjiang and a railway line linking Tibet with north-eastern China (Cohen 2001; Braun 1983). It was the fear of a nuclear-armed China that prompted India to conduct its own 'peaceful nuclear explosion' in 1974 (Kapur 2001; Abraham 1998) and undertake a round of military modernisation in the 1970s and 1980s. In 1998, after conducting a second round of nuclear weapon tests, India proclaimed itself a 'nuclear weapons state', primarily to establish a 'minimum credible deterrent' vis-à-vis China (*The Hindu* 2011a).

The modernisation drive within the PLA, particularly the PLA Navy's rapid development and growing power projection capabilities in the Indo-Pacific region (see Chapter 7), and Chinese muscle flexing in the South and East China Sea, began to ring alarm bells within the Indian government and military. The Chinese government invested massive resources aimed at transforming the PLA into a modern high-tech fighting force. It unilaterally declared an Air Defence Identification Zone (ADIZ) along its southern and eastern coastline and made territorial claims in the South China Sea and East China Sea, much to the consternation of China's neighbours such as Vietnam, the Philippines and Japan (Hsu 2014; Yoshihara 2012). The PLA Navy acquired nuclear-powered submarines, aircraft carriers, fixed-wing fighter aircrafts for the aircraft carriers and other assorted naval hardware. It started conducting training exercises for pilots designated to operate fighter aircrafts from the aircraft carriers, and it also started upgrading the communications and equipment of its personnel and began installing sophisticated electronic and radar equipment, designed to improve the targeting capability of its ships, submarines and naval fighter air-craft. US assessment of the PLA Navy's growth suggested that in the medium to long term Beijing would become capable of deploying substantial military power well beyond China's regional waters (*The New York Times* 2014; Raja Mohan 2012a, 2012b, 2010; Holmes et al. 2009). For India, particular concerns were the PLA Navy's growing presence in the Indian Ocean Region (IOR), increased Chinese submarine activity close to India's coastline, and the building and maintaining of ports in neighbouring states like Pakistan (Gwadar), Sri Lanka (Hambantota and Colombo), Bangladesh (Chittagong) and Myanmar (Coco Islands, Kyaukphyu). Indian security planners formed the perception that China was gradually encircling India strategically, which needed to be countered. This threat perception was reinforced by reports that the PLA Navy's counter-piracy task groups had made port calls in at least 12 IOR states for military-to-military engagements and resupply and replenishments. The Indian government viewed with particular concern the docking of two PLA Navy submarines in Colombo and Hembantota ports in Sri Lanka (Southerland et al. 2014; Singh 2011).

India's fear of Pakistan also increased in the post-Cold War era. In 1998, within a week of India's second nuclear tests, Pakistan carried out its own nuclear weapons tests, thereby confirming suspicions about its nuclear programme. Unlike India, Pakistan did not pledge a 'no first use' of nuclear weapons. Instead, Pakistan's nuclear doctrine advocated the first use of nuclear weapons in order to offset its conventional military inferiority against India (Chakma 2009). An accidental nuclear war in the event of a major crisis also could not be ruled out. Pakistan had actively supported the Sikh insurgency in the 1980s and the Kashmiri insurgency since the early 1990s. It had helped create and backed a plethora of Islamist groups, many of which were involved in insurgent activities in Indian Kashmir and other parts of India. In 1999, the Indian military even fought a brief border war with Islamist insurgents backed by Pakistani forces in the Kargil sector in Indian Kashmir, which further vitiated bilateral relations. The attacks on the Indian parliament and the Akshardham Temple by Pakistan-based and -backed Islamist militants heightened tensions and the two countries came to the brink of war again in November 2008 when suicide terrorists belonging to the Lashkar-e-Taiba, an Islamist militant group based in Pakistan, carried out a daring attack on the Indian port city of Mumbai.

India's security outlook and spending on defence were also influenced by the situation in Afghanistan. In Afghanistan, the Soviet military withdrawal in 1989 was followed by civil war until 1996 when the Pakistan-backed Taliban took power. In this civil war, New Delhi had supported the Northern Alliance, a largely Uzbek-Tajik-Hazara coalition fighting against the Pashtun warlords and the Pashtun-dominated Taliban. During the 1996–2001 Taliban rule the group's hostility towards India became obvious. A large number of Afghan mujahedeen, who had once fought against the Soviet occupying forces, were encouraged to infiltrate into Indian Kashmir where a separatist insurgency had started in 1989. In 1999, an Indian Airlines aircraft was hijacked by Islamist militants and flown to Kandahar in southern Afghanistan. Negotiations between the Indian authorities and the hijackers were complicated by India's lack of recognition of the Taliban regime and the Taliban's decision to surround the hijacked aircraft with its fighters in order to prevent Indian Special Forces from storming the aircraft and rescuing the passengers. The hijacking eventually ended after India released three militants serving time in Indian prisons. The Taliban's fall in 2001 and the subsequent US military occupation increased India's involvement in Afghanistan's development. As the US occupation gradually winds down, a resurgent Taliban could pose a serious threat to India's interests and assets in Afghanistan.

During the United Progressive Alliance (UPA) regime from 2004–14, Prime Minister Manmohan Singh and Defence Minister A.K. Antony publicly made the case for greater military spending to meet the threats posed by India's regional security environment and an uncertain global strategic milieu. Prime Minister Singh cautioned the country that a serious threat of nuclear weapons proliferation was confronting the Indian subcontinent and that the security of nuclear materials was a matter of grave concern. He also cautioned that India was faced with multiple threats, including the threat of non-conventional and cyber warfare. The prime minister argued that India's military forces must be equipped with the most modern means in order to meet the multitude of threats they faced (*The Indian Express* 2011; Bhowmick 2012). Defence Minister Antony argued that even after the change in leadership in Beijing, China's stance towards the boundary dispute with India was unlikely to change in the near future. He acknowledged the growing asymmetry in military power between India and China and spoke about India's need to build asymmetric warfare capabilities in order to counter threats from larger and more powerful forces perhaps acting in tandem on two or more fronts simultaneously. For this, he argued, the IAF must take steps to extend its strategic reach and be able to operate effectively far away from the Indian mainland. He further suggested that India must develop and integrate its capabilities in space-based military assets, air defence, surveillance, modern fighter aircraft and advanced weapons systems (*The Indian Express* 2009). He called for India to develop its nuclear weapons capabilities in order to maintain a minimum credible deterrent against China (*The Times of India* 2013b; Katoch 2013b; Baweja 2013).

Defence procurement and modernisation

To speed up the Indian military's development and modernisation drive, the Indian government paid attention to expanding defence relations with a large number of countries. India's economic liberalisation, which unleashed the country's economic potential and produced growth rates of around 8.5 per cent on average from the early 1990s, made it possible to allocate more resources to the military even though military expenditure as a percentage of GDP did not increase significantly.

Brian Hedrick of the Strategic Studies Institute of the US Army War College has argued that the imperative of procuring defence supplies from multiple sources forced India to jettison its long-cherished foreign policy posture of 'non-alignment' in favour of a more pragmatic posture of 'poly-alignment'. This shift allowed New Delhi to establish defence-specific bilateral agreements with 26 different countries by 2008, most of which were with established or emerging global leaders in the field of armaments production and New Delhi hoped that they would be willing to transfer the latest weapons technologies and production licences to India. The Indian military also held joint exercises with a number of foreign militaries, most notably the annual Malabar exercises with the US military. India also articulated its willingness to forge strong ties with IOR littoral states, offer active leadership in regional and global multilateral organisations and commit strongly to peacekeeping operations (Hedrick 2009: 49–50).

India's military and defence ties improved dramatically with the USA. During the Cold War, India was often at loggerheads with the USA, which it blamed for supporting Pakistan and opposing India's position across a range of international issues (Chaudhuri 2014). The end of the Cold War and the onset of India's economic liberalisation started a thaw in bilateral relations, but India's nuclear weapons tests in 1998 put the brakes on the relationship at least temporarily (Raja Mohan 2003). Under President George W. Bush, the USA began to see India as an 'anchor' around which stability in the IOR could be built and sustained over the next few decades. The joint military exercises and regular strategic dialogues were resumed and American defence sales to India started to increase. In the period 2001–13, American companies sold an estimated \$13 billion worth of military hardware to India (Hardy 2013).

India also actively worked to strengthen its strategic relations with Russia, which continued to be the Indian military's principal supplier. The IA entered into negotiations with the Russian government to procure T-90 main battle tanks and for the IAF the Sukhoi-30 MKI fighter aircraft. The IN acquired the overhauled and refitted aircraft carrier, INS *Vikramaditya*, and several stealth frigates from Russia. It also acquired on lease a nuclear-powered submarine, the INS *Chakra*, from the Russian Navy.

Apart from the USA and Russia, India established strong defence collaboration with Israel, Australia, Japan, Singapore, Vietnam and several European states. Prime Minister Singh visited Japan in May 2013, whilst in August 2014, newly elected Prime Minister Narendra Modi visited Japan. A key outcome of these visits was a strategic convergence between the two countries that they needed to work together to ensure the stability of the Asia-Pacific region in the face of a militarily aggressive China. Japanese Prime Minister Shinzo Abe advocated that India and Japan should institutionalise and increase the frequency of joint naval exercises. Japan also indicated that it was willing to sell to India the highly advanced amphibious aircraft ShinMaywa US-2, which has both civilian and military applications (*The Times of India* 2013c).

In June 2013, then Defence Minister Antony met with his Australian counterpart, Stephen Smith. In the following year, Australian Prime Minister Tony Abbott visited New Delhi and declared that Canberra was willing to sell uranium to India. This visit was followed by Indian Prime Minister Modi's visit to Australia in November, the first by an Indian prime minister in three decades. The two sides acknowledged the need to deepen the India-Australia strategic partnership by stepping-up military-to-military exchanges, holding regular bilateral dialogues on maritime security and planning a joint naval combat exercise in 2015 to build confidence and familiarity between the two navies (*The Times of India* 2013d).

India's projected defence procurements over the next five years are ambitious and, if carried out, would significantly boost its military's conventional war-fighting capabilities. The IA has plans to raise a new Mountain Strike Corps in the east and support it with an upgraded attack helicopter fleet and basic infantry, artillery and armoured equipment (Clary and Narang 2013). The Army plans to purchase the T-90 main battle tank, which would offer a significant upgrade from India's current and ageing stock. No new gun has been inducted into the IA since the Bofors kickback scandal of the 1980s; this may change if the Army gets the go ahead from the Ministry of Defence to procure ultra-light howitzers for its artillery programme (Behera 2013: 2). The Army also has plans to import assault rifles, along with mini unmanned aerial vehicles

(UAVs), shoulder-fired rockets and surveillance sensors (Katoch 2013b). With the development, testing and induction of the BrahMos cruise missile, the Army's air-defence system has received an urgent overhaul (Katoch 2013b). In September 2013, India successfully tested the long-range Agni-V ballistic missile for the second time. Capable of carrying multiple nuclear warheads, the induction of the Agni-V ballistic missile would give India's Strategic Forces Command the capability to strike targets in far-flung places.

The mainstay of the IAF has been the MiG-21 fighter, which has been in service for over 50 years. The IAF's squadron of Mirage 2000 fighters have also become antiquated. Under the modernisation plan, therefore, the IAF plans to build a fleet of 42 squadrons and acquire new ultra-modern fighter aircraft such as the Sukhoi-30 MKI fighters, French Rafale fighters and Boeing Apache Longbow attack helicopters (Behera 2013: 2). The IAF has also expressed an interest to develop jointly with Russia a fifth-generation Sukhoi PAK FA fighter (Clary and Narang 2013). In September 2013, the IAF's ability to move troops and weapons swiftly to the battlefront received a boost with the induction of the first US-built C-17 Globemaster III heavy-lift transport aircraft. The IAF plans to procure several more C-17 aircraft and also the Boeing CH-47F Chinook heavy lift helicopter (*The Times of India* 2013f). The IAF further plans to buy several Airbus A330 Multi Role Tanker Transport aircraft, flight refuelling aircraft and airborne early-warning systems in deals worth $20–25 billion (Behera 2013: 2).

The IN has launched an ambitious expansion plan to better protect India's long coastline and project power into the IOR and beyond. Its annual expenditure has increased from $181 million in 1988 to $6.78 billion in 2012 (Hardy 2013). Prime Minister Narendra Modi and his Defence Minister Monohar Parikkar emphasised the vital need for India to build up its navy and quickly approved various acquisition plans totalling almost $8 billion (NDTV 2015). The bulk of this expenditure has been earmarked for acquiring and upgrading the IN's submarine and surface fleets. The INS *Arihant*, the indigenously built nuclear-powered ballistic missile submarine, was inducted in 2013. Capable of carrying nuclear-capable ballistic missiles, the INS *Arihant* is undergoing sea trials and is to be commissioned in 2017–18 (*The Times of India* 2013h). For India's sea-based nuclear deterrent to be fully operational, however, it will need at least three more nuclear submarines (Mason 2012).

In August 2013, India's first indigenous aircraft carrier, the 20,000-ton INS *Vikrant*, was launched. Capable of carrying MiG-29K fighter aircraft, Tejas Light Combat Aircraft and anti-submarine and reconnaissance helicopters on its 2.5-acre flight deck, the INS *Vikrant* is expected to enter into service in 2018 (*The Times of India* 2013e). The *Vikrant*'s bigger sister ship, the INS *Vishal*, is under construction. In November 2013, India acquired its second aircraft carrier, the INS *Vikramaditya*, from Russia (Clary and Narang 2013; *The Times of India* 2013g). The INS *Vikramaditya* will provide the IN with additional power-projection capabilities. The IN has also inducted several stealth destroyers into the force. The latest, the 6,800-ton INS *Kolkata*, was commissioned in August 2014 and recently successfully test-fired its main weapon, the BrahMos supersonic cruise missile (*The Times of India* 2015).

The IN has also developed new bases and modernised existing ones. The Navy plans to build a new strategic base near Rambilli on the Seemandhra coast close to Visakhapatnam, the headquarters of the Eastern Naval Command. Once completed, this state-of-the-art base will have underground pens to protect nuclear submarines from spy satellites and enemy air attacks. The Navy is also expanding the Karwar naval base on the coast of Karnataka in order to create strategic depth and operational flexibility on the western seaboard. The new ports along with the upgraded facilities in Andaman, Mumbai and Visakhapatnam will provide the IN with the ability to project substantial force in the Arabian Sea, the Bay of Bengal and the Indian Ocean (*The Times of India* 2013a).

The Indian military's strategic outlook

The IA's essential battle plan vis-à-vis Pakistan is based on the so-called 'Cold Start' doctrine, developed in the 1980s in the context of the debate within the Indian establishment over how to prevent Pakistan from going nuclear, after intelligence reports suggested that its nuclear weapons research programme was at an advanced stage (Ganguly and Hagerty 2005: 53–58). The essence of the Cold Start plan is to have highly mobile strike corps of mechanised and armoured infantry backed by airpower that can strike pre-emptively and surgically with lighting speed deep into Pakistani territory, without the need for elaborate and time-consuming mobilisation (Ladwig 2007). The plan has been revised and updated multiple times

While the basic contours of the Cold Start doctrine remain at the core of the Army's strategic thinking, the IA is gradually carrying out organisational and operational changes in order to become a more agile and potent force, capable of simultaneously fighting a two-front war with China and Pakistan while carrying out major counterinsurgency operations in border areas. General V.K. Singh, former chief of army staff, explained that the focus of the Army 'is now shifting from being an adversary-specific force to a capability-based force, able to fight across the spectrum – in the mountains, in the desert, night and day, in the hot summer or harsh winter' (Gokhale 2011). In an operational sense, this means that the Army is going to be organised and deployed in a way that would allow different theatres to be functionally independent of each other and operate without having to borrow each other's resources.

The IA's Cold Start doctrine and the capability-based approach were put to the test in May 2011 during a six-day joint exercise with the IAF in the Rajasthan desert near the Pakistan border. During the exercise, known as Operation Vajayee Bhava (Be Victorious), defensive corps along the border with Pakistan were converted into 'pivot' corps and given enhanced blitzkrieg-style offensive capabilities under the concept of integrated battle groups (IBGs) – division-sized forces comprising armour, artillery and aviation assets which can swiftly strike across the border before one of the main three strike corps, located deeper inside India, is able to mobilise. This was followed by a two-month military exercise in November–December 2011, Operation Sudarshan Shakti, when the Army successfully integrated its satellites and UAVs into the IBGs to provide real-time battlefield pictures and information to the corps commanders. In addition, real-time links between sensor and shooter were tested and information shared among platforms and personnel (Gokhale 2012). The aim of the exercise was 'to initiate transformation and maintain continuous offensive capabilities with a networked headquarters supported by intelligence, surveillance, and reconnaissance acting as the nerve-centre of operations' (*The Hindu* 2011b).

The Cold Start doctrine is essentially, then, an offensive military doctrine that is designed to strike Pakistan with lightning speed in the event of crisis, to catch its military by surprise and destroy it, and to capture large swaths of Pakistani territory which can be used as a bargaining chip in post-war nego-tiations (Kapila 2004). For this strategy to work, it would require strong, courageous and resolute political decision making at the highest levels of government. Critical assessment of the doctrine, however, suggests that while India has the military capacity to implement the strategy, it may lack the poli-tical will to do so. This impression was strengthened by Indian military inaction particularly in the aftermath of the 2002 parliament and the 2008 Mumbai attacks by Pakistan-based and -sponsored terrorists. It is as yet unclear how the current Narendra Modi-led Indian government would react if a Mumbai-style attack by Pakistan-based terrorists or a major escalation of firing and encroachment by Pakistani forces across the Line of Control (LOC) in Kashmir were to happen. As far as Pakistan is concerned, however, its govern-ment and its military have made it clear that any attempt by India to oper-ationalise Cold Start against Pakistan would be met with nuclear weapons. Hence, Pakistan has refused even to consider a nuclear 'no first use' policy vis-à-vis India (Raina 2014).

With an eye on the China land frontier, the IA has created two mountain divisions and a mountain strike corps, which are mostly deployed in defensive positions. To prepare better for a potential land war with China, the IAF has also developed high-altitude airfields, which can be used by fighter jets as well as heavy-lift cargo aircraft. In the Ladakh sector, where the Pakistan and China frontiers converge, India has introduced an armoured regiment and has plans to add a further armoured brigade to the Leh plateau. The increasing Indian mili-tary offensive capability in mountainous terrain along the Sino–Indian border means that India can better resist any serious transgressions of the border by the PLA and can even launch a serious counter-attack against the Chinese military positions in Tibet. The Indian military's strategic thinking and manoeuvres seem to indicate that its main aim vis-à-vis China is to ensure that the PLA can no longer 'surprise India' and 'teach India a lesson', as it did during the 1962 Sino–Indian border war. It also signals to the Chinese that any aggressive move against India would result in substantial 'costs' (Ahmed 2014).

The IAF's acquisition plans suggest that it is gearing-up to play a range of offensive and defensive roles in the future. A priority area for the IAF is to acquire multi-mission fighters such as the French-built Rafale or the Russian-built Sukhoi-30 fighter jets. These expensive multi-mission fighters can act as force multipliers for the IAF and be used in offensive roles, particularly in air-to-air combat operations. These aircraft can carry nuclear warheads, thereby providing India with air-launched nuclear capability. The planned acquisition of these aircraft also suggests that the IAF envisages that it may have to play offensive combat roles in theatres beyond India's immediate neighbourhood in the future. To support the operations of its multi-mission fighters, the IAF has given attention to acquiring mid-air refuelling tankers and advanced surveillance and communication aircraft (Layton 2013). Expensive multi-mission fighters are, however, risky to use in ground-strike operations in tight tactical battlefields, such as the Indo–Pakistani and Sino–Indian land frontiers which are filled with air-defence weapons. Some analysts therefore suggest that the IAF ought to consider acquiring dedicated fighter ground attack (FGA) aircraft such as the Sukhoi-25 and Sukhoi-39, and precision guided munitions (PGM), along with attack helicopters such as the US-built Apache. During the 1999 Kargil war with Pakistan, air-to-ground strikes by the IAF's FGA aircraft neutralised Pakistan's air defences and destroyed enemy camps and bunkers, thereby allowing Indian ground troops to recapture enemy-held mountain ridges with minimal fatalities (Kanwal 2015).

Until the end of the twentieth century, the IN was little more than a glorified coast guard service. Although the IN had played an important role during the 1971 India–Pakistan war, it was nonetheless marginalised by India's security and political elites, which was reflected in its meagre budgetary allocation. Things started to change in the 1990s and picked up steam from early 2000 onwards. In 2007, the IN released the *Freedom to Use the Seas: India's Maritime Military Strategy* (Integrated Headquarters, Ministry of Defence – Navy 2007). This was followed in 2009 by the release of the *Indian Maritime Doctrine* (Integrated Headquarters, Ministry of Defence – Navy 2009). The 2009 document was published in the wake of the 2008 Mumbai terrorist attack. In the aftermath of the attack, the Indian government transferred the overall responsibility of coastal security to the IN and brought the State Coastal Police and Coast Guard under it.

Both documents spell out in considerable detail the IN's strategic vision in the twenty-first century. The IN sees itself as playing four key roles. First and most important, it envisages playing a *military* role, which would include providing sea-based nuclear deterrence, enforcing sea control and sea denial, implementing naval blockade, mounting special operations, coordinating combat operations with the other services and carrying out surveillance and power-projection operations. Second, the IN expects to conduct *naval diplomacy*, which would include Indian warships making port calls in the region and beyond and holding regular bilateral and multilateral naval exercises. The IN recognises the value of forward presence and soft-power projection through naval diplomacy and it wants to be viewed as an important and reliable partner by the major powers in the Indo-Pacific region. Third, the IN sees itself playing a vital role in ensuring India's *economic and energy security*. This may require the IN to secure India's offshore assets from seaborne threats, safeguard India's mercantile marine and maritime trade, ensure that vital sea lanes of communication (SLOC) remain open and protected from threats from enemy states, pirates and terrorists, and provide security to vital choke points through which large volumes of international trade pass. Finally, the IN is cognisant of its *humanitarian* role, which may include disaster-relief operations, evacuation of civilians from emergencies caused by nature, development or conflict, and providing non-combat support to the Indian diaspora (Holmes et al. 2009).

The Indian military's counterinsurgency doctrine and experience

The Indian military's experience with counterinsurgency (COIN) operations started in the immediate aftermath of independence but increased over the years, culminating in a massive operation in Jammu and Kashmir in the 1990s and 2000s.

In the immediate post-independence period, the main challenge came from Naga and Mizo separatists in India's far north-east along the border with Myanmar. Thereafter the IA had to deal with insurgents in Manipur, Tripura and Assam. As demands for COIN operations increased, the IA set up specialised training centres, such as the Jungle Warfare Training School in Dehra Dun and the Counter-Insurgency and Jungle Warfare School in Vairengte, to train its soldiers in counterinsurgency warfare (Rajagopalan 2000: 56). Over the years, the IA developed a COIN doctrine that was underpinned by two 'beliefs': one, that the Army's main task is to defend India's sovereignty against external enemies; and two, that fighting insurgents who are fellow citizens amidst civilian populations is a delicate task which requires sensitive and patient handling (Rajagopalan 2000: 44).

Underpinned by these two beliefs, the IA's counterinsurgency strategy incorporated three broad objectives. First, the IA tried to wear down the various insurgencies rather than try to score a decisive victory at any cost. The Army acknowledged that it is difficult and usually counterproductive to try to score an outright and decisive military victory against insurgents, since the costs of protracted military operations are often exorbitantly high, the operations usually exacerbate the social conditions that give rise to insurgencies, and such operations detract the Army from its main task, which is to protect India from external enemies. Second, the Army acknowledged that insurgencies are in their essence political problems and hence require political solutions; however, military force could be used to create an environment conducive to political resolution. Finally, the Army acknowledged that COIN operations must be strictly limited in terms of force in order to minimise civilian hardship and suffering, and to win the hearts and minds of the civilian population in insurgency-affected areas, which is essential in order to isolate the insurgents politically and induce them to agree to negotiations with the state (Goswami 2009; Rajagopalan 2008).

A central plank of the Indian Army's COIN operations, then, is to respond to shifting 'centres of gravity' in insurgency–counterinsurgency warfare. Analysts have argued that instead of a single centre of gravity, multiple and dynamic centres of gravity usually exist in insurgent warfare. Shimon Naveh (1997: 19), for example, has argued that in the battlefield multiple centres of gravity may exist and vary according to time, space and purpose. Joe Strange (1997: 43–48) agrees with Naveh that centres of gravity are dynamic and vary according to time and context; however, he divides centres of gravity into two main types: moral and physical. Moral centres of gravity in insurgent warfare include leadership, ideology, organisation and degree of popular support for the insurgency, while physical centres of gravity refer to insurgents' military, financial and diplomatic capability. Effective counterinsurgency must therefore be robust but flexible, and must operate in various ways using military and non-military means in order to neutralise the insurgents' multiple centres of gravity. The IA's COIN operations in recent times suggest that the Indian military and the Indian government accept and understand that insurgencies have multiple centres of gravity which vary across time and space and therefore a multipronged strategy is needed to deal with the phenomenon (Integrated Headquarters, Ministry of Defence (Army) 2004, 2006).

In essence, the Indian military and the Indian government have followed a four-pronged strategy towards armed insurgency (Ganguly and Fidler 2009). First, the Indian state has used the Indian military and paramilitary and police forces to weaken insurgent organisation and leadership and to reduce insurgents' capacity to wage war against the state (Bajpai 1997: 75–76). For instance, at the height of the Sikh insurgency in the Indian state of Punjab in the 1980s, the IA was ordered to enter the Golden Temple complex in Amritsar twice (Operation Blue Star, launched in June 1984, and Operation Black Thunder, launched in May 1988) to flush out and kill militant Sikh leaders who had taken up shelter there and were using the holy shrine as a sanctuary and operational nerve centre (Chadda 1997: 139). In the Indian north-east, too, the IA launched several use-of-force operations geared to reduce significantly insurgents' capacity to wage war. For instance, in the early 1990s, the IA launched Operation Bajrang and Operation Rhino against the United Liberation Front of Assam, which severely dented the organisation's military and political power. Similar Army operations against the Bodo, Naga and Manipuri insurgents have been launched in recent times in the north-east.

The most severe deployment of military force, however, occurred in the state of Jammu and Kashmir, where a violent separatist insurgency had started in the late 1980s. During the height of the insurgency in Jammu and Kashmir in the 1990s and 2000s, the Indian government authorised the deployment of forces from the IA, paramilitary units and the central police organisations. Together with the Jammu and Kashmir police, these forces were given a dual responsibility: to liquidate top insurgents and their support network within the state, and to stop the infiltration of insurgents into Jammu and Kashmir from Pakistan where most of the insurgent training camps were located (Wirsing 1994: 147). In order to liquidate top insurgents, to destroy their support networks within the state, and to protect people from insurgents' threats and violence, the security forces created and maintained 'secure zones', launched periodic cordon and search operations, administered both judicial (legitimate) and extrajudicial (illegitimate) punishments, and raised, trained and armed a small anti-insurgency force composed of captured former insurgents or *ikhwans* (Wirsing 1994: 154). To stop cross-border infiltration of armed insurgents, the IA launched border-sealing and counter-infiltration operations (Wirsing 1994: 147–154).

Second, to lift morale and strengthen the Indian security forces' hands in use-of-force operations against insurgent organisations and their leaders, the Indian government has enacted several pieces of legislation that have been termed draconian by human rights groups and lawyers. The most infamous amongst these is the Armed Forces Special Powers Act (AFSPA), which was initially introduced in the north-east in the 1950s but was later extended to Jammu and Kashmir in the 1990s, where it has remained controversially in operation until now. The AFSPA provides the security forces, among other things, with immunity from prosecution in the conduct of COIN operations in the so-called 'disturbed areas'. Another infamous piece of legislation that sought to strengthen the hands of the security forces was the Terrorist and Disruptive Activities (Prevention) Act, which remained active between 1985 and 1995. A third infamous piece of legislation was the Prevention of Terrorism Act, which was enacted in 2002 by the Bharatiya Janata Party (BJP)-led National Democratic Alliance (NDA) government. The Act was subsequently repealed by the Congress (I)-led UPA government in 2004.

A third strategy adopted by the Indian government involved concluding peace accords (such as the Punjab Accord and the Assam Accord) that contained specific provisions for resolving the insurgencies and rehabilitating the insurgents. In some cases the accords contained provisions for the protection of local ethnic identities and ethnic minorities. In other cases the accords devolved certain political and economic powers, such as the creation of local councils and the levying of local taxes and fees, to local areas. For instance, in Punjab, the Indian government kept the lines of communication with moderate Sikh leaders and political parties open through the accord. It eventually led to state elections in 1992 and the gradual elimination of armed secessionist insurgency in Punjab. Similarly, the Assam Accord helped to convince the Assamese student leaders to give up the path of violence and enter the political process. Both these accords, however, failed to resolve fully the root causes that alienated large populations in these states (Datta 1995).

A fourth and final strategy that the Indian military has adopted is to recognise the principle of people as the most important centre of gravity in COIN operations, which has led the military to adopt the posture of minimal use of force and to undertake welfare activities amongst alienated populations. The IA's COIN experience in the north-east, particularly people-centric welfare programmes under Operation Samaritan, played a central role in shaping its outlook towards civil-military partnerships aimed at winning the hearts and minds of alienated peoples in insurgency-affected areas.

That outlook was further tested and refined in Jammu and Kashmir. Operation Sadhbhavana (Goodwill) was launched in 1998 and in its initial years consisted of three main initiatives. First, the IA together with civil authorities organised and conducted local, state and national elections in Jammu and Kashmir aimed at kick-starting the state's moribund political machinery. Second, the IA took the initiative together with the state's civil authorities to revive Jammu and Kashmir's tourism industry, which is the lifeblood of the state's economy. Finally, the IA launched a major initiative to counter the negative propaganda against the state and the Indian military that was being carried out by the insurgents and the separatists. As part of this last initiative, school children from Jammu and Kashmir visited other parts of India and witnessed the Republic Day parade in New Delhi (Operation Sangam); children from other parts of India visited Jammu and Kashmir (Operation Maitree); and the Army took the lead in rebuilding schools that were damaged and destroyed by the insurgents (Operation Ujala). The Army also launched a programme called Siraj-un-Nisa, through which it aimed to provide women with basic computing and typing skills and also teach them about child care and mother-and-child health issues. Furthermore, the Army helped to form village self-help groups, used resources from the Border Area Development Programme to fund development projects, and involved local stakeholders in the design and implementation of these projects (Anant 2011: 12–13). More recently, during the devastating floods in Jammu and Kashmir in 2014, the Army initiated a major search-and-rescue operation under its hearts-and-minds initiative.

Problems and challenges

While significant progress has been made in transforming both the Indian military's weaponry and its ways of thinking, it remains bedevilled by certain problems and challenges. A key problem for the military and the Indian government has been persistent corruption allegations in India's military procurement, which has clogged up the process considerably and slowed down the further modernisation of the armed forces. For instance, in January 2014, the Ministry of Defence (MoD) cancelled an order with AugustaWestland, a UK-based subsidiary of the Italian conglomerate Finmeccanica, for 12 VVIP helicopters following allegations of bribery. The MoD also asked the Central Bureau of Investigation (CBI) to investigate allegations that global jet engine manufacturer Rolls Royce had committed financial irregularities to procure defence contracts to supply engines for the Hawk Advanced Jet Trainers (AJTs) being manufactured by BAE Systems in collaboration with Hindustan Aeronautics Limited (HAL) (*The Times of India* 2014). The MoD is further conducting an investigation into alleged irregularities in the proposed procurement of 145 M-777 ultra-light howitzers from the USA in a deal worth $847 million (Katoch 2013b). Although Defence Minister Manohar Parikkar has promised to come up with a transparent defence procurement policy, major defence acquisitions are likely to be delayed due to the need for greater scrutiny.

The Indian government's declared ambition to produce 70 per cent of India's required military equipment indigenously (up from the current 30 per cent) by the end of 2020 seems to be fanciful (CSIS 2011). Between 2006 and 2011, India overtook China as the world's largest arms importer; it received almost 10 per cent of the total volume of global arms transfers, with supplies from Russia alone accounting for 82 per cent of total arms imports (SIPRI 2011, 2012). Parikkar has conceded that India is a huge distance away from realising its 70 per cent target, but made it clear that self-reliance in defence procurement remains a steadfast objective.

The BJP government has articulated its desire to build and support a robust domestic defence-industrial base, but the government's efforts to attract private Indian firms to build aircraft for the IAF have received a lukewarm response. The main state-run defence aeronautics supplier is HAL, which has a patchy record. HAL had tried from the early 1980s to develop a light combat aircraft for the IAF but with little success. HAL was also the main reason why India's $15–20 billion deal with France's Dassault Aviation for 126 Rafale fighter jets has not yet materialised. The French company has raised serious doubts regarding the technological capabilities of HAL (its mandatory partner) to manufacture such a sophisticated fighter plane. The IAF also raised serious objections to HAL's prototype trainer jet as not being powerful enough, and expressed a desire to buy a cheaper and more efficient plane from a foreign company (Kotoky 2013). Delays in production, shoddy design and equipment and multiplying costs thus continue to dog the DRDO.

The IAF's and the IN's track record with accidents and mishaps has also taken the gloss off India's military transformation. The MiG-21 fighter has been nicknamed the 'flying coffin' after a series of accidents which attests to shoddy maintenance standards and the lack of proper pilot training. In recent times, however, it is the IN that has grabbed the headlines for the wrong reasons. Over a period of seven months from August 2013, the IN witnessed at least ten major accidents and mishaps involving warships and submarines. The most serious incident occurred in August 2013 when a major fire and explosion destroyed India's advanced diesel-electric submarine, the INS *Sindhurakshak*, and killed 18 sailors while it was docked at a high-security naval base in Mumbai (BBC News 2013). Then in February 2014 a major fire broke out on board the diesel-electric submarine INS *Sindhuratna*, as it was undergoing sea trials off the coast of Mumbai. In this accident, two of the ship's officers died and seven sailors were seriously injured. Taking moral responsibility for the accidents and mishaps under his watch, the Navy chief, Admiral Devender Kumar Joshi, resigned on 27 February 2014 (*The Times of India* 2014).

The Indian military urgently requires radical organisational changes in order to achieve greater synergy, integration and operational efficiency between the various services. Future wars are unlikely to be a single-service business. They are also likely to be short, intensive affairs which could require the simultaneous or sequential deployment of India's conventional, cyber, space and nuclear forces. The theatre of future wars could also be located far from Indian shores. In such a futuristic war scenario, synergy between the various services and their ability to operate jointly and efficiently will be vital. The Indian military's organisation, particularly its systems, processes, and command and control, should be such that it can be deployed quickly and effectively especially in faraway places. Equally crucial would be the configuration of the Indian military, particularly its operational and support roles.

In the aftermath of the Kargil war with Pakistan in 1999, the Kargil Review Committee had recommended the creation of a chief of defence staff of five-star rank to have operational command over the entire military and to act as a single point adviser to the minister of defence. This, the Kargil Review Committee argued, would facilitate the creation of an Integrated Theatre and Functional Command, which is necessary for fighting modern-day wars (Katoch 2013a).

However, analysts Bora and Bansal (2015) take a different approach and argue that a better way of reconfiguring the Indian military would be to follow the example of the US military. The US military has a chief for each service, whose responsibility lies with equipment, organisation and training, but not war-fighting. Operationally, the US military has divided the world into different geographical areas of responsibility (AORs), with each AOR under a combatant commander who has overall responsibility for all forces under his command and for all combat operations in his theatre. In addition, the US military has functional commanders for special operations, transportation and strategic weapons. Bora and Bansal argue that a similar operational and support matrix could be emulated by the Indian military. For instance, it could be divided into three geographical commands: an Eastern Command responsible for China and South, South-East and East Asia; a Western Command responsible for Pakistan and Central and West Asia; and a Southern Command responsible for littoral IOR/Indo-Pacific region, Africa and the Middle East. In addition, there would be functional commands for nuclear weapons/strategic forces and special operations. The responsibility for military operations would lie with the theatre commanders, who would hold four-star rank. This would negate the need for a five-star chief of defence staff. Instead, there could be a chairman and vice-chairman of joint chiefs of staff separate from the three service chiefs. The chairman of the joint chiefs of staff would act as a single-point military adviser to the MoD and the Prime Minister's Office.

Bora and Bansal (2015) also strongly argue for creating greater size parity between the three services of the Indian military, since 'disparity in size leads to disparity in egos, which makes a mockery of "jointness"'. Although perfect parity between a manpower-intensive Army and a machine-intensive Air

Force and Navy is impossible and undesirable, some force rationalisation could be worked out, keeping in mind future war scenarios and operational requirements. For instance, an entire corps (three divisions) of the Army could be trained in amphibious warfare, converted into marines, and placed under the Navy. Similarly, the Army and Air Force could jointly raise an air assault corps and put it under the operational control of the Air Force.

Bora and Bansal (2015) further argue that the role and mission of the Indian military are in need of urgent revision. The main role and focus of the three services must be on war-fighting against external enemies under different conditions and scenarios. Other operational tasks such as border protection, COIN operations, as well as humanitarian and relief services should be left with paramilitary forces, whose organisation, structure and operational capabilities should be revised and upgraded. Currently, the Indian military is often deployed to undertake many of these tasks, which may adversely affect the military's war-fighting capabilities. For instance, harsh COIN operations backed by draconian legislation such as the AFSPA which gives the security forces carte blanche have resulted in serious allegations of human rights abuses against the military by leading international human rights organisations. This has affected morale within the military and adversely affected its preparations for war-fighting.

Conclusion

India's military is slowly but surely transforming into a modern, integrated and specialised force with deep defensive and deterrent capabilities and a growing ability to project offensive power. This transformation has happened for several reasons: threatening developments within the region; an uncertain and unstable international security environment; the changing nature of war (conventional, non-conventional, cyber and nuclear) and the kinds of skills and organisation that will be required to fight such wars; perceptions of India's military and political elites and domestic security requirements. The process transformation has also been strongly influenced by India's economic rise.

There is an element of inevitability to this process, although it must be acknowledged that the global financial crisis did slow things down considerably. Still, India's defence spending remained steady at 2.5–3.0 per cent of GDP, and with the economy now gradually picking up and a new government in power with a clear mandate, the process of military modernisation and transformation is bound to speed up again. The process will involve astute leadership and decision making along three dimensions: What kinds of weapons will India need to develop, acquire and induct in the services in order to neutralise effectively conventional, non-conventional, cyber and nuclear threats to national security? What would be the best way to organise the Indian military so that it can achieve maximum synergy and perform its main task of defending the nation in the most effective way against all kinds of threats and war scenarios? What military strategy will underpin these changes and how can weapons, systems,

services and personnel be integrated seamlessly to achieve maximum efficiency, especially during combat operations? These questions do not have easy
answers and therefore the debate over these issues has been hard fought and
contentious. Over the next ten years, the picture is likely to become much
sharper and more distinct.

Bibliography

Abraham, I. (1998) *The Making of the Indian Atomic Bomb: Science, Secrecy and the Postcolonial State*, London and New York: Zed Books.

Ahmed, A. (2014, 22 August) 'Dissonance in India's Strategic Doctrine' *Foreign Policy Journal*. http://www.foreignpolicyjournal.com/2014/08/22/dissonance-in-indias-strategic-doctrine/ (accessed 18 February 2015).

Anant, A. (2011, October)*Counterinsurgency and 'Operation Sadhbhavana' in Jammu and Kashmir*, IDSA Occasional Paper No. 19, New Delhi: Institute for Defence Studies and Analyses, pp. 5–48.

Bajpai, K. (1997) 'Diversity, Democracy, and Devolution in India', in Brown, M.E. and Ganguly, S. (eds) *Government Policies and Ethnic Relations in Asia and the Pacific*, Cambridge, MA: The MIT Press, pp. 33–81.

Baweja, H. (2013, 23 April) 'India Moves in More Troops, Stand-off with China Escalates', *Hindustan Times*. http://www.hindustantimes.com/StoryPage/Print/1048784.aspx (accessed 23 April 2013).

BBC News (2013, 14 August) 'Indian Submarine Hit by Explosion at Mumbai Port'. http://www.bbc.com/news/world/-asia-23691324?print=true (accessed 26 February 2014).

Behera, L.K. (2013, 4 March) 'India's Defence Budget 2013–2014: A Bumpy Road Ahead', *IDSA Comment*, Institute of Defence Studies and Analysis, New Delhi, India. http://www.idsa.in/idsacomments/IndiasDefenceBudget2013-14_lkbehera_040313 (accessed 14 February 2014).

Bhowmick, N. (2012, 3 April) 'Enter the Elephant: India Looks to Overhaul its Military', *Time*. http://world.time.com/2012/04/03/indias-military-overhaul-through-export-and-import-defense-spending-a-priority/print/ (accessed 14 February 2014).

Bora, P. and Bansal, A. (2015, 19 February) 'Reconfiguring the Military', *The Indian Express*. http://indianexpress.com/article/opinion/columns/reconfiguring-the-military/99/ (accessed 19 February 2015).

Braun, D. (1983) *The Indian Ocean: Region of Conflict or Peace*, London: C. Hurst.

Chadda, M. (1997) *Ethnicity, Security and Separatism in India*, New York: Columbia University Press.

Chakma, B. (2009) *Pakistan's Nuclear Weapons*, London: Routledge.

Chaudhuri, R. (2014) *Forged in Crisis: India and the United States since 1947*, London: Hurst and Company.

Clary, C. and Narang, V. (2013, 16 September) 'Modernization and Austerity', *The RAND Blog* The RAND Corporation. http://www.rand.org/blog/2013/09/modernisation-and-austerity.html (accessed 18 November 2013).

Clausewitz, C. von (1989) *On War*, Princeton, NJ: Princeton University Press.

Cohen, S.P. (2001) *India: Emerging Power*, Washington, DC: Brookings Institution Press.

CSIS (Centre for Strategic and International Studies) (2011, 29 March) 'India's Defence Spending and Military Modernization', *Current Issues*, No. 24. http://www.csis.org/isp/dhg (accessed 25 February 2014).

Datta, P.S. (1995) *Ethnic Peace Accords in India*, New Delhi: Vikas.

Ganguly, S. and Fidler, D.P. (2009) *India and Counterinsurgency: Lessons Learned*, London: Routledge.

Ganguly, S. and Hagerty, D.T. (2005) *Fearful Symmetry: India-Pakistan Crises in the Shadow of Nuclear Weapons*, New Delhi: Oxford University Press.

Global Firepower (2013) *2013 World Military Strength Ranking*. http://www.globalfirepower.com (accessed 12 February 2014).

Gokhale, N. (2011, 25 January) 'India's Doctrinal Shift?', *The Diplomat*. http://thediplomat.com/2011/01/indias-doctrinal-shift/ (accessed 16 February 2015).

Gokhale, N. (2012, 17 January) 'India Military Eyes Combined Threat', *The Diplomat*. http://thediplomat.com/2012/01/india-military-eyes-combined-threat/ (accessed 16 February 2015).

Goswami, N. (2009) 'India's Counter-Insurgency Experience: The "Trust and Nurture" Strategy', *Small Wars & Insurgencies*, Vol. 20, No. 1 (March), pp. 66–86.

Gupta, K. (1971) 'The McMohan Line 1911–1945: The British Legacy', *The China Quarterly*, Vol. 47 (July–September), pp. 521–545.

Hardy, J. (2013, 2 June) 'India's Quiet, Big Naval Splash', *The Diplomat*. http://thediplomat.com/2013/06/indias-quiet-big-naval-splash/?allpages=yes&print=yes (accessed 20 February 2014).

Hedrick, B.K. (2009) 'India's Strategic Defence Transformation: Expanding Global Relationships', *Strategic Studies Institute, US Army War College*, pp. vii, 60. http://www.strategicstudiesinstitute.army.mil/ (accessed 24 February 2014).

The Hindu (2011a, 10 November) 'India's Military Modernization "To Contain China": PLA Daily'. http://www.thehindu.com/news/international/indias-military-modernisation-to-contain-china-pla-daily/article2615757.ece?css=print (accessed 4 December 2013).

The Hindu (2011b, 6 December) '"Sudarshan Shakti" Aims to Transform Armed Forces'. http://www.thehindu.com/news/national/sudarshan-shakti-aims-to-transform-armed-forces/article2692709.ece (accessed 16 February 2015).

Hoffmann, S.A. (1990) *India and the China Crisis*, Berkeley, CA: University of California Press.

Holmes, J.R., Winner, A.C. and Yoshihare, T. (2009) *Indian Naval Strategy in the Twenty-first Century*, London: Routledge.

Hsu, K. (2014) 'Air Defence Identification Zone Intended to Provide China Greater Flexibility to Enforce East China Sea Claims', *U.S.-China Economic and Security Review Commission Staff Report*. http://origin.www.uscc.gov/sites/default/files/Research/China%20ADIZ%20Staff%20Report.pdf (accessed 16 February 2015).

The Indian Express (2009, 16 November) 'India Should Build Asymmetric Warfare Capabilities: Anthony'. http://www.indianexpress.com/story-print/542221/ (accessed 4 December 2013).

The Indian Express (2011, 12 October) 'Threat is Up, Both Global and Regional: PM'. http://www.indianexpress.com/story-print/858638 (accessed 4 December 2013).

Integrated Headquarters, Ministry of Defence (Army) (2004, October) *Indian Army Doctrine.*

Integrated Headquarters, Ministry of Defence (Army) (2006, December) *Doctrine for Sub-conventional Operations.*

Integrated Headquarters, Ministry of Defence (Navy) (2007) *Freedom to Use the Seas: India's Maritime Military Strategy.*

Integrated Headquarters, Ministry of Defence (Navy) (2009) *Indian Maritime Doctrine*. INBR-8.

Kanwal, G. (2015, 12 February) 'Air Power and Future Battlefields: India's Needs', *Institute of Peace and Conflict Studies*, Article No. 4833. http://www.ipcs.org/article/india/air-power-and-future-battlefields-indias-needs-4833.html (accessed 17 February 2015).

Kapila, S. (2004) 'India's New "Cold Start" War Doctrine Strategically Reviewed', *South Asia Analysis Group*, Paper No. 991. http://www.southasiaanalysis.org/paper991 (accessed 16 February 2015).

Kapur, A. (2001) *Pokhran and Beyond: India's Nuclear Behaviour*, New Delhi: Oxford University Press.

Katoch, P.C. (2013a, 19 June) 'Elusive Military Transformation', *Indian Defence Review* (online edn). http://www.indiandefencereview.com/print/?print_post_id=11612 (accessed 4 December 2013).

Katoch, P.C. (2013b, 16 August) 'The Dilemma: Military Modernization in India', *Fair Observer*. http://www.fairobserver.com/article/dilemma-military-modernizatio n-India (accessed 18 November 2013).

Kavic, L.J. (1967) *India's Quest for Security: Defence Policies, 1947–1965*, Berkeley and Los Angeles, CA: University of California Press.

Kotoky, A. (2013, 9 October) 'Ministry Row Latest Blow to India's Defence Modernization', *Reuters*. http://www.reuters.com/assets/print?aid=USL4N0HZ2HS20131009 (accessed 4 December 2013).

Kumar, V. (2014) 'India Will Be Fourth Biggest Defence Spender by 2020', *The Hindu*, 14 February. http://www.thehindu.com/news/national/india-will-be-fourth-biggest-defence-spender-by-2020/article4393957.ece (accessed 14 February 2014).

Ladwig, W.C., III (2007) 'A Cold Start for Hot Wars? The Indian Army's New Limited War Doctrine', *International Security*, Vol. 32, No. 3, pp. 158–190.

Layton, P. (2013, March) 'Indian Air Force Ramps up Combat Capability', *Defence Today*, pp. 20–22. http://www.academia.edu/2711676/Indian_Air_Force_Ramps_Up_Combat_Capability (accessed 18 February 2015).

Mason, S.A. (2012, 22 August) 'From Dyad to Triad: What India's Nuclear Developments Mean for Pakistan', *WMD Junction*, James Martin Centre for Nonproliferation Studies. http://wmdjunction.com/120822_india_pakistan_nuclear.htm (accessed 20 February 2014).

Maxwell, N. (1970) *India's China War*, London: Cape.

Naveh, Shimon (1997) *In Pursuit of Military Excellence: The Evolution of Operational Theory*, New York: Frank Cass.

NDTV (2015, 18 February) 'PM Modi Clears $8 Billion Plan for Warships to Counter China: Report'. http://www.ndtv.com/india-news/pm-modi-clears-8-billion-plan-for-warships-to-counter-china-report-740627?pfrom=home-lateststories (accessed 19 February 2015).

The New York Times (2014, 1 January) 'China's First Aircraft Carrier Completes South China Sea Drills' http://www.nytimes.com/reuters/2014/01/01/world/asia/01reuters-china-carrier.html?ref=world&_r=0&pagewanted=print (accessed 2 January 2014).

Raina, H. (2014, 10 December) 'India Must Clarify its Strategic Doctrine to Avoid Miscalculation with Pakistan', *International Affairs Review*. http://www.iar-gwu.org/content/india-must-clarify-its-strategic-doctrine-avoid-miscalculation-pakistan (accessed 16 February 2015).

Rajagopalan, R. (2000) '"Restoring Normalcy": The Evolution of the Indian Army's Counterinsurgency Doctrine', *Small Wars and Insurgencies*, Vol. 11, No. 1 (Spring), pp. 44–68.

Rajagopalan, R. (2008) *Fighting Like a Guerrilla: The Indian Army and Counterinsurgency*, London: Routledge.

Raja Mohan, C. (2003) *Crossing the Rubicon: The Shaping of India's New Foreign Policy*, New Delhi: Viking.

Raja Mohan, C. (2010, 18 August) 'PLA Power Projection takes it Far from China to Indian Ocean', *The Indian Express*. http://www.indianexpress.com/story-print/ 661753/ (accessed 4 December 2013).

Raja Mohan, C. (2012a) *Samudra Manthan: Sino-Indian Rivalry in the Indo-Pacific*, Washington, DC: Carnegie Endowment for International Peace.

Raja Mohan, C. (2012b, 26 September) 'India and China's First Aircraft Carrier', *The Indian Express*. http://www.indianexpress.com/story-print/1008218/ (accessed 4 December 2013).

Singh, M. (2011, 17 December) 'China Base a Threat to India Navy?', *The Diplomat*. http://thediplomat.com/2011/12/china-base-a-threat-to-india-navy/ (accessed 16 February 2015).

SIPRI (2011, 14 March) 'India World's Largest Arms Importer According to New SIPRI Data on International Arms Transfers'. http://www.sipri.org/media/pressrelea ses/2011/armstransfers (accessed 25 February 2014).

SIPRI (2012, 19 March) 'Rise in International Arms Transfers is Driven by Asian Demand, Says SIPRI'. http://www.sipri.org/media/pressreleases/2012/rise-in-interna tional-arms-transfers-is-driven-by-asian-demand-says-sipri (accessed 25 February 2014).

SIPRI (2013) *Yearbook*. http://www.sipri.org/search?SearchableText=SIPRI+Yearbook +2013 (accessed 25 February 2014).

Southerland, M., Koch-Weser, I. and Zhang, A. (2014, December 22) 'China-India Relations: Tensions Persist Despite Growing Cooperation', *U.S.-China Economic and Security Review Commission Staff Report*. http://origin.www.uscc.gov/sites/defa ult/files/Research/Staff%20Report_China-India%20Relations–Tensions%20Persist%20 Despite%20Growing%20Cooperation_12%2022%202014.pdf (accessed 16 February 2015).

Strange, J. (1997) *Centres of Gravity & Critical Vulnerabilities, Perspectives on Warfighting No. 4*, Quantico: Marine Corps University.

The Times of India (2013a, 26 March) 'India Readies Hi-Tech Naval Base to Keep Eye on China'. http://timesofindia.indiatimes.com/india/india-readies-hi-tech-naval-ba se-to-keep-eye-on-China/articleshow/19203910.cms?prtpage=1 (accessed 26 March 2013).

The Times of India (2013b, 9 April) 'Antony Warns Army Against Threats from China, Pakistan'. http://timesofindia.indiatimes.com/india/Antony-warns-Army-aga inst-threats-from-China-Pakistan/articleshow/19450161.cms?prtpage=1 (accessed 9 April 2013).

The Times of India (2013c, 30 May) 'India, Japan Join Hands to Break China's "String of Pearls"'. http://timesofindia.indiatimes.com/india/India-Japan-join-hands-to-brea k-Chinas-string-of-pearls/articleshow/20341060.cms?prtpage=1 (accessed 30 May 2013).

The Times of India (2013d, 6 June) 'India, Australia to Strengthen Defence Ties to Contain China'. http://timesofindia.indiatimes.com/india/India-Australia-to-strength

en-defence-ties-to-contain-China/articleshow/20452688.cms?prtpage=1 (accessed 6 June 2013).

The Times of India (2013e, 7 July) 'India's First Homegrown Aircraft Carrier Set for "Launch", Will be Operational by 2018'. http://timesofindia.indiatimes.com/india/indias-first-homegrown-air...-will-be-operational-by-2018/articleshow_b2/20951030.cms?prtpage=1 (accessed 22 July 2013).

The Times of India (2013f, 2 September) 'IAF Inducts its Biggest Transport Aircraft C-17 Globemaster III'. http://timesofindia.indiatimes.com/india/IAF-inducts-its-biggest-tra...ort-aircraft-C-17-Globemaster-III/articleshow/22222667.cms?prtpage=1 (accessed 4 December 2013).

The Times of India (2013g, 16 November) 'Indian Navy Gets INS Vikramaditya as it Seeks to Bolster Defence Capabilities'. http://articles.timesofindia.indiatimes.com/2013-11-16/india/44137322_1_indian-navy-mig-29k-ins-vikramaditya (accessed 18 November 2013).

The Times of India (2013h, 4 December) 'India's First N-Sub to Head for Sea Trials in Feb-March'. http://timesofindia.indiatimes.com/india/indias-first-N-sub-to-head-for-sea-trials-in-Feb-March/articleshow/26814064.cms?prtpage=1 (accessed 4 December 2013).

The Times of India (2014, 27 February) 'Navy Chief Admiral D.K. Joshi Quits After Another Submarine Fire, Government Quickly Accepts Papers'. http://timesofindia.indiatimes.com/india/Navy-chief-Admiral-DK-Josh...fire-govt-quickly-accepts-papers/articleshow/31061435.cms?prtpage=1 (accessed 27 February 2014).

The Times of India (2015, 15 February) 'Supersonic BrahMos Successfully Test-fired from INS Kolkata'. http://timesofindia.indiatimes.com/india/Supersonic-BrahMos-successfully-test-fired-from-INS-Kolkata/articleshow/46248399.cms (accessed 16 February 2015).

Vertzberger, Y.I. (1984) *Misperceptions in Foreign Policymaking: The Sino-Indian Conflict, 1959–1962*, Boulder, CO: Westview Press.

Wirsing, R.G. (1994) *India, Pakistan, and the Kashmir Dispute: On Regional Conflict and its Resolution*, New York: St Martin's Press.

Yoshihara, T. (2012) 'China's Vision of its Seascape: The First Island Chain and Chinese Seapower', *Asian Politics and Policy*, Vol. 4, No. 3, pp. 293–314.

10 Smart power, military transformation and the US-Philippine joint Balikatan exercises

Pauline Eadie

Introduction

> Contrary to what many critics think, the US military has been building schools and clinics – for military and political ends – for over 100 years.
>
> (McNernay 2008: 191)

The Philippines, as a case study, offers a useful counterpoint to the chapters on Japan and China in this collection. As a consequence of its defeat in the Pacific theatre of World War II, Japan has lacked international military legitimacy. Meanwhile chronic underfunding and a preoccupation with domestic insurgency have challenged the international reach of the Armed Forces of the Philippines (AFP), and the Philippines cannot compete with the technological modernisation of the Chinese military. Consequently, the recent 'Asian pivot' of US foreign policy may inevitably force the Philippines further into the protective arms of the USA, not least because of ongoing territorial disputes with China in the South China Sea. The transformation of the military, as far as a transformation can be identified, in all three countries can only be fully understood against the backdrop of the influence of the USA.

The joint Balikatan 'shoulder-to-shoulder' exercises are bilateral US-Philippine military exercises that have run annually since 1991, with a suspension between 1995 and 1999. They offer a useful lens through which to assess the dynamics of the US-Philippine military relationship within the changing international security environment. The Balikatan exercises, run under the auspices of the 1951 Mutual Defence Treaty, are aimed at, first, promoting interoperability between US and Filipino forces and, second, enhancing the capabilities of the AFP. The US and Philippine militaries have enjoyed a close, if sometimes uneasy, relationship since Spain ceded the Philippines to the USA under the terms of the Treaty of Paris at the end of the 1898 Spanish–American War. The Philippines merits investigation as one of the oldest and closest allies of the USA in South-East Asia.

This chapter assesses the extent to which the concept of 'smart power' offers a useful framework through which to analyse the evolution and character of the Balikatan exercises. Parallels can be drawn between the evolution of smart power as a concept and the dynamic between technological and social military transformation. By using the Balikatan exercises as a case study, this chapter examines the extent to which contemporary challenges to the military, including the need to craft effective counter-terrorism strategies, have heralded a transformation in military practice. This is intended, in some measure, to address Christopher Layne's critique that, related to smart power, soft power 'needs to be subjected to empirical testing to determine the validity of its claims and the robustness of its causal logic' (Layne 2010: 68). In this case, Layne (2010: 67) defines 'smart power' as new and improved 'soft power'. It will be shown that an evolution, rather than a transformation, of military tactical planning has taken place under Balikatan in line with the logic of smart power thinking. It will also be argued that this evolution has been social rather than technological. An assessment of this process is important as the USA has a track record of using the Philippines as a testing ground for polices that are later rolled out elsewhere. This has been the case in Vietnam, Iraq and Afghanistan. The Balikatan exercises are significant beyond the context in which they are currently executed.

Moreover, they are illustrative of the broader US-Philippine relationship. They mirror the state of play between the two countries and also their wider foreign policy objectives in South-East Asia and beyond. The Balikatan exercises are not only valuable as a means to embed the bilateral governmental US-Philippine alliance but also as a means to send a message elsewhere. This message is that the USA has an ongoing military presence in maritime South-East Asia and that it is a strong ally of the Philippines. China, which has a vested interest in the South China/West Philippine Sea, and terrorist networks operating throughout South-East Asia, can be regarded as the primary target of that message. Thus the Balikatan exercises reflect the strategic objectives of the USA in South-East Asia.

Joseph S. Nye Jr is widely seen as the key architect of soft/smart power. Therefore, particular reference will be made to his work and his critics. Nye (Armitage and Nye 2008: 3) identified three specific principles of smart power: standing, allies and civilian tools. These will be used to structure an analysis of the Balikatan exercises. The application of these principles will also address contextual intelligence. Nye defines this as 'an intuitive diagnostic skill that helps a leader to align tactics with objectives to create smart strategies in varying situations' (Nye 2008: 87).

Key aspects of smart power thinking will be highlighted and mapped against the Balikatan relationship. The 'smartness' of the Balikatan exercises will be assessed in terms of the simultaneous 'uni-', 'multi-' and transnational relations that Nye (2004: 136) defines as 'a complex three dimensional chess game'. Smart tactics will be addressed in terms of sensitivity to specific local environments (micro), national sensibilities (meso) and macro-level influence and the inter-play between these levels will be identified. It will be shown that the Balikatan exercises are a useful empirical testing ground for the strengths and weaknesses of smart power. It will be argued that historically and strategically the Philippines has been a smart choice for a US military part-nership. It will also be shown that US contextual intelligence is evidenced to a greater extent in this case than has been seen elsewhere. This offers the opportunity for important lessons to be learnt.

Lastly, the dynamics of the Balikatan exercises have been both hindered by spoilers and aided by unforeseen opportunities beyond its control. Spoilers include the cases of 'Nicole'[1] and Jennifer Laude,[2] and opportunities include Typhoon Ondoy and Typhoon Yolanda (*Philippines Daily Inquirer* 2013). Similarly, smart power is not the sole remit of states; the non-governmental forces that smart power is deployed to counter also adopt smart power strategies. Smart power is part of the terrorist arsenal. Force and attraction are deployed in a fashion that mirrors the tactics of states. Consequently, smart power, like military force, operates in a competitive asymmetrical environment.

It will be argued that the USA is pushing at an open door with the Philippines given that approval ratings for the USA are so high. Statistics show that despite a vocal minority opposed to the ongoing US-Philippine military relations, Filipino approval and trust in the USA is consistently high relative to that shown in other countries. However, US strategy has not merely evolved to keep an already allied state on side. The 'audience' for the Balikatan exercises includes, but is not limited to, the civilian and military Filipino population; the exercises are also aimed at countering what Nye (2013) has termed 'the rise of the rest'. In conclusion, it will be argued that the Balikatan exercises can be seen as a contextually intelligent, if not transformative, way to address at least partially these diverse challenges simultaneously.

The AFP and the limitations of transformation

The extent of the reliance of the AFP on the USA became evident in 1992 subsequent to the termination of the Military Bases Agreement. The closure of the bases coincided with the end of the Cold War and a sea change in the strategic priorities of the USA. During the Cold War, the USA had funded the AFP to the tune of US$200 million annually, equating to '67% of the AFP's acquisition and maintenance costs' (Nye 2013). The AFP's financial woes were compounded by the fact that 80 per cent of its remaining defence budget was allocated to personnel costs (Joint Defence Assessment 2001: 41). Over the next decade the AFP faced further problems as its armoury disin-tegrated due to a lack of spare parts or new equipment. The experience of the AFP post-Cold War stands in sharp contrast to the 'Revolution in Military Affairs' being enjoyed by militaries elsewhere. For the AFP there was no discernible technological transformation.

Nevertheless, under former President Gloria Macapagal-Arroyo (2001–10) the Philippines pledged to upgrade its military capabilities via the Philippine Defense Reform (PDR) programme and the Capability Uplift Programme (CUP) (Chalk 2014). However, the financial inadequacy of the AFP was subsequently highlighted by wide-ranging accusations of corruption and graft

(Mangahas 2011; Santolan 2011) which culminated in a congressional inquiry in 2011. A number of plunder charges were filed against former military generals.

Similarly, in his 2013 State of the Nation Address President Benigno Aquino III also declared his wish to modernise the AFP; however, he noted that budgetary constraints would make this a problematic endeavour. Nevertheless, he announced plans in 2014 to modernise the military under the Philippine Defence Transformation Roadmap 2028. Since 1986, Philippine presidents have been obliged to walk a fine line with the military as the AFP are politicised and played a key role in bringing down President Marcos in 1986 and President Estrada in 2001 (Yabes 2009). This also goes some way to explaining the level of commitment to military salaries even in the face of budgetary constraints.

Unusually, perhaps, for an archipelago, the bulk of Philippine defence spending has historically been allocated to the Army. This is because the primary threats to the Philippine state, notably the ideologically communist New People's Army (NPA) and Islamic aligned Moro Islamic Liberation Front (MILF) and the Abu Sayaff Group (ASG), are domestic. However, the MILF and the ASG have known links to al-Qaeda and Jemaah Islamiyah. Their operatives trained alongside the mujahedeen in Afghanistan. The porous borders of the Philippine archipelago have allowed terrorist networks to use the country as a hub through which to channel arms and finance across South-East Asia.

In 2014 the Philippine government pledged 'a 2015 defence budget of PHP115.5 billion (USD 2.6 billion), which according to official figures is a 29% increase over military spending in 2014' (Grevatt 2014). However, the 'Philippine Army will receive PHP41.2 billion while the Philippine Air Force and Philippine Navy have been allocated PHP14.6 billion and PHP13.3 billion respectively' (Grevatt 2014). This indicates that either the Philippine government continues to view internal insurgency as its primary military challenge, or that it can rely on its allies (the USA) to help counter external threats.

The long-standing threat of domestic insurgency has meant that the Philippines is well versed in protracted low-intensity conflicts 'where there are no fronts, no campaigns, no bases, no uniforms, and no respect for the territorial units of the state' (Cruz de la Castro 2010: 154). Such wars of attrition are notoriously difficult to counter with hard power. The shift to a 'smarter' approach, at least in relation to the ASG, will be cross-referenced to the 'social' transformation of the military and expanded upon later in this chapter. The next section will outline smart power as a concept and as a policy option.

Smart power

Nye 'developed the term smart power in 2003 to counter the misperception that soft power alone can produce effective foreign policy' (Nye 2010: 224). For Nye, smart power is a combination of hard and soft power designed to consolidate US standing in the world, meet challenges alongside 'capable and willing allies' (Armitage and Nye 2008: 3), and draws on the idea that 'civilian tools can increase the legitimacy, effectiveness, and sustainability of US government policies' (Armitage and Nye 2008: 3). On the other hand, hard power rests on 'inducements ("carrots") or threats ("sticks")' (Nye 2004: 5), whilst soft power is about 'an attraction to shared values and justness and duty of contributing to the achievement of those values' (Nye 2004: 7; Nossel 2004). Nye argues that hard and soft power are closely related; operating as a combination of command and co-optive power. Smart power forms the basis for 'an integrated grand strategy that combines hard military power with "soft attractive power" to create Smart Power [which is] a framework for guiding the development of an integrated strategy, resource base and tool kit to achieve US objectives' (Nye 2004: 7).

Smart power is transformative to the extent that it identifies the need to get the balance right between hard and soft power. Since 9/11, at least, the hard power strategy of the USA has contradicted and undermined its soft power rhetoric. The inclination to resort to tactics of 'shock and awe' and to 'find out who did this [the 9/11 attacks] and kick their ass' – reportedly stated to Vice President Dick Cheney by President George W. Bush during a conversation on Air Force One on 9/11 (Summers and Swan 2012: 85) – is not concomitant with the notions of seduction and attraction (Nye 2004: 8) related to soft power. Controversial aspects of the conduct of the 'war on terror' such as the Iraq War in 2003 and the use of torture have widely eroded trust in the USA. As Armitage and Nye (2008: 4) have noted, 'when our words do not match our actions, we demean our character and moral standing and diminish our influence'. Clearly, in terms of the balance between soft and hard power and the realisation of smart power, the USA still has work to do.

Smart power as a policy initiative

Armitage and Nye (2008: 3) argue that smart power 'is a framework for guiding the development of an integrated strategy, resource base and toolkit to achieve US objectives, drawing on both hard and soft power'. Nye (2010: 225) also argues that smart power 'has evaluation built into the definition'. Thus, smart power is presented as an operational strategy against which success, failure or even transformative capacity can be tested. However, it is less clear how effective balancing between hard and soft power and the successful exercise of smart power can be measured. Layne has argued that 'the term soft power these days is so expansive that it can be said to include just about everything including the kitchen sink [and military power]' (Layne 2010: 58). He posits that smart power is no more than soft power 2.0 (Layne 2010: 67), and that this conceptual development further undermines soft power as an evaluative device.

Despite its entry and establishment into the political lexicon of foreign policy, smart power continues to lack clarity. The balance between hard and soft power is a constantly shifting dynamic. Hard power tends to subdue and alienate, characteristics that sit awkwardly in relation to the alleged seduction and attraction of soft power. Indeed. Armitage and Nye acknowledge that 'foreign policy decision-making is too fractured and compartmentalized [...] with no overarching strategy or budget' (Armitage and Nye 2008: 4) that integrates differing instruments of soft power. When considering the failings in Armitage and Nye's thesis, Gelb (2009: 69) notes that smart power 'is a mechanical combining rather than a genuine blending'. He blames 'the two gut impulses of American foreign policy – the power of love and the love of power' (Gelb 2009: 72) for the inadequate fusion of US hard and soft power.

Nye has also been criticised for using characteristics that are more commonly seen at the level of individuals, i.e. attraction and seduction, and extrapolating them to the aggregate level of the state. Rather than say that a state or its values are attractive or seductive, it might be more realistic to argue that acquiescence to another state's foreign policy message is more likely to be driven by a simple cost-benefit analysis. Also if smart power is hailed as a success within specific contexts, how can you systematically identify why that policy was successful? Nye suggests measuring the influence of soft power based on polls or focus groups; however, Layne (2010: 56) argues that societal or public response to soft power does not necessarily translate into foreign policy. Consequently, how do you isolate which components, or configuration of components, were key to the success of smart power? Also, how do you assess whether a policy will be sustainable?

Nye goes some way to answering these questions by citing the importance of contextual intelligence: 'an intuitive diagnostic skill that helps a leader to align tactics with objectives to create smart strategies in varying situations' (Nye 2008: 87). Contextual intelligence involves 'the identification of trends in the face of complexity and adaptability while trying to shape events' (Nye 2008: 88). Arguably, contextual intelligence is emotional intelligence at the aggregate level. It involves seeing the world as it really is and not as one wants it to be. It is about identifying the fears, hopes and aspirations of others and working out how to capitalise on these successfully.

Smart power will not work unless the combination of hard and soft power is crafted in response to the context in which it is to be deployed. Misaligned hard and soft power strategies are further evidence of weak or only partial contextual intelligence. Contextual intelligence is about understanding 'the different values involved in an issue and how to balance what is desirable with what is feasible' (Nye 2008: 88). Contextual intelligence involves political skill, good timing and the ability to capitalise on opportunity. It requires reflexive skill when dealing with spoilers so that policy is not completely derailed. Moreover, it is of key importance for military strategists as poor contextual intelligence makes for inadequate strategy.

Systematic empirical testing, of the kind advocated by Layne, can help to clarify the importance of contextual intelligence and why strategies succeed or fail in this respect. There is value in assessing the Balikatan exercises within this framework. Previous studies have tended either to approach the exercises from the stance of disapproval (often based on sovereign interference) or approval (based on pragmatic materialism). The aim of this chapter is to make a useful intervention in the nexus between smart power rhetoric and actual policy. Key questions to be addressed in the next section will include: What does the USA want? What does the Philippines want? How have the Balikatan exercises helped them to achieve these aims? These questions will be addressed in relation to Armitage and Nye's themes of standing, allies and civilian tools. However, first it will be shown that the very existence of the US-Philippine Balikatan partnership is an obvious example of contextual intelligence.

Contextual intelligence: why the Philippines?

In 1902 Lieutenant General Arthur MacArthur, Jr, who became military governor of the Philippines, testified to the US Senate that 'the archipelago affords an ideal strategic position. It is the stepping stone to commanding influence – political, commercial and military supremacy in the East' (US Congress Senate Committee on the Philippines 1902: 867). This statement has held true throughout the twentieth and into the twenty-first century. The fortuitous geography of the Philippines, as a gateway to the Pacific, mainland Asia and maritime South-East Asia meant that the USA maintained an enduring interest in the archipelago. Nye's themes of allies and standing offer us a useful framework through which to examine the importance of the Philippines to the USA.

For over a century, the Philippines has been a staging post for US interventions in Asia. Post-independence, the USA secured continued access to military installations, including Clark Air Base and Subic Bay, by virtue of the 1947 Military Bases Agreement. The agreement ran until 1991. The USA-Philippine post-colonial relationship was further consolidated in 1951 with the signing of the Mutual Defense Treaty that remains in force today. The Balikatan exercises are an indication of ongoing commitment to this treaty.

In 1991, the Philippine senate voted to reject an extension of the Military Bases Agreement and closed down the US bases. Their decision was taken amid mass public protests that were part of a broad-based anti-bases movement. Critics argued (Simbulan 2009: 152) that the bases agreement violated the Philippine Constitution by compromising its sovereignty and undermining the independence of its foreign policy. In the event, the USA was helped on its way by the eruption of Mt Pinatubo in June 1991. The volcano caused extensive damage to the bases.

Despite all US military personnel withdrawing from the Philippines, the allied relationship continued under the provisions of the Mutual Defence Treaty. US troops were back to take part in the first Balikatan exercises within a few months of the cessation of the Military Bases Agreement. Notwithstanding the suspension of activities between 1995 and 1998 as the Visiting Forces Agreement (VFA) was being negotiated, US troops have been a semi-permanent presence ever since. The alliance was further consolidated by the ratification of the VFA in 1998. The VFA limits visiting US soldiers to non-combat roles and explicitly denies the USA permanent bases in the Philippines. It also legislates for which national laws (US or Philippine) US troops are subject to under various criteria.

There exists an embedded, although not static, logic of cooperation between the USA and the Philippines. Therefore, if the USA aims to adopt smart power strategies in South-East Asia it makes sense to work with the Philippines because of the longstanding allied relationship and track record of military cooperation. Also, approval ratings for the USA are consistently high: 2013 figures from the Pew Research Global Attitudes Project (2013) show that 85 per cent of Filipinos have a favourable opinion of the USA. In answer to the question 'How much influence is the USA having in the way things are going in our country?' some 90 per cent of Filipinos polled said a great deal/a fair amount. In other words, the USA has a great deal of influence in the Philippines, but the vast majority of Filipinos do not mind this. Somewhat ironically, given the termination of the bases agreement in 1991, only 19 per cent of Filipinos think that the USA should have fewer bases, the lowest figure of all countries polled (Chicago Council on Global Affairs 2007).

Layne claims that public opinion does not significantly affect the foreign policy of a state; however, there is some evidence in the Philippines that it does. The US military bases were shut down in 1991 in the face of mass public opposition and in 2004 President Macapagal-Arroyo withdrew from the Coalition of the Willing as a result of public outrage over the kidnapping of Philippine overseas foreign worker Angelo de la Cruz (Eadie 2011). Public opinion in the Philippines has a track record of conversion into mass mobilisation, not least in 1986 and 2001 when the Marcos and Estrada regimes were respectively ousted. Therefore, it makes sense for the USA to target smart power initiatives at the level of the Philippine public as well as the government. Public opinion matters.

In the local (micro) context, specific attitudes to the Balikatan exercises broadly reflect wider Filipino attitudes to the USA. The first Balikatan exercises post-9/11, in 2002, were marked by a sharp increase in US troop numbers in both Luzon and the Muslim-dominated Sulu archipelago. Approval ratings for the US troop presence were highest in Muslim Mindanao (the Sulu archipelago runs south-west from Mindanao which is the home of the ASG). Of the 90 per cent of Mindanaoans aware of the exercises, 73 per cent were in favour of them continuing (Pulse Asia Media Release 2002).

The popularity of troops was perhaps due to the military providing public services such as schools and roads with a degree of competency unlike that of the local and national government (Cragin and Chalk 2003). Mindanao is 'a highly destitute area compared with the rest of the Philippines and one in which it is generally accepted that Islamic communities have suffered the most' (Cragin and Chalk 2003: 16). The national government has a long history of discrimination against the Muslim south in the Philippines and the

USA played an 'historical role as a foil to the relentless interference and intervention of the Philippine central state' (Cragin and Chalk 2003: 16). Local *datus* or chiefs joined forces with the US military in the early twentieth century to agitate against central national control of Moro Mindanao (Abinales 2004: 5–6).

Standing

General Arthur MacArthur noted that 'the Philippines are the finest group of islands in the world. Its strategic position is unexceeded by that of any other position on the globe' (in Etzold and Gaddis 1978: 229). The archipelago served as a staging post for Korea and Vietnam during the Cold War and its strategic position 'at the door of all the East' (Docena 2007) is no less important today. The southern tip of the Philippines has close proximity to Malaysia, Indonesia and the rest of Muslim South-East Asia, whilst China lies to the west across the South China Sea. The Philippines is uniquely placed to assist the USA in the consolidation of its standing in the Asia-Pacific region.

Patterns of financial military assistance since World War II mirror this relationship. Peaks in military assistance coincide with, for example, the Communist Revolution in China (1949), the Korean War (1950–53), the Cuban Missile Crisis (1963), the Vietnam War, the 1973 oil crisis, and the Soviet–Afghan War (1979–89), which coincided with the high tension of the 'second Cold War'. Funding rallied post-9/11; however, expenditure is now only a fraction of what it was during the Cold War (Docena 2007).

Over time the Philippines has capitalised on the hegemonic aspirations of the USA. Post-9/11 the USA faces actual or perceived military, economic and ideological challenges to its hegemony from both China and al-Qaeda. Both of these actors have contributed to the so-called Asian pivot that marks the reorientation of US strategic attention away from the Middle East and towards the Asia-Pacific.

The Balikatan exercises operate in a multifaceted sense. They utilise both hard and soft power and as such their operation can be tentatively considered 'smart'. The Philippines is geographically important for the USA. This importance is embedded in terms of both material cooperation and social trust. The Philippines is contextually intelligent for the USA. The domestic audience is, notwithstanding a vocal minority in opposition, on side. However, the Balikatan exercises operate at two levels of smart power. One is internal, primarily but by no means exclusively soft, and designed to counter the domestic and transnational threat of terrorism. The other is outward facing, primarily hard and aimed at China. The Balikatan exercises have been designed to attract local communities away from the lure of radicalisation. They also aim to send a warning shot across the bows of China and highlight that the USA is a presence to be reckoned with in the Asia-Pacific. The Balikatan exercises are designed to attract and deter simultaneously. This will be expanded upon in the following section.

Transnational terrorism and the ASG[3]

In terms of smart power, transnational (macro) relations are arguably the hardest to control and measure as 'power is chaotically distributed and diffuses to non-state actors' (Nye 2009). Therefore, the articulation of a 'national agenda' is difficult to craft, regulate and defend in the face of both transnational challengers and a multifaceted audience. Non-state actors include terrorist organisations and their growing influence can be classified as 'the rise of the rest'.

In 2002, there were two rounds of exercises: Balikatan 02-01 and 02-02. Over 4,000 US troops were involved in the exercises. Balikatan 02-01 was 'specifically designed to counter terrorism' (Narcise 2003: 21).

Terrorists operating in the Philippines – i.e. Ramzi Yousef, Jamal Khalifa and Khalid Sheik Mohammed – were known to have links to al-Qaeda and Osama bin Laden (Summers and Swan 2012: 220–232; Ressa 2011). Yousef, known as 'The Chemist', made and delivered the bombs that were used in the first attack on the World Trade Center in 1993. The exercises were aimed at the ASG and targeted the group's stronghold, the island of Basilan. The ASG is a splinter group of the MILF, which is in turn a splinter group of the Moro National Liberation Front (MNLF). Ideological differences between the MILF and the MNLF led to a split in 1996. The USA has tended to let the Philippine government manage their own relations with the MNLF and the MILF. Both groups seek an autonomous Bangsamoro region in the southern Philippines. A peace agreement was signed with the MILF in October 2012, although more recently the MNLF has orchestrated sporadic violence in Zamboanga City in an alleged attempt to undermine the peace agreement with its erstwhile comrades. The word 'group' should be treated with caution in the case of the ASG, as membership is shifting and decentralised.

Terrorist groups, like states, consolidate standing and foster allies, including some state regimes, through smart power strategies. Transnational support networks ensure the exchange of ideas, money and material goods. States and terrorist groups have both built networks of influence to sell the primacy of their agenda. This is facilitated by international telecommunications. As Nye (2009) notes, 'success is the result not merely of whose army wins but also whose story wins'.

Maria Ressa has argued that assessing why someone becomes a terrorist has to involve an understanding of social context. Consequently, her assessments of the social networks that drive and maintain terrorist organisations are akin to Nye's call for contextual intelligence and the social transformation of military activity. Terrorist activity has to be seen within the social environment that sustains it. This includes education, family ties and material well-being or lack thereof. Ressa argues that terrorist networks are consolidated through blood as well as ideological ties. There are patterns of inter-marriage between families known to have spawned terrorists, making allegiance familial as well as ideological. A localised understanding of these social networks is crucial to intelligence gathering and smart military strategy.

The ASG operates primarily as a kidnap for ransom group. Whilst there are clear links between the ASG, al-Qaeda and Jemaah Islamiyah and radical Islamists, evidence indicates that the media, the Philippine government and the USA have arguably constructed the ASG as a 'terrorist' organisation. When interviewed by this author, few people referred to the ASG as terrorists. Carol Pagaduan-Araullo of the left-wing group BAYAN called them 'basically a bandit group with no political agenda' (Eadie 2008d). Philippine Senator Aquilino Pimentel called them 'kidnappers or hoodlums' (Eadie 2008a), and Joel Virador of the left-wing party Bayan Muna commented that they were a 'creation of the US government' (Eadie 2008b). This view corresponds with the claim of journalist Mark Bowden (2007), in his article 'Jihadists in Paradise', that 'after 9/11, everything changed. No longer was Abu Sayyaf just an obscure group of kidnappers; it was now a regional arm of the international Islamist menace'.

Even Asim Mangkabon Absar, otherwise known as Abu Hurayra, the ASG member who drove the boat used to kidnap over 20 hostages from Dos Palmas resort in Palawan in 2000 including American missionaries Martin and Gracia Burnham, described the ASG as 'bandits' (Eadie 2010b). He claimed that the ASG procure weapons from local politicians and that the split from ransom money from kidnapping was typically 60/40 or 50/50 between the politicians and the ASG. He claimed that the politicians in the Sulu archipelago use the ransom money as campaign funds during elections.

Senator Juan Ponce Enrile (Eadie 2010a) did refer to the ASG as terrorists; however, he also noted that they are driven by a 'desire for segregation and the dismemberment of the Philippines; they chose to camouflage this with religious belief'. The USA designated the ASG as terrorists and used the vehicle of the Balikatan exercises to pursue them. Arguably they constructed the enemy they wanted in order to justify their favoured strategy – a scenario later repeated in Iraq writ large.

Interview evidence indicated that ASG kidnappings were undertaken primarily for the ransom money. Many interviewees also commented that some of the ranks of the AFP were taking kickbacks from the ASG. That is, the Army were taking a cut in the ransom money and in return the ASG were able to continue their activities unhindered by military intervention. Bai Ali Indayla of Suara Bangsamoro (Eadie 2008c) made reference to a priest who told the media that the 'AFP gives money and guns to the ASG'. Many people referred me to the book *In the Presence of My Enemies*, written by kidnap victim Gracia Burnham (2010). In her book Burnham notes that 'oddly the AFP didn't pursue us. As time went on we noticed they never pursued us. A battle was one thing, but pressing on for capture didn't seem to be on their agenda. This was one of the continuing mysteries of our ordeal' (Burnham 2010: 95).

The events of 9/11 also meant that the continuing ordeal of the Burnhams, who spent a total of 377 days as hostages, became a priority for the US government. Local intelligence finally brought an end to their ordeal. The alignment of US technology and 'smart, trustworthy [Filipino marine] corpsmen who spoke the local languages without accent and were plugged into the islands' families and clans' (Bowden 2007) led to a showdown with the ASG. Sadly hostages Martin Burnham and Ediborah Yap died in the shoot-out, with Gracia Burnham surviving. Solid human intelligence skills, contextual intelligence, opportunities to capitalise on disagreement within the ASG and modern technology ultimately exposed the kidnappers. Hard power alone would have been no match for the kidnappers.

The Balikatan exercises in 2002 were unusual in that they allegedly had 'live targets'. Usually a government deploying counterinsurgency forces to third-party states has the choice of either 'deploying its own troops to conduct operations within the host country, or to limit its support to training, advice and assistance in the hope that the security forces of the host nation are sufficiently capable and reliable to conduct operations on their own' (Ucko 2009: 11). In this case, the rules of engagement were blurred, if not transformed. Critics argued that existing treaty obligations had no 'provisions for the deployment of foreign military forces, advisers, foreign military trainers or coordinators in actual combat operations' (Simbulan 2002). Under the VFA US troops did not even have the authority to return fire in self-defence.

Civilian tools

Post-9/11 the Balikatan exercises transformed their remit towards development work. The provision of social goods such as schools and medical care are akin to the civilian tools that inform soft power. However, such services were not just driven by benevolence. Along with routines of social care came opportunities for human intelligence gathering, at clinics 'villagers casually volunteered information about the insurgents while their children were being treated for scabies, malaria, and meningitis, and having their teeth pulled' (Kaplan 2005: 166). Consequently, the effective provision of these social goods helped to build community-level trust in the military and disrupt the 'friendly sea' in which the ASG swam in the southern Philippines. As well as providing the military with the wherewithal to hunt the ASG down, the Balikatan exercises were also aimed at disrupting their local support base. This can be related to the contextual intelligence of smart power that, in some cases, relates to very specific localities.

In an interview in 2012 Major General Juancho Sabban confirmed that the Balikatan exercises had moved away from tactical only-based training and towards development work. He framed this in terms of moving the centre of gravity (i.e. the loyalty of the population) away from terrorist groups. The aim of the exercises, at least in part, was to attract the local population away from the influence of the ASG. He claimed that strategies rolled out in Sulu and Basilan were later rolled out in Iraq and Afghanistan. Meanwhile, Robert Kaplan notes that, where possible, US troops kept to the background and allowed the AFP to take the credit, the objective being to 'legitimize the Philippine military among the islanders' and undermine the influence of the ASG (Kaplan 2005: 167).

However, Sabban acknowledged that US troops were diverted from the Balikatan exercises in 2009 to help with the typhoon Ondoy (Ketsana) relief efforts (GMA News 2009). Similarly, the US military was at the forefront of relief operations (Lum and Margesson 2014) in the aftermath of typhoon Yolanda (Haiyan). The US military has been praised for a non-partisan and efficient operation in comparison with local efforts. Many local government units simply collapsed given the destructive force of Yolanda and the national government response lacked credibility and coordination.

Critics argue that the USA is killing two birds with one stone by developing infrastructure projects in the southern Philippines. Building roads and bridges, runways and ports helps the local population with the movement of goods and services. However, these projects simultaneously enhance troop movements, and when these projects are focused on areas such as Basilan, soft power coincides with the consolidation of US friendly military installations. This arrangement flies in the face of the Constitution of the Philippines and the VFA. However, high trust and popularity ratings suggest that the USA has succeeded in attracting the majority of Filipinos to its cause. The effective exercise of smart power and contextual intelligence has allowed the USA to conduct the 'war on terror' in the Philippines in ways that have caused widespread condemnation elsewhere.

As well as addressing transnational terrorist threats and the localised threat of the ASG, the Balikatan exercises have also been used to manoeuvre the USA into areas of strategic importance regarding Chinese influence in the region. In this respect the Balikatan exercises are also outward facing, an issue that will be addressed in the next section.

China and the Asian pivot

The Balikatan exercises have evolved, if not transformed, in the face of complex transnational and international pressures. This is Nye's three-dimensional chess game. Strategies have been designed to counter alleged transnational terrorist networks that are also capable of weaving their own brand of smart power. Local 'terrorist' groups have been subsumed into the overall threat of ideologically driven Islamist terrorism. Smart power strategies have sought to undermine the ideological, social and material lure of groups such as the ASG. The US military is ostensibly operating as an allied partner in military training and civil-military programmes; however, a by-product of the Balikatan exercises is the consolidation of the US presence in South-East Asia.

In 2012, the Balikatan exercises were held in Palawan, which is the nearest Philippine landmass to the hotly contested Spratly Islands in the South China Sea. A cynic might surmise that the Balikatan exercises were designed to remind the Chinese that the USA was engaged in the area, a phenomenon that was welcomed by the Philippine government given that the capacity of the AFP to repel any serious incursions by the Chinese is limited. The AFP is 'underfunded, ill-equipped and, with the exception of its special forces, poorly trained. The air force flies virtually no combat aircraft worth that designation, and the navy's ships are Vietnam War vintage and barely seaworthy' (Sheldon 2011: 4). President Benigno Aquino mooted the possibility of upgrading the AFP in his 2013 State of the Nation Address. However, this is easier said than done (Jacobson 2013), with funding being a key issue. The alternative for the Philippines is to make itself indispensable to US strategic aims in South-East Asia. In terms of military reach, the Philippines remains of key importance to the USA as its ports and airfields are the only adequate facilities within 500 nautical miles of the centre of the contested South China Sea (Cliff et al. 2007). The USA wants a safe haven within 'the dragon's lair' (Cliff et al. 2007: 47) and the Philippines wants to be seen to have a powerful ally in the face of China.

Vietnam, China, Brunei, the Philippines, Malaysia and Taiwan have all made territorial claims to the Spratly Islands (Dzurek 1996). The interested parties seek to secure access to potential oil and gas reserves and control some of the busiest shipping lanes in the world. The official position of the USA is that it has no interest in the South China Sea dispute. However, China's recent substantial investment in military hardware and claims to the Spratlys mean that the USA would be denied freedom of navigation in the South China Sea and the Western Pacific in the event of an escalation of tensions (Glaser 2012). This would be a significant hindrance to the US Asian pivot, which seeks to rebalance US interests towards the emerging 'economic centre of gravity' (Schiavenza 2013) that is the Asia-Pacific.

Significant attention has been paid to the South China Sea issue in the academic literature (Raine and Le Mière 2013; Schofield and Storey 2011); however, for the purposes of this chapter it will suffice to note that the physical presence of US troops and hardware has been referenced as ballast against Chinese aspirations in the Spratly Islands. For instance, much has been made of the presence of US warships docking in Subic Bay (Gurney 2013). It is against this backdrop that the Balikatan exercises in Palawan were described as 'provocative' (Symonds 2012). Philippine and US officials denied that the exercises were aimed at China, but 7,000 troops busied themselves in simulating the retrieval of an island territory from 'militants' (Symonds 2012) – exactly the type of scenario that could occur if China started throwing its weight around over the Spratly Islands.

Also in 2013, for the first time, the Chinese were invited to a series of desk exercises organised under the auspices of the Balikatan exercises at Camp Aquinaldo in Quezon City. The exercises were focused on humanitarian assistance and disaster relief and described as 'confidence-building' (Kwok 2013) measures. Australia, Indonesia, Japan, Malaysia, New Zealand, Thailand, South Korea and Vietnam also sent representatives to the desk exercises. In 2014, the exercises focused on non-traditional threats, especially in relation to national disasters, as a response to typhoon Yolanda, and the defence of Philippine territory. According to Albert del Rosario, the foreign secretary of the Philippines, the exercises were designed to 'bolster the preparedness of the Philippines and the United States to deal with tensions "due to excessive and expansive maritime and territorial claims" and "aggressive patterns of behaviour" – a thinly veiled reference to China's increasingly assertive behaviour in the region' (Panda 2014).

In relation to smart power, the outward-facing nature of the Balikatan exercises relates to standing. According to the rubric of smart power they capitalised on a conducive local context (micro), played to the national sensibilities of the Philippines over China (meso), and also faced outwards to the regional and international (macro) nature of the contest over the South China Sea. The Balikatan exercises were perhaps akin to a display of military hardware and capabilities. The audience was China.

Conclusion

For Nye the pursuit of power and hegemony are only partial explanations of foreign policy and military strategy. It is not enough simply to have a lot of power; a calculation must be made on 'which forms of power behaviour are most likely to succeed?' (Nye 2011: 208). There may be asymmetry in power between the USA and the 'rest'; however, simply throwing one's weight around will not counter sub- and transnational actors that wield both irregular forms of hard power and technologically facilitated soft power.

Smart power comes into play when hard and soft power strategies are aligned and reinforce each other. In order for this to succeed, the deployment of smart power has to be credible to the audience. Smart power strategies can be targeted at states, but this is not necessarily the case. Smart power can target civilians, through public diplomacy initiatives, military protection and the provision of material well-being. Such initiatives can attract publics to the agendas of foreign powers and away from the siren call of 'the rest', whoever they may be.

Smart power also needs a degree of subtlety. US Ambassador Philip Goldberg argued, at a time when negotiations were underway for a greater rotational military presence in the Philippines, that Yolanda highlighted the need for a US-Philippine framework agreement on defence and humanitarian issues (GMA News 2013). Goldberg's thinking correlates closely to the notion of social military transformation explored throughout this book. Goldberg's sentiments show the importance of not just contextual intelligence but also timing and opportunity in the deployment of the smart power arsenal. Condoleezza Rice stated that the 2005 Indian Ocean tsunami 'was a wonderful opportunity to show the world the compassionate side of the United States, which has responded with a massive military aid effort and millions of dollars in private donations for the ravaged countries' (News 24 Archives 2005). However, Rice was subsequently criticised for her cynicism and lack of focus on the victims of the tsunami. Thus, whilst crisis can offer opportunity, overtly pursuing national agendas in times of crisis is not necessarily smart.

Critics argue that smart power is nothing new and that the concept is just a combination of old strategies rebranded in the face of the multiple challenges of a complex international environment. Also states do not have the monopoly on smart power. Transnational actors and even individuals are able to capitalise on modern technology to openly and swiftly challenge and falsify the agendas of states and to disseminate counter-agendas. Smart power has also been criticised as being little more than a sound bite that lacks a track record of empirical testing. Smart power has been adopted as a rhetorical device by policymakers, such as Hillary Rodham Clinton, but is it any more than an aspiration?

This chapter has tracked the joint US-Philippine Balikatan exercises against the concept of smart power, specifically in relation to allies, standing and contextual intelligence. It has found that the exercises have transformed their remit from tactical-only operations towards civil-military development projects. This has heralded a social transformation in military activity in the Philippines. This trend could be described as smart power as it meets the criteria of 'the intelligent integration and networking of diplomacy, defence, development and other tools of so-called "hard and soft" power' (Nye 2008: 208). Effective smart power demands social 'smartness' from the military. Consequently, the evolution of smart power can be cross-referenced to both the technological and social transformation of the military. Instead of (or as well as) chasing local insurgents, the Balikatan exercises have disrupted the friendly sea in which the ASG swims. The Balikatan exercises have undermined local patterns of complicity between the ASG, certain elements of the AFP and the local population by the provision of infrastructure and humanitarian initiatives. This has gone some way to transforming the historically hostile relationship between the AFP and civil society in the Philippines. It has also reduced the reliance of the local population on the 'terrorist' groups that maintained loyalty through a mixture of threat and coercion based on the distribution of ransom monies.

As a result of the 2002 Balikatan exercises, the ASG was routed from its stronghold in Basilan. However, critics counter that the ASG has simply set up shop on the neighbouring island of Sulu. They also argue that infrastructure projects such as roads and airports are designed to allow ease of access for US military hardware rather than to improve local livelihoods. It is difficult to isolate the effectiveness of smart power and to quantify its effect. It is extremely hard to isolate and measure the extent to which smart power works as an instrument of de-radicalisation. Allegiance to the aims and values of the USA may be driven by short-term material calculations as opposed to any fundamental shift in allegiance.

The Philippines – specifically the Muslim south – is a contextually intelligent place for the USA to deploy smart power in South-East Asia as levels of trust in the USA are high. However, trust can be fleeting, and in relation to soft power it is hard to quantify as it is essentially based on emotion. It may also be dependent on events beyond the control of governments. For instance, the cases of Nicole and Jennifer Laude struck a chord in the Philippines not just to the extent that Filipinas were abused, but because the abuse effectively represented an assault of Philippine sovereignty under the provisions of the VFA. Therefore, the message of benevolence and partnership was compromised. On the other hand, environmental disasters, such as typhoon Ondoy and, more recently, Yolanda, have presented opportunities for the USA decisively to present a positive public image to the Philippine public. Post-Yolanda the Philippine government was condemned by its own population for political in-fighting over relief efforts whilst images of US aid parcels, delivered by the US military, bearing the words 'from the American people' were being beamed around the world. Comment forums in the Philippine media repeatedly stated 'God Bless America'.

What the USA wants out of its smart power initiatives with the Philippines is contested. The USA denies that its activities are designed to counter Chinese ambitions in the region; however, given the so-called Asian pivot, this claim is questionable. It is not unreasonable to claim that the Balikatan exercises go some way to reinforcing US standing in South-East Asia. Historically the Philippines has been a critical US military outpost in the Pacific and the Balikatan exercises have been used as a 'smart' way to leverage access to Philippine territory. The Philippines is in no position to counter Chinese encroachments on Philippine territory in the South China Sea alone. The only state that can realistically counter Chinese ambitions in the region is the USA. The Balikatan exercises allow the USA a smarter way to signal their presence. The USA has shown both smartness and opportunism in the Philippines. Their activities have been 'smart' in that the context they are operating in has, mostly, been receptive to a mix of compatible soft and hard power.

Both states have been opportunist in terms of their relationship. The Philippines rapidly signalled support for the USA post-9/11 and signed up to the Coalition of the Willing, ostensibly to be a good ally in the 'war on terror' but in reality to capitalise on its loyalty. Not for nothing has the Coalition of the Willing also been called the Coalition of the Opportunists. Meanwhile, the USA has capitalised on Philippine insecurities over the South China Sea, the ongoing Muslim insurgency in the southern Philippines and the recent devastation wrought by typhoon Yolanda.

Notes

1 Lance Corporal Daniel Smith, a US serviceman, was convicted of raping a Filipina named 'Nicole' in 2006 when on leave from military exercises. He was sentenced to 40 years in jail but his conviction was subsequently overturned in 2009. Activists claimed that the case reflected the inequalities inherent in US-Philippine relations more broadly (Cerojano 2009).
2 US Marine Joseph Pemberton was arrested for the murder of transgender Filipina Jennifer Laude in October 2014 in an Olongapo hotel room whilst on leave from his ship (Capozzola 2014).
3 The Communist Party of the Philippines' armed wing, the NPA, was designated a foreign terrorist organisation in 2002 by the USA. However, the Balikatan exercises have not targeted the NPA to the extent that they have the ASG, possibly because they are not an Islamic-derived organisation. The ASG was designated by the USA a foreign terrorist group in 1997, and is regarded as the most violent group operating in the Philippines (Cronin 2004: 4–7). The ASG has alleged links to the MNLF and

the MILF; however, these groups are not designated terrorist organisations by the USA. The USA has publically adopted a hands-off stance in relation to these groups, as the former has managed some level of reconciliation with the Philippine government and the latter signed a Framework of Agreement on the Bangsamoro on 7 October 2012 after long-running peace talks.

Bibliography

Abinales, P. (2004) 'American Military Presence in the Philippines: A Comparative Historical Perspective', East West Centre Working Papers, Politics and Security Series, No. 7. http://scholarspace.manoa.hawaii.edu/bitstream/handle/10125/3639/PSwp007.pdf?sequence=1 (accessed 16 January 2015).

Armitage, R.L. and Nye, J.S., Jr (2008) 'Implementing Smart Power: Setting An Agenda for National Security Reform', Statement Before the Senate Foreign Relations Committee, 24 April. http://csis.org/testimony/implementing-smart-power-setting-agenda-national-security-reform (accessed 16 January 2015).

Bowden, M. (2007, 1 March) 'Jihadists in Paradise', *The Atlantic*. http://www.theatlantic.com/magazine/archive/2007/03/jihadists-in-paradise/305613/ (accessed 8 January 2014).

Burnham, G. (2010) *In the Presence of My Enemies*, Tyndale Momentum.

Capozzola, C. (2014, 26 December) 'The Killing of Jennifer Laude and US-Philippines Relations', *The Diplomat*. http://thediplomat.com/2014/12/the-killing-of-jennifer-laude-and-us-philippines-relations/ (accessed 3 January 2015).

Cerojano, T. (2009, 23 March) 'Philippines: US Marine Rape Conviction Overturned', *The Huffington Post*. http://www.huffingtonpost.com/2009/04/23/philippines-us-marine-rap_n_190454.html (accessed 2 January 2014).

Chalk, P. (2014) 'Rebuilding While Performing: Military Modernization in the Philippines', *Australian Strategic Policy Unit*. http://www.aspi.org.au/publications/rebuilding-while-performing-military-modernisation-in-the-philippines/SR68_Philippines.pdf (accessed 8 January 2015).

Chicago Council on Global Affairs (2007) *World Publics Reject US Role as World Leader*. http://www.worldpublicopinion.org/pipa/pdf/apr07/CCGA+_ViewsUS_article.pdf (accessed 15 October 2013).

Cliff, R., Burles, M., Chase, M.S., Eaton, D. and Pollpeter, K.L. (2007) *Entering the Dragon's Lair: Chinese Anti-access Strategies and Their Implications for the United States*, Santa Monica: RAND Project Air Force.

Cragin, K. and Chalk, P. (2003) *Terrorism and Development: Using Social and Economic Development to Inhibit a Resurgence of Terrorism*, Santa Monica: RAND.

Cronin, K. (2004) 'Foreign Terrorist Organizations', *CRS Report for Congress*. http://fas.org/irp/crs/RL32223.pdf (accessed 8 January 2015).

Cruz de la Castro, R. (2010) 'The twenty-first century Armed Forces of the Philippines: orphan of counter-insurgency or military geared for the long war of the century?' *Contemporary Politics*, Vol. 16, No. 2, pp. 153–171.

Docena, H. (2007) *At the Door of All the East: The Philippines in United States Military Strategy*. http://focusweb.org/content/door-all-east (accessed 8 January 2015).

Dzurek, D.J. (1996) 'The Spratley Islands Dispute: Who's on First?' *Maritime Briefing*, Vol. 2, No. 1. http://www.dur.ac.uk/ibru/publications/view/?id=232 (accessed 19 November 2013).

Eadie, P. (2008a) *Interview with Philippine Senator Aquilino Pimentel*, Pasig City, 3 August.

Eadie, P. (2008b) *Interview with Joel Virador of the left wing party Bayan Muna*, Davao City, 7 August.

Eadie, P. (2008c) *Interview with Bai Ali Indayla of Suara Bangsamoro*, Davao City, 8 August.

Eadie, P. (2008d) *Interview with Carol Pagaduan-Araullo of the left wing group BAYAN*, Quezon City, 11 August.

Eadie, P. (2010a) *Interview with Senator Juan Ponce Enrile*, Pasig City, 27 May.

Eadie, P. (2010b) *Interview with Asim Mangkabon Absar*, Fort Bonifacio, Manila, 8 August.

Eadie, P. (2011) 'Philippines Overseas Foreign Workers (OFWs), Presidential Trickery and the War on Terror', *Global Society*, Vol. 25, No. 1, pp. 29–47.

Etzold, T. and Gaddis, J.L. (eds) (1978) *Containment: Documents on American Policy and Strategy, 1945–50*, New York: Columbia University Press.

Gelb, L.H. (2009) *Power Rules: How Common Sense Can Rescue American Foreign Policy*, New York: Harper.

Glaser, B.S. (2012) 'Armed Clash in the South China Sea', *Contingency Planning Memorandum* No. 14, Council on Foreign Relations. http://www.cfr.org/world/armed-clash-south-china-sea/p27883 (accessed 19 November 2013).

GMA News (2009, 8 October) 'US Troops to End "Ondoy" Relief Work Saturday'. http://www.gmanetwork.com/news/story/174079/news/nation/us-troops-to-end-ondoy-relief-work-saturday (accessed October 2013).

GMA News (2013, 2 December) 'Ambassador Goldberg: Yolanda Proves the Need for a US-PHL Framework Agreement', *GMA News Online*. http://ph.news.yahoo.com/ambassador-goldberg-yolanda-proves-us-phl-framework-agreement-072938025.html (accessed 16 January 2015).

Grevatt, J. (2014, 31 July) 'Philippines Proposes 29% Defence Budget Increase', *HIS Jane's Defence Weekly*. http://www.janes.com/article/41426/philippines-proposes-29-defence-budget-increase (accessed 8 January 2014).

Gurney, M. (2013, 3 July) 'Worried Philippines Invite Back the Americans They Kicked Out', *National Post*. http://fullcomment.nationalpost.com/2013/07/03/matt-gurney-worried-philippines-invite-back-the-americans-they-kicked-out/ (accessed 19 November 2013).

Jacobson, R. (2013, 22 August) 'Modernizing the Philippine Military', *The Diplomat*. http://thediplomat.com/2013/08/modernizing-the-philippine-military/ (accessed 16 January 2015).

Joint Defence Assessment (2001) *Report of the Philippines Joint Assessment to the United States Secretary of Defense*, Washington, DC: Department of Defense.

Kaplan, R.D. (2005) *Imperial Grunts*, New York: Vintage.

Kwok, A.C. (2013, 14 April) 'China Joins US-Philippine Exercises for the First Time', *Interaksyon*. http://www.interaksyon.com/article/59487/china-joins-us-philippine-balikatan-exercises-for-the-first-time (accessed 19 November 2013).

Layne, C. (2010) 'The Unbearable Lightness of Soft Power', in Parmar, I. and Cox, M. (eds) *Soft Power and US Foreign Policy: Theoretical, Historical and Contemporary Perspectives*, London and New York: Routledge.

Lum, T. and Margesson, R. (2014) 'Typhoon Haiyan (Yolanda): US and International Response to Philippines Disaster', *Congressional Research Service Report*. http://www.fas.org/sgp/crs/row/R43309.pdf (accessed 2 January 2014).

Mangahas, M. (2011, 22 February) 'On EDSA's 25th, Corruption Devours the Armed Forces', Philippine Centre for Investigative Journalism. http://pcij.org/stories/on-edsas-25th-corruption-devours-the-armed-forces/ (accessed 8 January 2015).

McNernay, M. (2008) 'CIMIC on the Edge: Afghanistan and the Evolution of Civil-military Operations', in Ankersen, C. (ed.) *Civil-Military Cooperation in Post-Conflict Operations: Emerging Theory and Practice*, London and New York: Routledge.

Narcise, S., Col. (2003) 'Republic of the Philippines – United States of America Visiting Forces Agreement: Balikatan Exercises', USAWC Strategy Research Project, Pennsylvania: US Army War College.

News 24 Archives (2005, 19 January) 'Tsunami "an Opportunity" for the US'. http://www.news24.com/World/News/Tsunami-an-opportunity-for-US-20050119 (accessed 16 January 2015).

Nossel, S. (2004) 'Smart Power', *Foreign Affairs*, March/April. http://www.foreignaffairs.com/articles/59716/suzanne-nossel/smart-power (accessed 5 January 2014).

Nye, J.S., Jr (2004) *Soft Power: The Means to Success in World Politics*, New York: Public Affairs.

Nye, J.S., Jr (2008) *The Powers to Lead*, Oxford: Oxford University Press.

Nye, J.S., Jr (2009) 'Get Smart', *Foreign Affairs*, July/August. http://www.kantiana.ru/eu4u/Summer_school_2013/Get_Smart_791B7B73109AA.pdf (accessed 2 January 2014).

Nye, J.S., Jr (2010) 'Responding to My Critics and Concluding Thoughts', in Parmar, I. and Cox, M. (eds) *Soft Power and US Foreign Policy: Theoretical, Historical and Contemporary Perspectives*, London and New York: Routledge.

Nye, J.S., Jr (2011) *The Future of Power*, New York: Public Affairs.

Nye, J.S., Jr (2013, 29 June) 'American Power in the 21st Century will be Defined by the "Rise of the Rest"', *The Washington Post*. http://www.washingtonpost.com/opinions/american-power-in-the-21st-century-will-be-defined-by-the-rise-of-the-rest/2013/06/28/f5169668-dced-11e2-9218-bc2ac7cd44e2_story.html (accessed 2 January 2014).

Panda, A. (2014, 6 May) 'US Philippines Begin Annual "Balikatan" Military Exercise', *The Diplomat*. http://thediplomat.com/2014/05/us-philippines-begin-annual-balikatan-military-exercise/ (accessed 16 January 2015).

Pew Research Global Attitudes Project (2013) *Global Indicators Database, Opinion of the United States*. http://www.pewglobal.org/database/indicator/1/survey/15/ (accessed 15 October 2013).

Philippines Daily Inquirer (2013, 18 November) 'Aid Missions Boost US Troops' Image, Readiness'. http://globalnation.inquirer.net/91473/aid-missions-boost-us-troops-image-readiness (accessed 18 November 2013).

Pulse Asia Media Release (2002, 13 August) 'Survey Findings on Balikatan Continuation'. http://docs.google.com/file/d/0B3b9qPFV1cRDT1NrVjR0ei1KUUk/edit?pli=1 (accessed 15 October 2013).

Raine, S. and Le Mière, C. (2013) *Regional Disorder: The South China Sea Disputes*, London: International Institute for Strategic Studies.

Ressa, M. (2011) *Seeds of Terror: An Eyewitness Account of Al-Qaeda's Newest Centre of Operations in Southeast Asia*, New York: Free Press.

Santolan, J. (2011, 8 March) 'US Plays Key Role in Philippine Corruption Scandal', *World Socialist* online. http://www.wsws.org/en/articles/2011/03/phil-m08.html (accessed 8 January 2015).

Schiavenza, M. (2013, 15 April) 'What Does it Mean that the US is Pivoting to Asia: And Will it Last?' *The Atlantic*. http://www.theatlantic.com/china/archive/2013/04/what-exactly-does-it-mean-that-the-us-is-pivoting-to-asia/274936/ (accessed 19 November 2013).

Schofield, C. and Storey, I. (2011) *The South China Sea Dispute: Rising Stakes Increasing Tensions*, The Jamestown Foundation.

Sheldon, S. (2011) 'US-South-East Asia Relations: Deep in South China Sea Diplomacy', *Comparative Connections*. http://csis.org/files/publication/1102qus_seasia.pdf (accessed 16 January 2015).

Simbulan, R. (2002) 'The Renewed Phase of Military Intervention in the Philippines', *Anti-War*. http://www.indybay.org/newsitems/2002/02/04/1154451.php (accessed 16 January 2015).

Simbulan, R. (2009) 'U.S. Military Activity in the Philippines', in Lutz, C. (ed.) *The Bases of Empire: The Global Struggle against U.S. Military Posts*, London: Pluto.

Summers, A. and Swan, R. (2012) *The Eleventh Day: The Full Story of 9/11*, Ballantine Books.

Symonds, P. (2012, 26 April) 'US-Philippine Military Exercises Directed against China', *World Socialist* online. http://www.wsws.org/en/articles/2012/04/usph-a26.html (accessed 19 November 2013).

Ucko, D.H. (2009) *The New Counterinsurgency Era: Transforming the US Military for Modern Wars*, Washington: Georgetown University Press.

US Congress Senate Committee on the Philippines (1902) *Affairs in the Philippine Islands: Hearings Before the Committee, Washington*, Washington: Government Print Office.

Yabes, C. (2009) *The Boys From the Barracks, The Philippine Military After EDSA*, Pasig: Anvil.

11 Conclusion

Pauline Eadie and Wyn Rees

Western powers have been the drivers of military transformation. This is true of both technological and social military change. Western states have been the foremost military powers during the latter half of the twentieth century and their military confrontation with the former Soviet Union led them to innovate in military capabilities. The end of the Cold War provided a relaxation of global tensions. The strategic certainty of bipolarity collapsed, resulting in a fluid and unpredictable environment that placed varying demands on militaries around the world. In the immediate post-Cold War era military transformation was driven by technological innovation and social flux. States such as the former Yugoslavia, Somalia and Rwanda imploded along ethnic and racial lines. Saddam Hussein, fuelled by the seeming indifference of the USA, invaded Kuwait in 1990 in an attempt to retrieve territory that he claimed as rightfully Iraq's.

Extra-territorial military interventions were conducted for a variety of motivations including the defeat of inter-state aggression and liberal humanitarianism. Western militaries were required to consider how technology could be harnessed to expeditionary operations and how the military could be used to alleviate suffering in natural disasters as well as in post-conflict situations. Western powers, including the USA, are in relative decline and are facing challenge from other countries that look on the world from different perspectives. Whilst the USA remains the strongest military power, its prowess is subject to contestation. Meanwhile, the USA's European allies have been progressively reducing their military spending in a process that Washington regards as tantamount to demilitarisation.

According to Galbreath in this volume, the Revolution in Military Affairs (RMA) was made in the USA and the Europeans failed to catch up. The gap in technological effectiveness between the USA and its European allies grew over the course of the 1990s, resulting in tension within the North Atlantic Treaty Organization (NATO) because of the lack of European spending. This left the Europeans struggling to operate as effective NATO allies as their technological capabilities lagged behind those of the USA. In 1990 a NATO Summit called the 'Defence Capabilities Initiative' was held. The summit mooted interoperability between member states and across functions – humanitarian response, peace building or high-intensity war. However, the Europeans failed to reach the operational targets set by the USA. Consequently the military transformation debate is no longer dominated by the Western powers.

The emergence of countries such as China and India as major military powers has led them to develop their own ideas about defence transformation. These, as well as other Asian states, have sought to leverage high technology to enhance the capability of their armed forces. They observed and learned from Western experiences of post-Cold War conflicts. In particular, they watched the spectacular use of military technology by the USA in the first Gulf War. This event was a pivotal moment in terms of shaping the post-Cold War era for the USA and its military. It was indicative that the USA was willing and able to fight military campaigns that were not directly linked to its own national territorial survival: it was an extra-territorial war of choice. The USA, as the sole hegemon, would now defend its values and access to strategic natural resources against threats wherever it found them. The first Gulf War also allowed the USA to showcase its technological military superiority to a global audience under field conditions. 'Desert Storm' indicated the technological trajectory of future wars. It highlighted the importance of not just firepower but also information. Precise information allowed for resources to be used and controlled more strategically and for them to be deployed faster and with less risk. Technology made the US forces more efficient, lethal and less exposed to risk.

However, although the USA has been in the vanguard of transformation, there has been no simple process of other countries following, in a linear fashion, in its wake. Li describes the 'emulation' of the USA by the Chinese military, but all countries' approach to transformation has been shaped by their unique circumstances. History, economic strength, national strategic culture, alliance relationships and calculations of interest have shaped the approach of each country. The result has been that states have engaged in transformation to varying extents and at various speeds. The case of Japan exemplifies this point: its own unique constraints over the use of force restrained the government in Tokyo from pursuing military transformation. According to Hughes, this has now changed due to Japan's growing fears of both Chinese military power and the threat from a nuclear North Korea.

Ganguly has shown how India's military response to the end of the Cold War was dictated by a number of factors. India's strategic security was undermined by the collapse of its Soviet ally. The shared borders with its historical adversaries China and Pakistan challenged Indian national security. India was threatened by the aeronautical and maritime modernisation of China's People's Liberation Army and China's perceived encroachment of the Indian Ocean. India was also under threat from its erstwhile territory Pakistan and the Pakistan-sponsored Taliban regime in Afghanistan. India faced nuclear, conventional and asymmetric threats from its neighbours. In response, India forged collaborative agreements with a number of states including the USA, Russia and Japan. Since the end of the Cold War India has invested substantially in its military to secure both its regional environment and global identity as a significant military power.

Technological transformation

Military transformation has been a goal for many of the countries discussed in this volume. Transformation alters the posture of a nation's armed forces from one configured for static territorial defence, to one capable of overseas force projection. This makes the military potentially a more attractive and usable instrument of national power, a means of enforcing the will of the government. By making the military into a more agile and lethal tool, transformation increases its efficacy and the credibility of its use.

The US Air Force has been in the driving seat of these developments. The technologies of modern-day airpower have been well suited to the underlying ideas of transformation – namely, the ability to strike from long range with highly precise weapons, whilst minimising the risk of one's own casualties. The US Air Force was the architect of 'effects-based operations' and much of the doctrinal thinking that has accompanied transformation. Despite periodic bouts of anxiety within the USA that it is losing its edge to rivals, its lead in the field of transformation should not be ignored. The connectivity amongst the branches of its armed forces, the sophistication of its air-breathing and space-based reconnaissance assets, its lead in electronic warfare and the precision of its strike capabilities are formidable. Domination of conventional military issues by the USA is not likely to disappear in the near future as no country can compete.

Potential adversaries of the USA have carefully appraised its strengths and planned accordingly. As noted by Giles, Russia has been worried by US aerospace capabilities in particular, and since 2005 has been investing in modernising its military forces. Whilst Russia has sought to enhance its air force, it has also invested in nuclear capabilities as a means to offset US technological advantages. The firepower of 'Desert Storm' had a significant impact on Russia. Giles claims that there was an 'almost overnight' collapse in confidence in conventional Russian forces which led to the belief that nuclear weapons were now the only credible deterrence against the USA in the event of an attack.

Rex Li notes in his chapter on China that 'Desert Storm' forced a response from the Chinese leadership and military planners; it triggered China's own RMA. Li calls this an 'RMA with Chinese characteristics', with an emphasis on cruise and ballistic missile technologies plus advanced fighter aircraft. China has been trying to develop asymmetric capabilities that would render US long-range strike and carrier-based airpower less formidable.

The principal problem for allies of the USA has been to retain their relevance in the face of diverging technological sophistication. This gap has been exposed in conflicts such as Kosovo and Afghanistan, but will persist even when the fighting is over, due to the challenge of trying to ensure future interoperability with American forces. As a result, Galbreath refers to the UK, France and Germany as being 'both empowered and threatened' by the process of military transformation. Much will depend on the degree of investment that European states are prepared to make in their armed forces during periods of peace.

Procuring the necessary equipment is both expensive and time consuming, and the 2008 financial crisis has left defence ministries across Europe starved of funds. The trend towards shrinking military budgets looks likely to continue. Whilst transformation can be argued to enable more capable armed forces to emerge from a process of reducing the overall size of armed services, the likelihood is that capability will also be the victim of reductions in defence spending.

This is not to suggest that technological transformation offers a panacea for all types of threats. In reality, it is most suitable for high-end war-fighting capabilities where intense, inter-state conflict demands the most sophisticated armed forces. Ironically, this sort of conflict has been unlikely for Western forces over the last two decades. Only the two wars against Iraq in 1990–91 and 2003 came close to such a scenario, and the low technological proficiency of Iraqi forces made victory assured. It is only now, following Russian annexation of Crimea, that the possibility of large-scale inter-state war has returned to Western agendas. As Giles makes clear, Russia has continued to see the USA and Western European countries as the core threats to its national security, even though the idea has seemed unrealistic in Western capitals. The risk of war with a resurgent Russia is improbable but it is no longer something that can be discounted.

Yet inter-state war has not been an unrealistic prospect in Asia during the post-Cold War period. States have taken active steps to prepare for such conflict and have seen in Western transformation technologies the potential to gain advantages over their rivals. Ganguly explains how India has prepared itself for conflict against both China and Pakistan, whilst Hughes explores how Japan has begun to treat with greater urgency the threat from Chinese military power. The chapter by Rees also picks up the theme of growing disquiet in the Asia-Pacific region as major powers assert their interests. Even the USA is re-orientating its military capabilities towards that theatre in the expectation that a conflict involving one or more of the great powers could occur. The so-called 'Asian pivot' is an issue mooted in a number of chapters in this volume.

Where technological transformation has been found to be less relevant is in the prosecution of low-intensity operations. Such operations require large quantities of personnel to be conducted effectively, with patient and careful strategic direction. Along with conflicts involving paramilitary and irregular forces, it is these sorts of operations that have been the dominant experience of Western forces over the last two decades. The conflict against Iraq in 2003 saw its conventional forces defeated within a three-week offensive but it was followed by a protracted and costly engagement against insurgents comprising former members of the armed forces, Baathists, al-Qaeda and Sunni tribesmen. Similarly in Afghanistan, Western coalition forces found themselves fighting the Taliban and Pashtun tribesmen in a gruelling counter-insurgency campaign. Western forces had trained for high-intensity conflict but found themselves relearning the lessons of counterinsurgency. This provided a powerful lesson that high-value weapons platforms can be largely irrelevant against an opponent that chooses to fight asymmetrically.

The threat landscape of the future suggests that such hard-earned lessons should not be forgotten. Potential conflict presents a long and varied spectrum and technological transformation is only fully relevant in relation to a part of that spectrum. When fighting the armed forces of another state, then high-intensity warfare is a likely prospect. Yet the very dominance of that end of the conflict spectrum by the USA makes it likely that opponents will challenge the West in other ways. Adversaries are unlikely to fight by means that play to Western strengths. Rather, they will find other ways to mount challenges and opponents may just as likely be irregular combatants as the armies of another country. Conflict in cyber space offers another dimension, as does the kind of 'hybrid warfare' that was in evidence when Russian forces captured Crimea.

Social transformation

In addition to technological transformation, this volume has considered the role that military forces have performed in social transformation, such as rebuilding post-conflict societies and providing disaster relief. As the chapters by Kent and Stone and Özerdem illustrate, this has evolved into a complex landscape in which various types of governmental and non-governmental agencies interact with the military. The size, scale and frequency of these operations can present major challenges, and militaries are being called upon to adapt their cultures to interface with a variety of relief organisations.

The social transformation of the military has been driven by the notion that modern wars are principally about politics rather than military force. This is certainly true of counterinsurgency operations. Such operations involve a battle for 'hearts and minds' as opposed to the simple defeat of a clearly identified enemy. Consequently, modern militaries are involved in shifting the 'centre of gravity' of local populations in conflict zones away from insurgents and towards those tasked with peacekeeping and peace-enforcement operations. This has involved military personnel frequently taking on civilian roles which might include medical services, rebuilding civilian infrastructure and even taking over as schoolteachers when regular staff are not available. This has necessitated the military reconfiguring its relations with civilian agencies in order to build trust and social credibility on the ground. If implemented effectively, this 'soft' military activity can result in a rich stream of human intelligence that can be used to entrap local insurgents.

Social military transformation is also evident in post-disaster and post-conflict situations. Countries in Asia, such as Japan, have long taken an active role in peacekeeping and post-conflict stabilisation. As discussed by Hughes, Japan has provided peacekeeping personnel in Africa, the Middle East and Afghanistan, and has given disaster relief to Indonesia, Thailand and the Philippines. Japan has regarded such actions as a positive opportunity to address non-traditional security and human security concerns. Humanitarianism and a human security 'freedom from want'-driven agenda has allowed the Japanese to rehabilitate its post-World War II military identity without alarming its neighbours. Similarly, China has undertaken peacekeeping missions in Africa and is the member of the United Nations Security Council with the largest contribution to peaccekeeping operations. China has seen the potential of this activity to demonstrate that it is an actor on the international stage with its own priorities. In addition, the government in Beijing has taken a major role in anti-piracy operations off the Horn of Africa – another example of its willingness to utilise its armed forces for military operations other than war.

In this volume, Eadie has argued that the social transformation of the military is part and parcel of the notion of 'smart power'. She details the regular joint Balikatan exercises run between US and Filipino forces. She argues that the Philippines, which has been heralded as a 'second front in the "war on terror"', is a contextually intelligent location to practise the social transformation of the military as both the government and population of the Philippines are largely sympathetic to the USA. The common challenges of Islamist terrorism and the China threat underpin the US-Philippine military allegiance. Technological transformation is beyond the underfunded and antiquated Armed Forces of the Philippines and, therefore, Philippine national security continues to be well served by its longstanding alignment with the USA. The social transformation of the military does not mean that military strategists have abandoned the pursuit of national interests. It is, however, indicative that as states cannot dictate the conditions under which wars are fought, counterinsurgency is now an ideational as well as a material contest.

The states discussed in this volume have varied in terms of their engagement with the idea of the social transformation of the military. Their attitudes have been shaped by their sense of their own role in the world, their cultures and strategic ambitions. Once again, Western powers have been at the forefront of these efforts. The factors that have influenced their involvement have included the sophistication of their armed services and their political predisposition towards humanitarian interventions. This has been consistent with the dictum of Colin Powell, former chairman of the US joint chiefs of staff and secretary of state, that 'if you break it, you own it'. In the post-Cold War era, Western military forces have undertaken many operations into the internal security of other states, and along with disaster relief it has left them with a sense of obligation to repair the broken societies before they withdraw.

As discussed by Rees, it has been one of the ironies of Western policy that the USA has historically neglected the task of social transformation on the grounds that this would distract its armed forces from their war-fighting missions. Whilst the USA took an active role in providing post-disaster support in countries like Haiti and the Philippines, it sought to avoid post-conflict reconstruction roles in the Balkans and in post-2003 Iraq. Nevertheless, this strategy came to haunt American policy as demonstrated by the cases of Somalia, Iraq and Afghanistan. The USA learnt the lesson that it could not avoid these tasks and that the expectation of rapid entry and rapid exit operations was a mirage. There was little excuse for this mistake in the light of Western experience in both Bosnia and Kosovo, where the USA had been able to rely upon its European Union allies to foot the bill. Ignoring these lessons subsequently led the USA to pay a heavy price, in terms of blood and treasure, in the conflicts in Iraq and Afghanistan.

The future is likely to witness a more diverse range of both military and civilian actors involved in social transformation. As noted by Kent and Stone, armed forces have unique advantages in disasters because they possess personnel ready for deployment, their own means of transport and communication, as well as clear lines of decision making. As such, there is every chance that militaries will continue to be the first responders to crisis situations. Yet they may not be Western militaries; rather, they may be militaries from Asian countries. Added to this, the non-governmental organisations with which they will interact could be drawn from different parts of the world. In a post-Western age it may be Asian countries sorting out crises in their own regions.

This book has sought to explore how military forces from a selection of Western and Asian countries have evolved over the last two decades. Amidst a period of rapid technological change the armed services from these countries have sought to adapt themselves to new demands. This adaptation has inevitably involved organisational as well as operational reform. Competition for resources between different branches of the military still exists and military expenditure remains a key national security concern. States are now increasingly concerned with 'far' as well as 'near' enemies and the credibility of their long-range force projection. Ideational and asymmetric threats have forced states to reinvent military strategy so that threats can be responded to in innovative and agile ways. Militaries, often working in fluid and unpredictable environments, have faced challenges ranging from the shifting nature of armed conflict to the challenge of reconstructing societies damaged by war and disaster. There is every prospect that these changes will continue into the future, ensuring a dynamic field of study that will repay close attention.

Index

11 September 2001 – 9/11 67, 83, 193, 199
1984 Bhopal toxic gas crisis 21
1986 Chernobyl 21
2014 Ebola crisis 18, 22, 130
2016 World Humanitarian Summit 30

Abbot, Tony 172
Afghanistan: airpower in 68; counter-insurgency in 42, 70–3, 97; 34, 37–8, 97; development and 43; India and 170, 211; networks and 87; phases of conflict in 47; reconstruction of 34, 37–8, 43, 45–6, 52–4; US marines and 68; US-Japanese cooperation and 161;
aircraft carriers 64, 121, 135–6, 139, 155, 169
air force: Chinese 130, 132, 136, 138; French 93; Indian 167, 183; Philippines 192, 193, 202; Russia 109, 212; US 65, 67–9, 71, 75, 92
al-Qaeda 2, 192, 197–9
Allied Command Transformation (ACT) 5
anti-militarism 151
Aquino III, Benigno 192, 202
Arab Spring 54, 106
army: British 42, 87–8, 90; Chinese People's Liberation Army 119, 131, 133, 169, 173, 211; French 91, 93; Indian 167, 172, 174–8, 180, 183; New People's 192, 198–9; Philippine 192; Russian 102, 108–111; Sierra Leone; 42; US 64–75, 91, 173
Armed Forces of the Philippines (AFP) 189, 191–2, 199–202, 204
Asian Pivot 10, 189, 199, 201–2, 204–5, 213

Assam Accord 179
asymmetric war, warfare 75, 85, 96, 137, 139, 171, 211–16
Atlantic Command 5
Australia 12, 123, 162, 172

Balikatan Exercises 12–3, 189–209
Balkans 2, 98, 215
Baltic states 2, 101, 108
Battle: field 62–3, 65, 69–70, 72, 76, 81, 88, 175–8; space 63, 69, 84, 88–9, 92, 131
bipolarity 210
Bonn Agreement 52
Bosnia 2, 36, 46, 49, 216
Bush, George W. 66, 71, 79, 121, 172, 193

Cambodia 156
Camp Aquinaldo 202
catastrophic risk 23
ceasefire 42, 47
centre of gravity 72, 179, 200
civilian: casualties 138, 177; military partnership; 38, 50, 53, 159, 172, 183; peacebuilders 6, 51, 71–2; relief workers 18, 39–40, 43; tools; 200–01
Chang Ting-Chen (General) 6
China 119–47; India and 169, 171, 175; nuclear capability 103; Philippines and 189–90, 197; rise of 74, 148, 154–5; Russia and 103, 105; threat 103
Clark Air Base 195
Cold Start 174–5
Cold War 90, 100, 148, 150–4, 160, 197
constitution: Japan 148, 151–3, 157–9, 162; Philippines 195, 201
Constructivism 10

Constructivist perspective 125
counter-insurgency 70–3, 174–5, 177–9, 200, 214–15
Cuban Missile Crisis 197
Cyber-warfare 137, 155, 161, 170, 182–3, 214

Dayton Accords 2
defence: aerospace 99–100; agreements 12; air 133; European 80–83; German Ministry of 85–9; missile 132, 136; modernisation 119–20, 125, 138, 140, 171–4; NATO capabilities 82; planning; 83, 107, 137; policy; 66, 149; self 148, 152, 162; spending; 64–5, 103–5, 167, 183, 191, 213; territorial 160, 202, 212; UK Ministry of 87, 90
demilitarisation 8, 11, 40, 148, 151, 210
Desert Storm 123
development: activities 39, 46, 180; assistance 36, 43, 153; cross-sectoral engagement and 12, 51, 200, 204; economic 10, 128, 140, 155; human 54; peace building and 35, 52; programmes 41, 52–3; technological 10; digitisation 70

earthquake 28, 129–30
East-China Sea 122, 133, 135–7, 155, 169
East Timor 39–41, 156, 163
entrapment 154, 162, 214
expeditionary: coalitions 155; forces 80, 84–5, 89–93; operations 1, 3, 5, 139, 210; warfare 132, 139, 152

floods 129
Fukushima 20, 156

Germany 85–93, 149, 212
Giambastiani, Edward (Admiral) 5
global: community 18–19; financial crisis 1, 183; peace 130; risk 21; security (*see* security); strategic environment 168, 170; War on Terror, 67
Golan Heights 156
grand strategy *see* strategy
Gulf War, first 65–6, 68, 97, 153–4, 211

Haiti 27–8
Haiyan/Yolanda (typhoon) 28, 130, 156, 201
hegemony 149, 155, 157, 197, 203
Horn of Africa 215

Humanitarian: crisis; 20–21; sector; 23–32
Hussein, Saddam 65, 68, 210

India 28, 121, 158–9, 161–3, 167–188, 211
Indian Ocean 154
insurgency 73, 170, 178–9, 89, 192, 204
Iraq 40–6, 53–4, 65–6, 72–3, 75–6, 83–4, 90–2, 121

Japan 74–5, 122–23, 126, 134, 148–166, 169, 172
Japan Socialist Party 151

Kargil 170, 176, 182.
Kashmir 170, 175, 177–80
Koizumi, Junichiro 157
Kosovo 48–9
Kuwait 65, 68, 210

Lashkar e-Taiba 170
Liberal: Democratic Party (LDP, Japan) 151–2, 154, 156–8; humanism 210; peace 35–7, 53–4
Libya 54, 74, 81, 98–9
lift capacity 18
line of control (LOC) 175
logistical support 18, 154, 156, 161–2

Magapagal-Arroyo, Gloria 191, 196
market economy 36, 45
Marshall Plan; 35
military: budget 67, 213; build-up 112, 151; deterrence 164; exchanges 172; force 112, 140, 148; modernization 99, 119, 154–5, 169, 183; procurement 160, 180; tactical planning 190
Modi, Narendra 172–73, 175
Mozambique 156
Mujahedeen 170, 192
Mumbai attacks 175–6

National Diet (Japan) 157
national security 153–5
National Security Council (Japan) 159
NATO 81–3, 85–90, 92–4, 106–7
NATO Prague Summit 2002 5
navy: Chinese 129, 132, 136, 138, 155, 179; French; 93; Indian; 167, 169, 173–4, 176; Philippines; 192; Russian; 108, 110, 172; US; 67–69, 72, 75–6, 155
Neorealism 119–120, 123–5
Nepal 156

network centricity 63, 80, 84–90, 92–3
neutrality 151
New Komeito 158
NGOs 27, 36, 39, 49, 51, 53
non-nuclear principles; 153, 159
North Korea 65, 74, 154
nuclear: capabilities 103, 176, 212;
    deterrent; 133–4, 151, 154, 173, 176;
    parity; 9; power; 64, 99; status; 11;
    weapons (*see* also weapons of mass
    destruction); 100–3, 159, 169, 170–71,
    174–5, 182; tests; 169–70

Obama, Barack 73–4, 79, 121–23
offensive: capability 99–100, 102, 167–8,
    174–6; operations; 3, 75, 136; power
    155, 183
Owens, William (Admiral) 65, 85

Pacific Ocean 76, 134–5, 202, 205
Pakistan 28, 169–171, 174–76, 179,
    182, 211
Petraeus, David (General) 44, 70, 73
Philippine Defence Transformation
    Roadmap 2028 192
Philippine Defense Reform (PDR) 191
Philippines 74–5, 121–12, 156, 158, 169,
    189–209
Powell Doctrine 8
power: hard 193, 200; smart 189–209;
    soft 189–209
precision strikes/munitions 63–66, 68, 74,
    97, 99–100, 138–39
private: security companies 4; sector 17,
    22–3, 30, 32, 50, 53
procurement 99–100, 103–5, 160–61, 168,
    171–74, 181
Putin, Vladimir 99–100, 102–05

rearmament 96, 151–52
reconstruction 43–57,151–52, 156, 158,
    162, 215
relief 34–57, 70–71, 129–30, 201–2, 205
Revolution in Military Affairs (RMA)
    70, 79–95, 97, 119–20, 168, 191
revolutionary war 6
robotics 13
Rumsfeld, Donald 66, 89
Russia 64, 68, 96–116, 134–35, 167–68,
    172–73

sea lanes 126, 177
security *see also* national security: com-
    prehensive 150, 153, 155, 162, 164;

environmental; 30, 81, 128, 205;
    global; 80, 90, 150–51, 153–54, 156,
    161–62; non-traditional; 128, 135,
    149–50, 153, 163; regional; 150, 153,
    155, 162, 164
Senkaku Islands (Diaoyu Islands)
    122–23, 155
Shinzō Abe 157, 172
Smart power *see* power
South China Sea 74–5, 121–3, 133–34,
    201–3
South Korea 74, 123, 162, 202
Social Democratic Party of Japan 151
sovereignty 122–23, 126, 151, 177,
    195, 204
Soviet Union 85, 98, 102–03, 111,
    140, 168
Spanish American War 189
Spratly and Paracel Islands 123,
    201–2
strategy: counterinsurgency 177; exit 71;
    grand 79, 151, 157, 193; India
    maritime; 176; national security
    159; NATO 64, 90; naval 134;
    reconstruction 37, 42, 49, 51;
    US 8, 75, 151–52; smart power and
    193–94
submarines 74–5, 134–6, 173–4
Subic Bay 195, 202
Sudan 127, 130, 156, 163
sustainability 39–40, 47, 50–1,
    160, 193

Taiwan 74–5, 135–6, 138, 155
Taiwan Straits 121, 133, 155, 161–2
Taliban 66, 69, 72, 170, 211
technology: information 66, 90, 93, 131,
    168; military 120–1, 158–9, 199–200,
    210–11; nano 13
technological innovation 62, 83, 210
terrorism 67, 107, 139, 154, 197–200
Tibet 126, 169
Treaty: ASEAN 29; Paris 189; San
    Francisco Peace 151; START 102;
    Tilsit 111; USA-Japan Security
    151–52; Mutual Defense 195

United Nations 17, 35, 41, 129, 215
United Nations Charter 152
United States (USA): China and 119,
    121, 123, 136–9, 140; Europe and
    79–95; India and 171–2; Japan and
    149, 151–5, 157–164; technological
    transformation and; 4–5, 8–9, 61–79;

War in Iraq and 2, 4, 11; War in
    Afghanistan and; 11; Philippines,
    and; 189–205
USAID 26

War on Terror 67, 154, 193, 201, 205, 215
Weapons: air-defence 176; anti-satellite
    (ASAT) 137; conventional 105;
    high-tech 168; light 38; of mass
    destruction 100–3, 153–4, 168–71,
    174–5, 182; platforms 69, 72, 75;

precision 99, 212; programmes 63, 67,
    68, 76; smart 168; systems 62, 108–9,
    132, 137, 168, 183
winning hearts and minds 35, 177,
    180, 214

Xinjiang 126

Yoshida Doctrine 122–3, 155

Zedong, Mao 6, 131, 139